Sinatra
and the
Great Song
Stylists

# Sinatra
# and the
# Great Song
# Stylists

**KEN BARNES**

With contributions from STAN BRITT, ARTHUR JACKSON
FRED DELLAR and CHRIS ELLIS

LONDON
IAN ALLAN

First published 1972

ISBN 0 7110 0400 5

*For Anne*

© Ken Barnes 1972

Published by Ian Allan Ltd, Shepperton, Surrey and Printed in the
United Kingdom by A. Wheaton & Co, Exeter

01 12

# Contents

# Acknowledgements

The author gratefully acknowledges the help of the following persons, organisations and reference sources:

Barrie Anderton (English Representative of the International Al Jolson Society, and publisher of 'Jolsonography', the definitive fact guide to Jolson's career), Terry Bartram, Mike Batori (Reader's Digest Record Division), Moira Bellas (Reprise Records), Tony Bennett, *Billboard*, Stan Britt, David Britten (Reader's Digest Record Division), British Film Institute, Rodney Burbeck (RCA Records Press Office), Roy Burchell (*Melody Maker*), Sue Carling (Kinney Records), David Cavanaugh (Capitol Records, Hollywood, USA), Donald Copeman, Alan Dell, Fred Dellar (*New Musical Express*), Bob Drumm, Chris Ellis (EMI Records), Nick Handel (BBC Stills Library), Laurie Henshaw (*Melody Maker*), Arthur Jackson (*Hi-Fi News* and *Record Review*), Peter Jones (*Record Mirror*), Max Jones (*Melody Maker*), Michael Kennedy (World Record Club), George Kirvay (Rogers, Cowan & Brenner, Inc), Sandra King, Sally Lewis (Polydor Records), Michael Littman (CBS Records), Harry Roche, Christine Rothwell (CBS Records Press Office), Kay Rowley (CBS Records Production Dept), Peter Shephard (*Record Collector*), Fred May, Music For Pleasure, Phil Napier, Fred Nolan, Penny Probert (Andy Williams Appreciation Society), Harry Prosser, Anne Quirk, The Sinatra Music Society, Fred Wadsworth, Alec Wilder, Maggie Yuill.

# Foreword

Not because of my age but my taste do I deplore the passing of the accomplished singer of popular music. In this world of ordinary people, I prefer the extraordinary people. And the singers to whom this book is a tribute were, and the survivors are, extraordinary. Sad to say, the young listener doesn't seem to want them or the great songs they sang.

Reading about them, their careers and the songs they sang makes me feel not so much old as angry. For, as I said, I am not a champion of the ordinary or, God knows, the mediocre or the meretricious. All my life I have set my sights high and the devil take the hindmost. For I believe in the foremost, the foremost in taste, talent, sophistication, intensity, compassion, wonderment and joy.

That Frank Sinatra should stop singing is tragic; that Tony Bennett should continue is courageous and admirable. That some of the other names mentioned in this book should have deserted their heritage and their taste by singing trashy songs out of fear of losing their audience is unforgiveable.

And don't think that in this age of the least common denominator it is easy for Mr Bennett to pursue his dream and keep the faith. For where are the great songs? For every hundred acceptable songs written twenty years ago, there is, on occasion, one being written today.

I realise that in this age of obsession with the new, this self-hypnosis which sees the raddled old flesh of the Emperor as being bedecked in ermine robes, there is a strong likelihood that any disrespect for the tawdry, the pretentious and the bombastic may be viewed as the bitterness of a harness maker at an auto show.

On the contrary. My spleen is directed (in my role of harness maker) at badly designed and wretchedly fashioned machines.

Books appear about steam engines after they have been scrapped. My own book on American popular song (within the span of 1900 to 1950) appeared after all but a few truly professional song writers had died or quit. Mr Barnes's book appears when one rushes to hear Tony Bennett not only because he is a splendid singer and performer, but because there is practically no one else singing great songs.

Does the existence of this book imply that the great professional singer is shortly to become as obsolete as street cars?

If the public can develop a degree of taste and will demand quality in popular music and its interpreters, there will be great singers again, you may be sure.

It is possible that those among the popular music listeners who are too young

7

to have heard the great singers may not be aware that a very personal style was projected and perfected by each of them. This fact might have been slow to register with them since the listeners of the Sixties were subjected to and conditioned by, to put it as simply as possible, *productions*. Multiple recording devices and deceits, material which passed for song but sounded more like hard-sell slogans – and the selling was achieved through addle-pated political flim-flam, high decibel hysteria inducers; indeed, contrivance, science fiction reverberations and calculated monotony.

Naturally, there were exceptions. And these exceptions were always the basis of argument by enthusiasts of these amateur performers and their songs to prove their worth.

Years ago I asked someone in the music world how the popularity of the Andrews Sisters could be explained. He contended that any three high school girls in America could get together and sing as well. This belief, he felt, made hundreds of thousands of young women believe they were ready for the big-time. May I add that I've always believed that any Saturday night drinking group was sure they could sing as well as Mitch Miller's Sing-Along group. And maybe they were right.

I've brought this up by way of speculating about the immense popularity of the singing groups of the Sixties.

I have known many of the singers whose careers are discussed in this book: Frank Sinatra, Peggy Lee, Ella Fitzgerald, Andy Williams, Tony Bennett and others. And I've known them well enough to be able to state categorically that they were totally involved with perfecting their singing, their diction, polishing and focusing their style. It was no Lady Luck which gave them their stature. They worked, they listened, they considered, they decided and they sang.

These men and women were professionals. And that doesn't mean that they simply were paid for their work. It means that they understood the requirements of work well done: responsibility, authority, perspective, discipline, taste and style. Professionalism is a state of being. It's Mildred Bailey weeping while singing Willard Robison's *Old Deserted Farm* for the hundredth time because she was, in her heart, singing it for the first time. It's Mabel Mercer singing a concert with Bobby Short – with a fever of a hundred and four. It's Frank Sinatra making you believe that he just now, for the very first time, has found the magic of the song he's singing, which actually he's been singing for twenty years.

Professionalism is being grown-up – even if you're not old enough to vote.

The roster of names in this book is formidable. And definitive as it is, I, as an American, must be faithful to my memories by adding a few, just for the record: Marian Harris, one of the few of the singers of the Twenties who managed to break away from the rather stiff formality of the era; Helen Ward, probably the best of Benny Goodman's vocalists, excepting Peggy Lee; Jack Leonard, Frank Sinatra's predecessor in Tommy Dorsey's band and certainly an influence on Sinatra; Kenny Sargent, vocalist with the Casa Loma band and a very good one; Buddy Clark, a singer who mysteriously failed to achieve the recognition of which he was most certainly deserving; and, to drop further back in time, Red McKenzie, who, it is alleged, was Bing Crosby's ideal singer.

Tradition and continuity were part of life in the days of great singers. Without certain early singers, it is unlikely that the later ones would have developed and matured as they did. I know how sensitive composers, novelists and painters can be when it is suggested to them that their works bear the influence of predecessors. Only truly great (and therefore humble) creators can graciously acknowledge their early loves and models. It would be perhaps asking too much of those singers still alive to accept my convictions as to their stylistic sources. Let it suffice to say that only the very good ones borrowed from the very good ones. And candidly, solid seller of song as he was, I'm as glad no great singer sat at the feet of Al Jolson.

I'm extremely happy that Ken Barnes has seen fit to put this book together. It's high time the record was put into book form of the people who furthered the cause of the best of popular music and brought it's unique flavour, bitter-sweetness, lovingness, dreams and even its "Moon and June" to you and me.

*New York, June* 1972                                              ALEC WILDER

---

Mr Wilder is one of the most creative and respected personalities in American music. As a songwriter, he was responsible for such well known standards as *I'll Be Around, While We're Young* and *It's So Peaceful In The Country*. As a classical composer, he has written individual sonatas for every instrument in the orchestra in addition to numerous symphonic and operatic assignments. He has also composed original scores for films and TV. As an arranger, he has provided accompaniments for singers such as Mildred Bailey and Frank Sinatra. He is also the author of *American Popular Song – The Great Innovators* (Oxford University Press, New York, 1972).

# Part One

# The Songs, the Singers and the Styles (A Background History)

*What care I who makes the laws of a nation?*
*Let those who will take care of its rights and wrongs.*
*What care I who cares for the world's affairs*
*as long as I can sing its popular songs.*
  Irving Berlin—from the verse of *Let Me Sing And*
  *I'm Happy.*
  (Copyright: Francis Day & Hunter)

Whether one likes it or not, popular music is an integral part of our twentieth century culture. To welcome it may be purely a matter of choice but to ignore it is an impossibility.

If popular music, after all these years, is still looked down on as little more than a money-grubbing industry this is entirely due to false cultivation. We know that the whole sprawling history of this music has been a constant race between art and commerce – with commerce always a few steps ahead. But does this really matter? To be sure, singers, musicians and composers work for money – who doesn't? From all accounts, Wagner always insisted on being paid for what he did . . . and William Shakespeare was surely never a man to refuse the money. So it is quite wrong to always equate art with hunger and commerce with trash. For too long now, the popular music profession has been criticised for the wrong reasons just as its heroes and champions are often lionised for very much the wrong reasons. The object of this particular exercise is to take a fresh and, I trust, entertaining look at the progress of popular music in terms of the people who have made it come to life. The singers.

Approaching the subject in this way obviously calls for a good deal of discrimination. Singing, after all, is the most overcrowded profession in the whole of show business and for this reason it becomes difficult to define in simple terms just what it is that distinguishes a *great* singer from a merely good one. With so many microphones about sheer vocal volume is hardly a necessity (and, contrary to what many people may think, it takes real skill to properly use a microphone anyway). Nor is it particularly essential for a popular singer to possess an academically perfect tone. People who listen only for these qualities may very well overlook such vital considerations as stylistic flexibility, natural rhythmic phrasing or the rare ability to transform an apparently naïve lyric-line into a moving and communicative statement.

Natural musicianship and a good ear are, of course, staple requirements but they do not tell the whole story. The real magic generated by a *great* singer would seem to be based on qualities which are, let us say, *extra-musical*.

Like any other creative form, popular music has many faces; good, bad, honest, phony, artistic, amateurish and so on. Its general history is dotted with incident, which makes it interesting, and its overall progress is sometimes stimulated by innovation, which makes it exciting. Each individual area of popular music can usually point to a peak period – a *golden age* when everything went well and everyone was inspired. For instance, the golden age of songwriting was undoubtedly the 1930s when such composing giants as George

Gershwin, Irving Berlin, Jerome Kern, Cole Porter and Richard Rodgers were at the height of their creative powers. For big band enthusiasts, the golden age of swing lasted from around the mid-'30s to the mid-'40s when famous band-leaders like Benny Goodman, Count Basie, Artie Shaw, Woody Herman, Tommy Dorsey and Glenn Miller were all in top form and at the absolute peak of their popularity.

Singers, on the other hand, have always been a slightly different proposition. For one thing, there has never been a period in musical history when singers have not been popular, and for another, the general public have somehow always tended to take their vocal heroes pretty much for granted. Frank Sinatra, for instance, has been a household name for more than thirty years and he is still a solid commercial proposition. Should an achievement like this really be taken for granted? Of course not. In the transient world of the pop singer, Sinatra is a rarity. Or, to put it another way, one of a rare breed. Bing Crosby is another and the list goes on to include other durable personalities like Ella Fitzgerald, Perry Como, Peggy Lee, Tony Bennett and the late Nat 'King' Cole. All these fine singers share one quality in common with Frank Sinatra: the ability to withstand the ebb and flow of changing fashions – to remain artistic-ally relevant to the times.

This is where Sinatra and his contemporaries differ from the singers of other periods – other styles. So if popular singing is to be classified in terms of a golden age then it has to be from approximately the early '20s to the early '50s, for it was during this period that popular song interpretation developed from a some-what clumsy commercial function into something clearly approaching art.

To properly understand the evolution of popular singing and its many stylistic upheavals along the way, it is helpful for the reader to know something of the development and progression of the popular song. So by way of estab-lishing, in the broadest sense, a suitable atmosphere in which to appreciate the songs, the singers and the styles, this particular section of the book is given over to a kind of running narrative or "skim-history" of popular music from the turn of the century to the early 1950s.

# The Beginnings

Basically speaking, it is the vocalist who deserves most of the credit for the success of popular music. He has made life prosperous for both the songwriter and the musician, and he has helped to develop the commercial possibilities of the gramophone as a consistent form of home entertainment. Indeed, the first recording ever to sell a million copies featured, appropriately, the human voice. The year was 1903 and the voice belonged to Enrico Caruso singing *Vesti La Giubba* (*On With The Motley*) from Leoncavallo's celebrated opera *Pagliacci*.

To be fair, though, let us say that the singer, the songwriter, the musician and the gramophone constitute four interdependent factors in the making and marketing of popular music – but with the singer clearly representing the public's focal point.

Obviously times have changed radically since 1903. In those days it was a case of Caruso's magnificent voice struggling valiantly against the technical inadequacies of the period's primitive recording conditions, whilst these days it can so often be a case of the technical brilliance of modern recording conditions helping to disguise the vocal inadequacies of some young and inexperienced pop performer (it is a proven fact that the judicious application of echo in a modern recording studio can allow an indifferent vocalist something like a quarter of a tone latitude in pitch and this certainly makes it difficult to judge the singer's *true* ability).

From Caruso singing into an acoustic horn in the 1900s to the latest pop idol bellowing enthusiastically into an elaborate 16-track mixing console via the latest and most expensive microphone in the 1970s, here we have the two ridiculously mis-matched extremes of popular singing in the twentieth century. But between these two extremes lies a long and fascinating history of fluctuating social patterns, of song lyrics which on the one hand rhyme 'moon' with 'June' and on the other hand tell us all about the permissive society, drug addiction, pollution, the war in Vietnam and the over-publicised generation gap. In short a history of confusion, progression, retrogression and experiment in which the only stable factor has been the popular singer. His role may have undergone various desultory changes along the way but his function has remained essentially the same.

It is generally agreed – and certainly difficult to deny – that the natural birthplace of twentieth century popular music is America. Being a nation made up of so many different races and origins, it was natural that such a colourful cross-section of melodic and rhythmic influences should form themselves into a musical melting pot. The ingredients, multitudinous and varied, include accents, strains and inflections from all over the world. Some influences would recall Africa or the Caribbean whilst others were reminiscent of Western Europe or even Elizabethan England. In fact, there is probably no native musical element that America has not seized on and synthesized into its own mainstream of popular expression.

Out of this colourful hybrid of disparate sounds, certain distinctive patterns began to emerge around the end of the nineteenth century when the first identifiable forms of jazz and blues came into being. It is hard to say just when American popular music, as we now understand it, was born but for the sake of convenience let us say that the stylistic mechanism started to tick around the turn of the century. It was the era of horseless carriages, antimacassars and moustache cups, a time when families would gather around the living room piano and sing the sentimental and often naïve ballads of the day.

Most of these songs were of such simple construction that even the least musical member of the family was able to deliver the occasional solo passage without revealing his vocal shortcomings too painfully.

The excessive sentimentality of the 1890s – as typified by such songs as *A Bird In A Gilded Cage* and *She Is More To Be Pitied Than Censured* – was being supplanted by the lively sound of early ragtime. Ragtime, a simple musical practice of placing an *artificial* accent on the off-beat – anticipating or delaying the correct emphasis, came out of the South where the Negroes had been applying it for years.

A Negro named Ben Harney is sometimes credited with introducing ragtime to New York and thus to the whole country. In 1897 the Witmark Music Company published his *Rag-Time Instructor* in which Harney outlined the basics of syncopation using a slick line in 'modern' patter designed to 'convince' the potential buyer of the authenticity of his knowledge. Of Harney's many compositions in this vein, at least one, *You've Been A Good Old Wagon*, still survives (a good version of this sung by Dinah Washington appears on the Saga-Eros LP, *Back To The Blues*). But a more legitimate exponent of the ragtime style was the legendary Negro pianist and composer Scott Joplin whose famous *Maple Leaf Rag* was far and away the most significant published example of the ragtime *genre*.

The dawn of the twentieth century had a profound effect on America. Not just on its popular music but in practically every field of endeavour from industry and invention to politics and education. Americans suddenly became aware of their country's potential as a leading force in the new century. Novelists like Jack London and Frank Norris reflected this spirit in their writings, and Owen Wister wrote the first full length Western novel *The Virginian* around 1903. In 1910 the New York Metropolitan Opera staged the first performance of an American opera, Frederick Converse's *The Pipe Of Desire*. On a more popular level, famous impresario Florenz Ziegfeld set out to glorify the American girl by initiating the famous *Ziegfeld Follies*. And popular entertainer and composer George M. Cohan – who went to great lengths to tell the world that his birthday was July 4th (American Independence Day) even though his birth certificate insisted that the actual date was July 3rd – wrote, produced and starred in a whole string of musical comedies boasting strong American themes and loaded with patriotic characters waving star spangled banners.

It was a new era not just for patriotic drum-beating and spirited Sousa marches but for all facets of popular expression. The music publishers were enjoying such commercial prosperity that a million-copies sale of sheet music, previously a rarity, became almost commonplace. In 1910, an energetic Negro composer/pianist, Shelton Brooks, introduced one of his songs to a dynamic young singer named Sophie Tucker. Brooks himself had not had much luck with the song, but after Sophie had presented it at Chicago's White

City Park it was an immediate success and thereafter became permanently linked with her name. The song was *Some Of These Days*. Brooks also wrote two of Al Jolson's early songs, *Honey Gal* and *You Ain't Talkin' To Me*, but his biggest success apart from the Sophie Tucker hit was the well known *Darktown Strutters' Ball*.

In parallel with the popularity of the brass band concerts of John Philip Sousa, there was the full-scale emergence of Vaudeville (a sort of broadened continuation of the Minstrel Show tradition but in a more varied form of presentation) and its British equivalent, Music Hall. In the years prior to World War I, it was through the halls that most of the song hits of the day were established. At that time it was customary for a particular entertainer to acquire the exclusive performing rights to any song which they featured and it is a tribute to the talents of these early artists that so many of the songs from that era survive to this day. On the American side there was Norah Bayes (*Shine On Harvest Moon*) and Sophie Tucker (*Some Of These Days*) while in England there was Eugene Stratton (*Lily Of Laguna*) and the irrepressible Florrie Forde (*Down At The Old Bull and Bush*).

Incidentally, it is worth mentioning at this point that there was a much stronger relationship between Vaudeville and Music Hall than is now generally recalled, for such artists as Vesta Victoria (*Waiting At The Church, Daddy Wouldn't Buy Me A Bow Wow*) and Harry Lauder (*Keep Right On To The End Of The Road, I Love A Lassie*) were just as popular on the American circuits as they were in England. Also Ella Shields, who is still fondly remembered for her Cockney classic *Burlington Bertie From Bow*, was actually born in Philadelphia.

In 1911 the concept of ragtime, if not the actual application of it, inspired Irving Berlin to write *Alexander's Ragtime Band*. It became his first major hit and launched his career as America's first great songwriter of the twentieth century. On December 22nd, 1911, Al Jolson – who was then one of America's top Vaudeville artists – made his recording debut by cutting three titles for the Victor Talking Machine Company in Camden, New Jersey. This launched the recording career of America's first great song stylist of the twentieth century.

The impact of ragtime notwithstanding, much of American popular music before World War I was under a strong Viennese influence as typified by such composers as Victor Herbert and Rudolf Friml. But while many fine works emerged from these writers it was the new tradition established by Berlin and Jerome Kern which paved the way for other composing giants like Gershwin, Porter and Rodgers, all of whom were to make their initial contributions to musical history in the decade that followed.

With his 1914 composition *They Didn't Believe Me*, Kern made an immediate departure from previously accepted methods of songwriting. After a simple 4-bar opening statement, the chorus flowed for a further eight bars in quarter tones instead of proceeding to a 'logical' second 4-bar theme. The song went on to reach a climax through a key change and as it returned to pick up the main melodic thread, Kern introduced a further twist (heralded by the line " . . . and I'm certainly going to tell them") after which the song quietly ended in the conventional manner. Such a departure from the usual 32-bar format was a startling innovation. Yet the strange thing about Kern's work was that for all its technical complexity, most of his songs were reasonably easy to sing. In a sense he was able to make the worst singers perform the most wonderful key changing feats. Obviously his songs sounded a whole lot better when handled by an accomplished interpreter, but there were not too many of these around in 1914.

The same year saw the publication of W. C. Handy's *St Louis Blues*. This too was something of a departure from the traditional 12-bar blues form in that it contained three different sections each with its own melody and lyric theme. Two of these sections closely followed the accepted blues pattern of the 12-bar theme incorporating the 3-line verse. But the middle segment, in the minor key, bore more resemblance to a conventional popular song with its temporary shift into a tango rhythm – although Handy firmly claimed that the tango beat was an authentic Negro rhythm derived from a jungle dance called Tangana and therefore had every right to appear in a blues-based composition. (The public obviously agreed, for forty years after the publication of *St Louis Blues* Handy was still earning an extremely healthy annual income from sheet music and record royalties).

The various innovations that were taking place in songwriting were starting to demand a higher level of interpretation. The great songs were arriving. But where – apart from a small handful of distinctive stylists like Al Jolson and Sophie Tucker – were the great singers?

It was to take another fifteen years before this question could be effectively answered. But the seeds had been sown and the beginnings had been established.

# The Twenties—The Jolson Period and All That Jazz!

Following World War I with its surfeit of hit songs – good and bad – the music scene witnessed several radical changes most of which were dictated by the confusing social climate of the 1920s. The aftermath of the first World War had created a savage break with old pre-war social concepts. Jazz was becoming the accepted form of musical entertainment in some of the larger American cities. This was partly due to the efforts of the Original Dixieland Jazz Band (the first all-white jazz group) and partly due to the fact that New Orleans had suffered a decline as a capital of jazz in 1917 when the city's notorious red light district, Storyville, was closed by government order.

Soon after this most of the great jazz soloists and top bands drifted away from New Orleans, many of them settling in Chicago. These included Joe 'King' Oliver, Sidney Bechet, Freddie Keppard, the New Orleans Rhythm Kings and a truly brilliant young cornet player named Louis Armstrong. Soon Chicago became a flourishing mecca for top jazz talent and it was not long before many excellent white players arrived in Chicago, some to carry on the Dixieland tradition of New Orleans – others to create traditions of their own. Most notable of these was Bix Beiderbecke and his group, the Wolverines.

In a good many ways the 1920s paralleled today's permissive society. People discovered that they could behave more or less as they pleased so long as they remained reasonably within the law. Young people, particularly, enjoyed the luxury of testing the validity of practically every accepted social tradition. The result was a bawdy, rowdy rampage of sustained irresponsibility.

The social conflicts that were so much a part of the 1920s got off to a magnificent start in 1920 when Prohibition and women's suffrage – categorised by the eighteenth and nineteenth amendments to the American Constitution – became official facts within a very short time of each other. It was at this point that the parallels with our present-day society became so marked. Instead of smoking 'pot' the American youth of the '20s and his girl friend got their kicks out of a hip flask. Instead of belting down State Highways on a high-powered motor cycle and wearing a leather jacket, the teenager of the '20s disturbed the peace just as effectively by driving around in a souped-up Stutz Bearcat and wearing an over-sized racoon coat. Women found themselves liberated not only from the drudgery of the kitchen but also from the prejudices that had kept them out of the voting booths. Women also smoked in public, drank hard liquor in speak-easies, wore their skirts above the knees and even joined male drinking companions in the exchange of shady stories and 'blue' jokes.

Sex, or at least a commercialised representation of it, began to dominate the cinema screen in the persons of such idols as Rudolph Valentino, whose darkly Latin looks and drooping eyelids set feminine hearts aflutter, and Clara Bow, who was billed somewhat suggestively as the 'It' girl. Popular music, of course, was quick to reflect this extravagant atmosphere with its let's-live-for-today-and-screw-tomorrow philosophy in songs like *Ain't We Got Fun* and *Runnin' Wild*. Naturally, songwriters were also mindful of the American public's disapproval of Prohibition and this was mirrored in such songs as *If I Meet The Guy Who Made This Country Dry* and *It Will Never Be Dry Down In Havana*. But it was the gifted Irving Berlin who provided the cleverest and wittiest dissertation on the dry subject of Prohibition with *I'll See You In C.U.B.A.*

Family sing-songs around the living piano were still popular as a form of home entertainment but there were signs that other mechanical interests were beginning to take up more of their time. Gramophone records were starting to become the ultimate medium through which to sell music to the public. Electrical recording techniques had superseded the old acoustic studio methods, the disc had completely taken over from the cylinder and the general standard of sound reproduction had improved immeasurably. And it was in the early '20s that the names Louis Armstrong and Duke Ellington first appeared on records. One of the biggest stars in this medium – and indeed in any medium at that time – was Al Jolson.

Jolson, who made history in 1927 by starring in the first sound feature-film, thus becoming the first performer to sing on the screen, was undoubtedly the first of the great stand-up singers.

The public were all the time looking for excitement in their entertainment. To a large extent, talking films and jazz music provided it. But it would be wrong to say that all the music of the '20s was hot jazz and ragtime. There were still plenty of old fashioned ballads and genteel waltzes around just as there were still plenty of people who lived conventional and respectable lives. Occasionally one sensed that the wide vein of sentimentality which had been prevalent in the 1890s and the increasing popularity of jazz seemed to join forces in such songs as Ted Lewis's *When My Baby Smiles At Me* and the Jolson hit, *April Showers*.

Jolson, of course, could sell just about anything to the public. A performer of immense magnetism, his exuberant if somewhat strident delivery virtually overpowered audiences. Short on subtlety perhaps but, as his recordings still prove, long on excitement. But there had to be another way of singing the songs of the day and a dapper young saxophone-playing bandleader named Rudy Vallee came up with an alternative style which was to be known colloquially as 'crooning'. Not that he was the first to employ such a style (legend has it that the 1920s crooning style was first 'discovered' by a baritone named Jack Smith who turned up for work one night with a heavy cold – and the *unusual* quality of his singing pleased the audience so much that thereafter he was known as Whispering Jack Smith) but Vallee, with his wavy hair, winning smile and smartly tailored blazer was certainly the most prominent of the early crooners. His nasal tone and somewhat weak delivery (assisted by a hand-held megaphone) conquered feminine hearts and made a lot of money for Mr Vallee and his management.

Another singing bandleader of a more relaxed demeanour was Will Osborne who competed with Vallee in what music critic George T. Simon once referred to as the 'Single Nostril School of Crooning'.

This then, was the general standard of male singing in the middle-to-late '20s. Mildly amusing but not especially inspiring. When the public ear was not being serenaded by soporific crooners, it was being menaced by wooden baritones and pompous platform tenors. Little wonder then that Al Jolson stood out as such a giant. Things were substantially better on the distaff side with such stars as Helen Morgan, Ruth Etting, Annette Hanshaw, the dynamic Fanny Brice and the ever-popular Sophie Tucker. The jazz world also boasted some excellent talent in such eloquent stylists as Bessie Smith – still regarded as the greatest of all blues singers – the compelling Ethel Waters and the wonderful Mildred Bailey.

Undoubtedly the best selling vocalist on record at this time (1927 to 1928) was Gene Austin. An always likeable singer, though not a particularly vital stylist, Austin introduced two major songs to the standard popular repertoire – *My Blue Heaven* (1927) and *Ramona* (1928) – both of which became huge sellers making Austin not only a very popular entertainer but a very rich one too. Whatever his shortcomings, Gene Austin was certainly a better singer (on records anyway) than Rudy Vallee. And while neither singer did much to raise the over-all standard of song interpretation, both deserve a significant place in popular music history as stylistic pioneers.

Towards the end of the '20s, things began to take a turn for the better as a youthful baritone with the unusual name of Bing Crosby – who was working with the Paul Whiteman orchestra as part of a vocal-instrumental trio called The Rhythm Boys – began to attract attention.

As a song interpreter, Crosby's initial impact came like a breath of fresh air. His singing style was a peculiarly distinctive mixture of elements – it was folky but with more than a hint of big city sophistication, and it was jazzy yet decidedly sentimental. He had the look of an amateur performer yet he responded to on-stage conditions with all the shrewd hard-core timing of a seasoned vaudeville artist. As a song interpreter, it seemed there was no type of material that he could not handle effectively. In fact, young Crosby was very nearly the complete vocal embodiment of American popular music. At that time he was exactly what the songwriters needed, a sympathetic stylist.

As a professional entertainer, Crosby certainly carried an impressive set of credentials. His vocal apprenticeship in the Whiteman band was served in company with some of the greatest figures in musical history including such legendary musicians as cornetist Bix Beiderbecke and guitarist Eddie Lang, both of whom went on to achieve jazz immortality. Crosby claimed that his first real vocal influence was Al Jolson but, apart from a certain tendency towards emotional exaggeration in some of his early solo recordings, there was virtually nothing of Jolson's approach in his style. Other singers who had a more evident effect on Crosby were Louis Armstrong (whose wordless scat singing style prompted Crosby to insert similar phrases into his own recordings) and Mildred Bailey (whose brother, Al Rinker, was a fellow member of Whiteman's Rhythm Boys and a close friend of Bing's).

After some three years of recording in the subsidiary role of band vocalist with vocal refrain') with orchestras led by such personalities as Gus Arnheim, the Dorsey Brothers and, of course, Whiteman, Crosby was given his first solo recording with his name billed on the label above the orchestra. The year was 1929 and the song was *My Kinda Love*, but as a solo recording artist Crosby was not an immediate success and had to wait a further two years before gaining full recognition under his own name.

1929, of course, was the year that the 'roaring '20s' came to a grinding halt with the infamous Wall Street stock market crash. The whole of America was thrown into economic turmoil and millionaires had literally become paupers overnight as huge fortunes were scattered to the winds of change.

But whatever social calamities the '20s may have introduced, it had certainly been a colourful decade as far as popular music was concerned. Both songs and singers were at last assuming a twentieth century identity. It was an exciting decade, for the '20s had presented to the world not only an unrivalled vitality but also some of the most eloquent literary spokesmen that this century has known: Elmer Rice, Ernest Hemingway and F. Scott Fitzgerald – who perhaps more than any other writer symbolised the desperation, excitement and reality of that sprawling decade. And it was Hemingway who referred to the '20s as the 'lost generation'.

Lost, they may have been – but in terms of popular music just look at what they found!

Louis Armstrong, Ethel Waters, Mildred Bailey, Bing Crosby, Duke Ellington, Bessie Smith, Bix Beiderbecke, Eddie Lang and Fats Waller. Then think of the great songwriters who contributed to the '20s: Cole Porter, Rodgers and Hart, De Sylva, Brown and Henderson, Sammy Fain, Richard Whiting, Walter Donaldson and, of course, the Gershwins – George and Ira. Also, the introduction of radio had increased the reach and power of popular music and the cinema had learned to talk.

True, the 1920s did burn themselves out in many ways socially speaking. But artistically and technologically the decade left plenty behind to be remembered for.

# The Thirties—The Crosby Years and All Those Marvellous Songs!

The hectic mad-cap pace of the 1920s could not and did not endure with any strength of purpose beyond 1929 when the Wall Street market crash brought the decade to a screeching standstill. At this point, America found itself staring into the jaws of a terrible social and industrial Depression, life was no longer a bowl of cherries and lyrics such as *I'll Get By* (*as long as I have you*) really meant something.

This, then, was the condition of things at the start of the 1930s and it was to take America – and indeed the world – several years to pick itself up, dust itself off and start all over again – to paraphrase a well-known Dorothy Fields lyric of the '30s. Talking of lyrics, the work which perhaps most vividly reflects this period is the 1932 hit, *Brother, Can You Spare A Dime* (words by E. Y. Harburg, music by Jay Gorney). Popularised on an international scale by Bing Crosby, this might be accurately described as the first commercialised 'protest' song. Viewed in the context of the early '30s, this song still holds up as a fascinating piece of social comment.

Crosby, after several years as a band vocalist, was on the verge of big-time stardom at the start of the '30s. While his early solo recordings had not been particularly big sellers, his distinctive voice and unique style were starting to attract considerable attention. His big break came – as big breaks do, quite by chance – when one of his recordings (*I Surrender Dear*) was heard by William S. Paley, head of the CBS broadcasting network, while on an ocean liner trip to Europe in 1931. Paley was most impressed not only by the voice, but by the singer's unusual approach to music and lyrics. He immediately made a note of the singer's name and promptly wired instructions to the CBS Artists Bureau in New York to locate and sign Crosby for an exclusive radio series.

Meanwhile, Bing was in Hollywood where he had been making a minor impression in films having done a string of short comedies for Mack Sennett. His vocal reputation had increased considerably; so, too, had his recently acquired passion for golf. It was often thought that Bing would have made the big-time much sooner if he had not spent so much time on the golf course. And contrary to many press stories, Crosby's marriage in 1930 to film star Dixie Lee also slowed down his entry into the big-time. So in 1931, Bing Crosby headed for New York in response to the CBS request for his services and in September of that year began a fifteen-minute evening series which went out five times a week through the entire CBS network.

The effect was sensational. He was booked into New York's Paramount Theatre where he played to packed audiences. Hollywood, now a little more confident of his star potential, offered him parts in *major* films, and his recording career began to gather real momentum. Amongst the many fine songs he introduced at this time were *Out Of Nowhere, Sweet and Lovely, Wrap Your Troubles In Dreams* and *Stardust*.

His early feature films also yielded a further crop of marvellous songs, most of which became standards because he happened to sing them originally – *Please* (*The Big Broadcast* – 1932), *June In January* and *Love Is Just Around The Corner* (*Here Is My Heart* – 1934), Rodgers and Hart's *Easy To Remember* (from *Mississippi* – 1934) and *Pennies From Heaven* (from the film of the same name – 1936). But Crosby's biggest rival as far as the introduction of songs was concerned was a performer whose reputation rested more solidly on his dancing than on his singing – Fred Astaire.

Though it may not have seemed so at the time, history has revealed Astaire as the man who introduced more great songs to the standard repertoire than any other single performer in the whole history of popular music. True, Crosby was working with many top-class songsmiths like Johnny Green, Hoagy Carmichael, Ralph Rainger, Leo Robin, Sam Coslow, Jimmy Van Heusen, Johnny Mercer and even Rodgers and Hart on one occasion. But Astaire, in his various shows and films, was continually presented with the best of the best – Gershwin, Porter, Berlin, Kern, literally the greatest songwriting talent of all time. Think of the most famous songs by these eminent writers and you will discover that they were practically all written for Fred Astaire. A random list of these would include such gems as *Night And Day, Cheek To Cheek, Change Partners, S' Wonderful, They Can't Take That Away From Me, A Foggy Day, The Way You Look Tonight* and *A Fine Romance*. This list, of course, is by no means complete, but it does give a firm idea of the kind of songs that were passing through Astaire's hands at that time. His own peculiar renderings of them were equally delightful and certainly contributed towards their success. But it would not be untrue to say that the famous Astaire-Rogers films became box-office hits almost as much for the songs as for the charming and agile dancing of Fred and Ginger.

In the 1930s, radio had developed into one of the prime sources of home entertainment. Strangely enough in the late '20s and early '30s, the advent of radio had been blamed for the drastic slump in the sales of records (these days it seems to be quite the reverse). It seemed more likely that the Depression was the prime cause.

The recording industry, however, soon rallied and came back with a renewed commercial strength due to the introduction of the 35-cent 78 rpm disc, the electric-powered turntable and the widespread demand for the juke box. Radio stations were quick to appreciate that the listening tastes of the public were becoming geared to the sound of popular records. All that was needed to woo the public – and the advertisers – was a stack of the latest records and an articulate announcer with a friendly line in chatter. Thus, the disc-jockey (a term coined in 1937 by *Variety*) soon became as much a part of the music scene as singers and musicians.

Initially, the playing of records over the air was opposed by many record companies and the issue became a matter for the Supreme Court. The major recording companies maintained that the broadcasting of records constituted an infringement of copyright. But in the end the US Supreme Court upheld the right of all radio stations to use records for their programmes without paying the record companies. Of course, radio stations were required to pay a licence fee to the publishers who controlled the music, but this was a minimal expense. It is one of these amusing ironies that in later years, record companies were actually hiring people to ensure that their records were getting *maximum exposure on the air*.

To help satisfy this increasing public appetite for canned music, records came flooding onto the market. In 1933 the industry sold 10 million records, in

1938 the figure was 33 million and by 1941 it was estimated at 127 million.

The decade generally was rich in great popular compositions and has often been referred to, quite reasonably, as 'the golden age of popular song.' But apart from the indisputable excellence of the songs, the 1930s are just as vividly remembered as the start of the Swing Era which stretched roughly from 1935 to 1945, with slight overlaps at either end. It was the period in musical history that launched such influential and consistently popular musicians as Benny Goodman (who was dubbed 'The King of Swing'), Count Basie, Artie Shaw, The Dorseys – Tommy and Jimmy, Harry James, Jimmie Lunceford, Glenn Miller and a host of others whose names even today recall the high excitement of those swing-happy big band days.

But on the vocal front, Bing Crosby's influence as a stylist was becoming far more significant than anyone could have imagined. Somehow he managed to incorporate all of the qualities that audiences looked for in a popular singer. He was romantic, rhythmic, relaxed, his voice was tonally pleasing and – most unusual for a popular singer – he had a sense of humour, which was just what was needed in those Depression days of the early and mid-'30s. Undoubtedly, he was the dominant singing force of the '30s. Of course, he had rivals. Russ Columbo was one, Dick Powell was another. Columbo – who died so tragically in 1934 while cleaning a gun – was perhaps Bing's foremost competitor. Indeed, there were many people who believed that, had he lived, Columbo would have easily outstripped Crosby as an international star. Such a theory, however, could be regarded with some suspicion for while Columbo was undoubtedly a fine singer and a handsome fellow to boot, he lived stylistically very much in the shadow of Crosby, as did just about every other singer of the '30s. Dick Powell's appeal rested mainly on a fine clear tenor voice and boyish good looks, both of which were put to effective use in a series of popular film musicals, *Forty Second Street* (1933) and *On The Avenue* (1937) being amongst the best known. As a vocal stylist, Powell was pleasant but never distinctive and this may well have been the reason why, in his later years, he turned to straight acting and (quite successfully) to film directing.

Over in Britain, there was another warmly romantic and skilful balladeer by the name of Al Bowlly who was also being touted as a serious threat to Crosby's popularity. But in a world of would-be Crosbys (and Bowlly was just as Crosby-influenced as anyone else) it became more and more apparent that there was really only one Bing. He was to remain well-nigh invincible for close on thirty years.

But with so many singers doing their best to sound like Bing, public taste strayed somewhat understandably towards the hot and vital instrumental sounds of the big bands, and this was the real dawn of the Swing Era. Benny Goodman, with his 'King of Swing' banner proudly flying, led the way and the whole magical period was soon (pardon the pun) in full swing.

As a contrast to the high-powered excitement of eight brass, five saxophones and four rhythm every band was expected to project romantic elements too, so every band had to have its star vocalists. Chick Webb's band had Ella Fitzgerald, Benny Goodman's featured Martha Tilton and later Peggy Lee; Duke Ellington's had Ivie Anderson, Count Basie's had Jimmy Rushing and, at one time, Billie Holiday. And when trumpeter Harry James decided to leave Benny Goodman's band to form his own unit in 1939, he hired an eager young vocalist by the name of Frank Sinatra.

Like just about every other aspiring singer of the late '30s, young Sinatra was inspired by Bing Crosby but unlike the others his style was not a direct copy – although his 1939 recording of *Ciribiribin*, with the Harry James orchestra, did contain certain vocal inflections which could only have come from listening to Crosby. As for the remainder of his early recordings, these revealed the makings of a style which bore little or no resemblance to Crosby or any other singer. It was to take a few years for that style to properly crystallise, but right from the start it was apparent that the youthful Sinatra was no run-of-the-mill singer.

As the '30s neared their close, the popularity of the big bands gained momentum – in 1938 Benny Goodman had made history by giving the first jazz concert in New York's Carnegie Hall – and the Swing Era began to leap into top gear. Socially, of course, the decade had been spent largely in recovering from the dismal effects of the Depression and in a sense the big bands had probably helped to counteract much of the social gloom by livening up the airwaves with their infectious beat and driving enthusiasm. This indeed was the hey-day of the big bands and their general popularity carried well on into the 1940s. Several elements, however, tended to impede their progress and eventually bring them more or less to a standstill. One of these elements came in the awesome shape of World War II, the others were of a more human form . . . for, apart from the political turmoil and international confusion (or maybe because of it) the next decade proved to be the most interesting period in the development of popular singing.

# The Forties—The Sinatra Era and All Those Great Song Stylists

If the 1930s represented the golden age of the popular song then the 1940s can justifiably be termed the golden decade of the popular vocalist, for it was between 1940 and 1950 that more good and distinctive singers emerged than at any other time in musical history. And the fact that so many of these artists are still operating today is creditable evidence of their ability to communicate with all kinds of audiences.

In the late '30s and early '40s band musicians often viewed singers as a necessary evil. At first some bands would not hire singers as such; instead the leader would hand out the occasional vocal chorus to a member of his personnel. Or, conversely, a leader would not hire a singer unless he could also play an instrument. Generally speaking musicians tended to look down on vocalists who did nothing but sing – sometimes, though, with good reason.

Because of this general situation (and because no one likes being looked down on, least of all a singer), conditions on the vocal front began to improve. Young Frank Sinatra was one of the first of this new breed of band vocalist. And in 1939 no one had to tell Harry James how good a singer Sinatra was. A good musician like James knew, just by listening.

It was June of 1939 when Harry James, who had formed his band only four months before, was playing an engagement at New York's Paramount Theatre. In between shows Harry was resting in his hotel room listening to the radio (local station WNEW) when he suddenly found himself impressed by an un-named singer on the show. At that time James was looking for a male singer to work with his band. He already had a female singer but he had not been fortunate in finding anyone good enough to fill the male spot.

The voice on the radio remained unidentified but James did learn that the band was Harold Arden's and it was broadcasting from a spot called the Rustic Cabin in Englewood, New Jersey.

The next night James travelled over to the Rustic Cabin and asked the manager where the singer was. "We don't have a singer," he was told. "We do have an M.C. though, and he sings a little bit." The M.C.'s name was Frank Sinatra.

"I asked Frank to come on over the next day and see me at the Paramount," recalled James in a *Billboard* article. "He did and we made a deal . . . There was only one thing we didn't agree about right away. That was his name. I wanted him to change it. I thought it would be too hard for people to remember. But Frank had other ideas."

Sinatra's name had, in fact, become slightly familiar to people who had been tuning in to any one of several independent radio stations around the New York area. The eager young kid from Hoboken, New Jersey, had already gained a sizeable slice of exposure as a member of a group called the Hoboken Four who had won first prize in a Major Bowes Amateur Hour contest. But Frank decided to go it alone for a while and he was making every effort to be heard as much as possible. Radio was the answer and because the exposure was more important to him than money, he offered his services for nothing.

Jimmy Rich, who accompanied most of the singers on WNEW, recalls young Sinatra well – and with affection. ". . . Frank always seemed to make himself available whenever there'd be an opening. He was a pusher, always polite but he was always interested in himself too. I remember, I'd come out of my office and he'd be standing there to see the head of continuity or anybody who would listen to him. Somehow he'd get past the receptionist and there he was!"

On these broadcasts, Frank often sang with just Rich's organ as an accompaniment. Rich recalls that he had a good ear – also a very strong will. Says Rich, "I'll never forget the time he insisted upon doing *Begin The Beguine* in the original key. For some reason or other he felt he could sing it like a tenor. That meant he had to hit a high G. He insisted he could do it and I kept insisting he shouldn't. We rehearsed it his way several times, but by the time the broadcast came on, his voice was so tired that he settled for singing it two tones lower." (It is worth noting, though, that later in his career Sinatra was hitting top G with confident ease – and even topping it by soaring up to an A flat in his version of *All The Things You Are*.)

Recalling this early period of his career in a 1965 article for *Life* magazine, Sinatra wrote, "When I started singing in the mid-1930s everybody was trying to copy the Crosby style – the casual kind of raspy sound in the throat. Bing was on top, and a bunch of us – Dick Todd, Bob Eberly, Perry Como and Dean Martin – were trying to break in. It occurred to me that maybe the world didn't need *another* Crosby. I decided to experiment a little and come up with something different. What I finally hit on was more the Italian *bel canto* school of singing, without making a point of it. That meant I had to stay in better shape because I had to sing more. It was more difficult than Crosby's style, much more difficult."

After staying with the James band for six months – during which time he cut ten sides (his first commercial recordings) – Sinatra's voice was brought to the attention of the great Tommy Dorsey who was looking for someone to replace Jack Leonard in the male singing spot. Harry James knew what such a break would mean to Frank (he also knew that Frank's young wife, Nancy, was pregnant and that the Sinatras needed the kind of money that Dorsey could afford to pay) so he let the singer out of the contract which still had five months to run. It was a gesture Sinatra never forgot. "Frank still kids about honouring our deal," said Harry James more than twenty years later. "He'll drop in to hear the band and he'll say something like 'Okay, boss' – he still calls me boss – 'I'm ready anytime. Just call me and I'll be there on the stand.' "

A few weeks before Sinatra joined the Dorsey outfit the leader had signed a fine vocal quartet called the Pied Pipers. One of its members, Jo Stafford, recalls that when Frank sang along with the group he doubled her lead line an octave lower and this produced a voicing somewhat akin to that used by Glenn Miller's reeds. "He was very well liked in the band," she remembers, "and he certainly worked hard to fit in. Most solo singers usually don't fit too well into a group, but Frank never stopped working at it and, of course, he blended beautifully with us. He was meticulous about his phrasing and dynamics. He worked very hard so that his vibrato would match ours. And he was always conscientious about learning his parts."

Frank, of course, had to *learn* his parts because, unlike every member of the group, he didn't read music. "If I learned to read music," he once said, "it would probably louse up my feeling."

During the two and a half years or so that Sinatra spent with Dorsey, his singing certainly contributed to the band's overall success. This was further evidenced by the fact that Sinatra's voice was heard on no less than 83 of the band's recordings between 1940 and 1942.

But if Dorsey had any reason to thank Sinatra, Sinatra had more reason to thank Dorsey for the stylistic and musical education he received while singing with the band. The experience improved his musicianship and general phrasing as well as providing a launching pad to a successful solo career. As a result of listening to Dorsey's superb trombone solos with their *legato* phrasing and beautifully executed *glissandi*, not to mention the leader's incredible breath control, Sinatra eventually managed to incorporate many of the same qualities into his own singing. Consequently his style of song interpretation began to take a definite shape. His new found ability to sing long unbroken phrases enabled him to draw more attention to a lyric by *underplaying* the sentiments and placing the emphasis only on key words. The general effect, while free from cheap dramatics, tended to softly jolt the listener into appreciating the story line. To Sinatra, a song was not merely a collection of notes, bar lines and words to fit, it was a story that needed to be told with as much expression as possible. Not all of the stories he was asked to 'tell' were interesting (he was occasionally loaded with some pretty poor songs – *Snooty Little Cutie*, *I'll Take Tallullah* and *Dig Down Deep*, for instance) but he always did his best to give them a polish which they lacked on the printed manuscript. But when he applied this approach to good songs like *I'll Never Smile Again*, *There Are Such Things* and *Without A Song* the results were, and still are, beautiful to hear.

When Sinatra left Dorsey amid a barrage of publicity and teenage idolatry his place was taken by another ex-Harry James singer, Dick Haymes. Like Sinatra, Haymes had much to commend him – a warm voice with natural musicianship and an easy charm that scored with the fans. The wealth of top class vocal talent to be heard in front of most of the big bands at this time was quite staggering in that many of the singers became major solo stars in their own right – Perry Como (from the Ted Weems band), Doris Day (first Bob Crosby's then Les Brown's band), Peggy Lee (Benny Goodman's orchestra), Sarah Vaughan and Billy Eckstine (both from the Earl Hines band) and Anita O'Day (who sang with the bands of Gene Krupa and Stan Kenton). It must also be remembered that Bing Crosby had started out as a band singer back in the '20s with Paul Whiteman, and in the '30s, the great Ella Fitzgerald had received her vocal grounding with Chick Webb's band.

But the '40s was really the decade when the solo singer came to the fore. It was an exciting period of stylistic ferment and general progress. Bing Crosby's 'bu-bu-bu-boo' manner of crooning was already being considered corny – even Crosby himself was no longer doing it, although many of his die-hard imitators still were. But just by way of proving that he was not *passé* Bing proceeded to turn out more million-selling discs in the '40s than in any other decade in his long and illustrious career (including, of course, the biggest selling record ever made, *White Christmas*).

Unquestionably the most important contributing factor to the extreme popularity of vocalists during the '40s was World War II. The war had introduced so much confusion, pressure and personal loneliness into people's lives that the soothing and therapeutic qualities of a well sung sentimental ballad such as *You'll Never Know* or *I'll Be Seeing You* served as moral ammunition to families and loved ones who were countries and oceans apart. Top British singer Vera Lynn had been dubbed the 'Forces' Sweetheart' and the appealing warmth of her friendly voice singing such soft-centred songs as *We'll Meet Again* and *Yours* were as much a part of the second World War home front as ration cards, Anderson shelters and Winston Churchill's speeches.

In 1941, during a heavy air raid, the popular Al Bowlly was killed when a bomb exploded near his London flat in Jermyn Street. Before achieving fame in his own right, Bowlly had been a popular mainstay of the Lew Stone orchestra. And when Ray Noble formed his American band, Al had joined him in the USA for about 18 months in the mid-'30s. He returned to Britain a more popular artist than ever. Amongst the many fine compositions he helped to popularise were *By The Fireside*, *The Touch Of Your Lips* and that truly classic ballad *The Very Thought Of You* – these three songs, incidentally, were all penned by Ray Noble.

After Vera Lynn, the best of Britain's contingent of female singers during, and immediately following, the war was Anne Shelton. Like Miss Lynn, she had gained her early experience with Ambrose and his orchestra, one of Britain's most celebrated dance bands. Hers was a voice of pleasing quality, a good range and natural charm. When Bing Crosby visited London in 1944, it was she who joined him on a broadcast for a delightfully impromptu duet version of Irving Berlin's *Easter Parade*, the recording of which still rests today in the vaults of the BBC. Not that it was a particularly outstanding performance but it did make interesting listening for the wily manner in which Bing effected a key change (after Miss Shelton had opened the song in her key) to suit his own range. The mark of a sly old 'pro', you might say.

The increasing popularity of singers and the social effects of the war were not the only reasons for the impending decline of the big bands. Another damaging factor presented itself in the form of James C. Petrillo, president of the American Federation of Musicians, who in his infinite wisdom decided to call a strike against the recording companies in his scheme to win royalties as well as session fees for accompanying musicians. Seen in a sensible light Petrillo's demands were tantamount to industrial blackmail. Demanding a perpetual royalty on every record made by his members was exactly the same as having every carpenter, bricklayer and plumber share in the rental of any building they helped to erect.

When these unreasonable demands were rejected, all instrumental recording was banned for the greater part of 1943 and Petrillo himself proudly announced that the strike had cost his members about seven million dollars in fees.

The strike took place just as Frank Sinatra and a few other former band vocalists were about to embark on solo recording careers, but with no musicians to handle the accompaniments the outlook was extremely dull at first, *until someone realised that the ban only affected musicians*. The problem was suddenly solved in an ingenious way, and the first singer to benefit from it was Dick Haymes. Instead of singing against an orchestral background, Haymes recorded his songs in a choral setting supplied by a group of singers calling themselves the Song Spinners. One of the songs on this session, *You'll Never Know*, became a million-seller for Haymes.

Sinatra soon entered the studios under the same conditions. The arrangements for the 16 Bobby Tucker Singers were written by Alec Wilder whose sensitive scoring for the voices skilfully overcame the lack of instruments and created a superb setting for Sinatra's elegant vocals. Wilder recalled that at one of these sessions there appeared a visitor in full evening dress. It was none other than Richard Rodgers who had left an important dinner engagement to attend the session simply because he had heard that Frank was going to record one of his songs, *Oh, What A Beautiful Morning*, from his new show *Oklahoma*. As it turned out, Frank was also recording another of his songs, *People Will Say We're In Love*, from the same show.

Bing Crosby's recording of *Sunday, Monday Or Always* from his 1943 film *Dixie* was also produced with choral accompaniment; in Bing's case it was the Ken Darby Singers. Sinatra also made a fine recording of this song, but it was the Old Groaner who collected the gold disc.

It was more than two years before the record companies foolishly agreed to Petrillo's absurd demands. But as far as the livelihood of the big bands was concerned the damage had been done. The vocalists had not only supplanted the bands in the studios, they had radically influenced public taste too. Record buyers, not being exposed to the delights of swinging band sounds on new records, had turned away from swing in favour of sentimental ballads. Petrillo's victory, which scarcely proved to be in the best interests of his members anyway, turned out to be rather short lived. The record manufacturers may have capitulated but the paying out of royalties to each individual member of a recording orchestra was later declared illegal by government order. So that was that!

It had been a costly strike on both sides. The musicians had forfeited millions of dollars in fees during their long absence from the recording studios, and there was no evidence to suggest that the recording industry ever retrieved a single penny of the millions paid directly to the union before the government stepped in and put matters to rights.

As the big bands started into their decline – generously assisted by the so-called "experimental" sounds of certain bandleaders who seemed to be doing their conscientious best to drive audiences away from the dance floor – and indeed the theatre – so the market for popular singers expanded. Even second-rate singers, some of them fugitives from first-rate bands, were finding it possible to earn a healthy income in a solo capacity, but fortunately it was the more musicianly singers who eventually emerged as the biggest sellers. Such considerations as tone, range, accuracy of pitch, feeling for lyrics and thoughtful phrasing (not to mention personality and/or sex appeal) were regarded as the prime requirements for the successful singer, which meant that the door to top-flight stardom was wide open to artists like Sinatra, Haymes, Perry Como, Doris Day, Dinah Shore, Mel Torme, Billy Eckstine, Margaret Whiting, Jo Stafford and ex-jazz pianist Nat 'King' Cole; but tightly shut to anyone who could not quite measure up to such standards. This is not to imply that all the popular music of the '40s was perfect, far from it. All manner of dreadful recordings were foisted on the public, from nauseating harmonica trios to treacly light orchestras and one-finger pianists. But the general level of singing during this decade was encouragingly high, musically speaking. And there are still plenty of recordings on the market to prove the point.

Naturally, Hollywood was quick to spot the expanding market for vocalists. Crosby was already a major film attraction and it didn't take long before the name of Sinatra was also seen on cinema frontages. To be honest, though, most of Frank Sinatra's films from this early period are best forgotten. MGM's *Anchors Aweigh* – made in 1944 – was an exception. The first of three musicals in which he co-starred with the ebullient Gene Kelly, it had a zest and pace that his previous films had sorely lacked. The plot, of course, was no literary masterpiece with Sinatra donning a sailor suit and competing with the agile dancing of shipmate Kelly for the hand of soprano Kathryn Grayson. Although it was Kelly who won the girl, Frank was able to console himself with some fine ballads (written by Jule Styne and Sammy Cahn) such as *I Fall In Love Too Easily* and *What Makes The Sunset* – all exquisitely wrapped up with excellent orchestrations by his musical director Axel Stordahl. And in 1945, Dick Haymes was happily – and profitably – serenading Betty Grable in a pleasant techni-coloured fable called *Diamond Horseshoe* with first rate songs such as *The More I See You* and *I Wish I Knew*. The following year the on-screen Haymes was competing with his former boss Harry James (who had also turned screen actor) for the fair hand of Maureen O'Hara in a romantic triangle with music titled *Do You Love Me?*

In 1947, Doris Day became an overnight box office sensation in her first film *It's Magic* (US title, *Romance On The High Seas*) and subsequently collected her third gold disc award for her million-selling version of the film's main song

*It's Magic.* Perry Como also appeared successfully in three or four films as did the baby-faced, but very talented, Mel Torme. So the singing was good, the songs were good and if the films were not exactly masterpieces it didn't really matter. The important thing was that the fans all over the world were able to see, as well as hear, their idols in action. And that made everybody happy. Especially the film companies!

Of course, this blissful state of affairs couldn't last forever and as the 1950s loomed ominously ahead, the smooth complexion of popular singing began to gather an embarrassing wrinkle or two. Younger audiences were now demanding a change of pace from the chocolate-box romanticism of the '40s. Frank Sinatra and Dick Haymes were starting to slip both at the box office and at the record counters. Perry Como might easily have followed suit had he not developed an aptitude for delivering corny little novelty tunes with clickety orchestrations and clackety vocal groups. In addition to this, Como also scored a huge personal success on television. Two other singers who managed to avoid commercial disaster were Doris Day, whose bubbly personality and screen popularity kept her record sales healthy, and Billy Eckstine, whose big deep voice and wide vibrato seemed even more suited to the '50s than to the '40s so his fame just increased.

# The Fifties — The Gimmick Years.. Sobs, Tears and All

What music fans were looking for at the start of the '50s was something with more of a kick in it. Big bands might have provided it, but bookers and promoters were not prepared generally speaking to take a chance of lining up big units of sixteen to twenty players. The cost of road trips had increased and following the break-up of many a top band most musicians were quite content to concentrate on studio work for a living and go home to their wives and families like normal people.

One of the most popular sounds on record at the start of the '50s was the virile muscle-bound voice of Frankie Laine, of whom Bob Hope quipped: "It's easy to see why people buy his records – it's the first time they've ever seen a foghorn with lips." Much more extreme than Laine – who was basically a good singer anyway – was the 'crying' (sobs, tears and all) of Johnnie Ray. Then there was the calculated corn of Guy Mitchell whose recordings (replete with French horns and handclapping choruses) dealt with such fascinating subjects as 'coconuts', 'red feathers', 'shirt cuffs' – and a certain 'pawnshop around the corner in Pittsburgh, Pennsylvania'. Yes, the fabulous '50s had certainly arrived and things had certainly changed – and not really for the better.

But while all this was going on, what was Mr Crosby doing? As usual he was still turning out hit records just as he had been doing for the previous twenty years. For him changing fashions seemed to present no problems. He was a law unto himself. Although by the early '50s even his most ardent fans were aware that the celebrated voice was beginning to get a little frayed at the edges. But the charm and enthusiasm were still there, and there was no other vocalist in the world who could match him for personality.

Sinatra seemed to have been hit harder than any other major singer by the commercial and stylistic eccentricities of the early '50s. His private domestic affairs – which, of course, did not remain private – probably had as much to do with his fall from favour as did changing trends. Indeed, one news columnist of the early '50s even posed the sniping question: "Does anyone know of a more boring person in show business than Frank Sinatra?" Yet through sheer determination and shrewd judgement the much-maligned balladeer managed to launch himself back into the limelight, but this time as a much more dynamic personality. Gone was the sentimental mildness of the previous decade and in its place a more resilient and potent image which found its vocal outlet not in the cheap juke box fodder of the '50s but in the sophisticated and jazz-tinged songs of Cole Porter, Gershwin and Rodgers, etc. When he did record new songs they reflected, in the main, his abiding policy of sensible lyrics, fine tunes and tasteful orchestrations. His acting career, too, gained momentum from his Academy Award-winning performance in the 1953 film, *From Here To Eternity*. Sinatra was heading for the top once more. And he was doing it by presenting quality, which meant that he was more or less standing alone. But a breakthrough of an unusual nature was coming.

As the sentimentality of the '40s (which despite its faults had given us some of the most talented singers the profession has ever known) reluctantly gave way to the prevailing gimmickry of the '50s, the commercial exploitation of the long-playing record did much to appease the more sensitive record buyers, for it was through the medium of the long player that they began to discover the full measure of Sinatra's vocal talent – and Ella Fitzgerald's, Peggy Lee's, Nat Cole's and Mel Torme's. Thus, the record market of the '50s split itself into two diametrically opposed factions. On the one side, the callow mass market of the pop single, and on the other the more discerning (and more expensive) LP market with its encouraging emphasis on quality repertoire and generally gimmick-free talent. But while singers like Sinatra, Cole and Peggy Lee were able to enjoy equal success on both albums and singles, there were actually very few of the *accepted* singles artists who were capable of crashing into the then revered LP market. One who did manage to make the transition, however, was Tony Bennett. After a string of Frankie Laine-like hits, he suddenly emerged as a highly *original* and sensitive purveyor of quality material.

Obviously the aimless meandering of the singles market could not sustain itself indefinitely without at least some vague sense of direction and in 1954, with the arrival of the newly-coined 'rock 'n' roll' era, it found a very definite direction in which to go. First in the driver's seat was Bill Haley and his group the Comets. The sound and spirit of Haley's outfit (which was the first significant forerunner of the '60s pop groups) may have been utterly lacking in subtlety but it was undeniably lively and exuberant. So with public taste being what it was, Haley became an immediate sesnsation.

Hot on the heels of Haley's triumph came a young ex-truck driver from Tulepo, Mississippi, whose effect on the teenage record buyers of the '50s was destined to alter the whole course of popular singing . . . and whose talent was to become a subject of lasting controversy. Elvis Presley had arrived! The year was 1956 and the recording that started it all was *Heartbreak Hotel*. After this, things were never quite the same again. But that's quite another story belonging not to the golden age of popular singing but to the hey-day of rock 'n' roll.

The coming of the rock age meant the beginning of the end for the great song stylists. But did it, really? The big beat, admittedly, made the going rough for many a fine ballad singer, but true professionals have a way of surviving. Quality can never really be swept aside by fashion because, whatever the current trend may be, there is always a section of the great public who respond to a good song, well sung. To sing well is to entertain, and entertainment is an extremely difficult art. Difficult because it calls for communication. The singers whose careers are dealt with on the following pages have all, in some degree, mastered that art because they came out of a period in musical history where the dividing line between art and commerce was not as noticeable as it is today. No doubt they have had a little help from their friends the songwriters, and from that marvellous little invention of Mr Edison's. But it is an arrangement which has certainly proved beneficial to all of us who love and enjoy popular music.

KB

# Part Two

# *The Great Individualists*

*All good things which exist
are the fruits of originality.*
John Stuart Mill (1806–1873)

*. . . the father of Pop songs in our
time, the pioneer who put just about every
performer today in his debt. Al taught us
the power of 'taking care of biz' when it
comes to entertaining an audience.*

Tony Bennett

# Al Jolson

Although he has been dead for more than twenty years, Al Jolson's influence can
still be felt in so many areas of show business. Some regard him as the greatest
entertainer who ever lived while others swiftly dismiss him as the most embarrassing ham of all time. Therefore, in approaching Jolson as a subject it is as well
to keep both viewpoints in mind without subscribing to either.

Jolson is a show business legend. But more than that he has become a sort of
apotheosis of the American vocal entertainer. Indeed his life would appear to
recapitulate all the legendary situations of American show business. Everything
about him seemed to be at least two and a half times larger than life. When he
sang a sad ballad of loneliness he would wring every last drop of pathos from
the lyric then, in almost fanatical desperation, he would metaphorically shake
the song back to its senses and start all over again with a reprise that would make
the first chorus sound like a pale rehearsal. On the happier songs his big rolling
baritone voice would shoot each lyric line full of adrenalin, smearing a note
here bending a phrase there and taking the climactic note up a further octave
to create an electrifying aura of gleeful corybanticism. When he laughed it was
a rollicking, roaring belly-laugh. When he cried – and he frequently cried
too – he displayed a dejected and forlorn side to his nature that, some might say,
bordered on the masochistic. Yet without these qualities he would not have
been the magnetic on-stage personality that he was.

Contrary to what Hollywood would have us imagine, Jolson didn't look a
bit like Larry Parks. Also his life story was jam-packed with incident and
colourful far beyond the mindless commercial scribblings of a film scriptwriter.

He was born Asa Yoelson on May 26th, 1885 in the village of Srednike,
Russia. He was the youngest of five children born to Rabbi Moses Reuben
Yoelson and Naomi Cantor Yoelson.

As a child, Asa received orthodox religious instruction from his father which
also included a solid vocal foundation and musical appreciation. Asa took to
singing as naturally and instinctively as other children learned to talk. Strangely
enough his elder brother, Hirsch (who later became an entertainer, Harry
Jolson) didn't respond quite so effectively to the vocal tuition.

In 1890 Rabbi Yoelson emigrated to America with a promise that he would send for the rest of the family as soon as he had sufficient money, which was not for another four years. In 1894, Mrs Yoelson joined her husband in America, taking the children with her. The family settled in Washington, DC (it is sometimes inaccurately stated that Al Jolson was born in Washington). The following year Asa's mother died and he was so grief-stricken that he went out of the house and did not return home until the next day. It was the first time in his life that he had suffered such a profound sense of loss.

A year later, Rabbi Yoelson married again and this apparently threw the household into a state of flux. Asa and Hirsch – who had now Americanised their names into Al and Harry – left home on several occasions in order to establish themselves in show business, initially as amateur entertainers singing in saloons and clubs. Their occasional sojourns away from home took them to places like New York and Baltimore.

With the Spanish-American war dominating the headlines in 1898, young Al attempted to enlist for combat and was accepted instead as a singing mascot by the 15th Pennsylvania Volunteers. When they sailed for Cuba he was left behind. Nursing a spirit of lost adventure the enthusiastic 13-year-old joined a travelling circus. Later, when the circus folded, he was arrested while singing in the streets of Baltimore and imprisoned for vagrancy.

Back again in his home town of Washington, DC he visited the Bijou Theatre and purely on impulse sang from the audience during Eddie Leonard's act. Leonard offered to take him into the act, but he declined. Some time later in the same year (1899) he again sang from the audience during Aggie Beeler's act – and this time he accepted an offer to tour with her Villanova Burlesque Company. This took him to New York and to what has been officially credited as Al Jolson's first fully professional stage appearance. October 16th, 1899, the first of three performances in a mob scene from Israel Zangwill's *Children Of The Ghetto* at the Herald Square Theatre on 35th Street.

The next year he toured with Fred E. Moore's vaudeville act as a boy soprano. But he was forced into early 'retirement' due to his voice changing.

In 1901, with his larynx still awkwardly between registers, he decided to take up whistling till his vocal chords made up their mind. During this period, he teamed up with brother Harry to form an act called 'The Hebrew and The Cadet' and sustained this and other specialty acts both singly and together throughout a series of reviews and burlesque one-nighters, eventually becoming well known as talented individuals. Harry employed a black-face routine for the first time in 1902, which was some time before Al began using it. Years later, Harry was often accused of blacking up to cash in on his brother's success.

Al's first marriage, to Miss Henrietta Keller of Oakland, California, took place in San Francisco in 1906 amid the din of repair work following the infamous earthquake. It was at this time that Al was said to have first coined his famous catch-phrase "You ain't heard nothin' yet!"

With his bride accompanying him, Jolson toured the mid-West as a successful solo act. During that season his salary rose in a series of jumps from $75 all the way up to $250, which was commensurate with the way his popularity was increasing. So confident was he that he placed ads in all the trade papers saying "You never heard of me – but you will!" They did. Subsequent stints with Lew Dockstader's Minstrel Show (in which he eclipsed the popularity of the show's veteran stars, Dockstader and Neil O'Brien) helped to build him into a top-line vaudeville attraction.

During these years of touring the popular circuits, Jolson developed a shrewd business approach off-stage which effectively supplemented his on-stage professionalism. In his autobiography, *Call Me Lucky* Bing Crosby, an ardent teenage fan of Jolson, recalled seeing the star in such shows as *Sinbad* and *Bombo* and made the following observations:

> "Although Jolson was the star of those shows, he spent most of his time when he wasn't on stage rushing out to the box office and counting the take. The star of a show which penetrated that far into the hinterland had to be a businessman as well as a performer.
>
> "Later, when I got to know and work with Al, he remembered how industrious he'd been on those hegiras so far from Broadway, and we laughed at it. He didn't remember the lop-eared lad named Crosby who watched his every move, but I remembered him vividly."

Parallel with building up his stage career, Jolson kept a watchful eye on all areas of contact with the public. He had made his first phonograph recording on December 22nd, 1911 for the Victor Talking Machine Company in Camden, New Jersey. The titles at this session were *That Haunting Melody* – a George M. Cohan composition which he had introduced a month previously in a show called *Vera Violetta* – a piece of trivial nonsense entitled *Rum Tum Tiddle* and a parody of the old song *Asleep In The Deep*. Apart from the purely historical significance, this session is also worth recalling for an amusing story which maintains that Jolson could not record without first being strapped into a strait-jacket, the reason being that he was such an animated performer that he simply could not keep still while singing into the acoustic horn.

Another area of communication in which Jolson excelled was publicity. He was forever dreaming up new ways of putting his name in front of the public. A typical incident being the November 23rd, 1911 edition of *Variety* which carried the following ad. devised by Al himself:

> "*Everybody likes me. Those who don't are jealous!*
> *Anyhow, here's wishing those that do and those that*
> *don't a Merry Christmas and a Happy New Year –* "
> Al Jolson

The same ad. was repeated a year later on November 25th, 1912.

Being the flamboyant character he was, Jolson was responsible for several show business innovations, not least of which was his insistence on having a special runway built from the stage to the auditorium of New York's Winter Garden theatre so that he could get closer to the audience. This was arranged for the March 1912 opening of his show *The Whirl Of Society*. He also inaugurated special Sunday night concerts at the Winter Garden for show business people who had to work the rest of the week. It was actually claimed, though, that the owners really installed the runway so that the audience could get closer to the near-nude show girls and that the Sunday night concerts were inaugurated in order to milk one more box-office turnover per week by presenting the show in street clothes and calling it a 'concert'. In this way they managed to overcome New York's 'blue' laws against Sunday performances.

There is another amusing story – which some claim to be absolutely true – concerning the origin of Jolson's famous down-on-one-knee pose. It was the opening night – February 6th, 1913 – of Jolson's show *The Honeymoon Express* at the Winter Garden. In the middle of a song Jolson became troubled by an ingrowing toe-nail and in an attempt to relieve the pain he dropped to one knee. The effect was sensational and the audience broke into spontaneous applause. Thus, another famous Jolson trademark was born. (Actually the whole thing sounds like one of Al's own publicity brainchilds).

During the next ten years Jolson consolidated his position as the golden boy of the Broadway set. His prestige as a star performer coupled with his abiding interest in politics brought him into frequent personal contact with the United States President Woodrow Wilson, who was a great show business fan and a fervent Jolson admirer. This meant that Al could often come home to visit his family in Washington, DC and stop by on the way to have breakfast with the President of the United States.

At a 1918 benefit show, Al followed the great Caruso, saying to the audience; "You ain't heard nothin' yet!" This obviously delighted the Jolson fans, but raised the hackles of the opera critics. The two singers later met privately and Jolson sang for Caruso, who was reportedly so impressed that he offered Jolson an operatic career at the Met. Fortunately for Broadway – or fortunately for the Metropolitan opera fans, whichever way you care to look at it – Jolson declined Caruso's offer.

In 1919 his marriage ended in divorce and three years later he married again, this time to actress Alma Osborne. In 1923 he began his long association with songwriter Harry Akst (of *Dinah* fame) who became his regular accompanist. The same year saw him starting work on his first silent film *Mammy's Boy* with the renowned film director D. W. Griffith, but Jolson was so disappointed and depressed with the initial results that he fled to Europe to avoid completing the film. His excuse being that he was "a rotten actor." Griffith sued the singer for breach of contract and won his case three years later in a New York court. Jolson was unable to convince the jury that he was a rotten film actor and a verdict for $2,627.28 was returned against the singer. 1926 was also the year in which his second marriage went on the rocks.

1927 was indeed a much better year in that it represented the high water mark of the entire Jolson career. He starred in the film *The Jazz Singer* – the first full length sound production – and in doing so created history by ushering in a new era in entertainment . . . the talkies!

The whole world was now at his feet and through the medium of talking pictures the Jolson legend became an international fact instead of a show business myth that only penetrated from the footlights to the box office and made the newspapers occasionally, Jolson was being seen – and heard – in every country in the world.

Following the stupendous success of *The Jazz Singer*, things got better and better for Al Jolson both professionally and privately and in 1928 he married popular actress and film star Ruby Keeler the same month (September) as the premiere of his second film, *The Singing Fool*.

And what a colourful premiere it was, taking place at the Winter Garden, New York on September 19th with special giant-size silver tickets featuring a black face silhouette of Jolson and selling for $11 top price. Those theatres wired for sound had been showing a special one-reel advance publicity film starring Al himself. Those not wired for sound closed for modification and quickly reopened with *The Singing Fool* as their premiere talkie. The results made Jolson richer and more famous than ever.

When Ruby Keeler opened in *Show Girl* at New York's Ziegfeld Theatre on July 2nd, 1929, Al – in true blue showbiz style – sang *Liza* to her from the audience just as he had been doing in the show's pre-Broadway run in Boston.

With his always larger-than-life approach, Jolson's mass appeal on stage as well as on the screen was based on his singing style which seemed to reach out and grab the listener by the lapels, thrust a tear-stained handkerchief into his hand and say pleadingly "Won't you join me in a good weep – surely, sir, you had a mammy once. Or maybe you've got a sonny boy at home right now who loves you and needs you. Go to him – but not until I've finished this song." During the making of the film *Say It With Songs*, Al gave a press interview in which he explained the effect behind such songs as *Sonny Boy* and *Mammy*:

". . . of course, they aren't real life. In real life Sonny Boy would generally rather sock you on the jaw than climb on your knee. Most of the Mammies, instead of having hands all toil-worn for me and that sort of thing, are stepping out with their boy friends having a good time. But that's just the very reason why the public loves 'em. If they were really like that, pictures like *The Singing Fool* and songs like *Mammy* wouldn't disturb a handkerchief. The public wants life as it'd like it to be, not as it is. They feel that Sonny Boys on knees and toil-worn Mammies are the way things ought to be, the way they would like things to be."

In 1935, after seven years of marriage, Al and Ruby adopted a seven-weeks old baby boy to make up for the child Al couldn't have. They christened him Al Jolson, Jr. Four years later he came home from 20th Century Fox studios where he was filming *Swanee River* to find his wife had left him and taken their son with her. She filed for a separation charging the singer with extreme cruelty leading to mental and physical suffering.

A month later Jolson fell ill and the following month the court granted Ruby a divorce giving her custody of the child.

By 1940 Jolson had become a very pathetic figure. No longer active in films or radio, he planned a big Broadway comeback with a show co-produced by himself and George Hale. He engaged Ruby Keeler for the cast in the feeble hope that his magnetic appeal before an audience would win her back. In out-of-town try-outs of the show he even took to telling the audiences, warm, sentimental anecdotes of their marriage which Ruby bitterly referred to as "personal remarks." Of Jolson's pitiful emotional state she was heard to say, "I can't understand Al's strange attitude." During the show's pre-Broadway run in Chicago she finally walked out.

When the show, which was called *Hold On To Your Hats*, did open on Broadway it proved to be a success. Jolson won both the critics and the public whilst the show itself received plaudits on almost every level. Hollywood quickly made bids for the screen rights, although they wanted it without Jolson.

During the run of *Hold On To Your Hats*, Al contracted psychosomatic grippe and pneumonia but nevertheless kept the show going. He installed microphones along the footlights in order to save his voice, but was finally forced to close the show after 158 continuous performances. He then went off to Florida alone, morose and dejected. The news came that Ruby Keeler had married again and had changed their son's name from Al Jolson, Jr to John Lowe, Jr.

World War II and the need for stars to entertain the troops overseas helped to snap Jolson out of his melancholia and gave him a new sense of purpose. Headlining USO camp shows his travels encompassed Alaska, the Aleutian Islands, England and Ireland. Further tours, with Harry Akst at the piano, took in the Caribbean, North Africa and Sicily.

On returning from a particularly gruelling tour of approximately 120 shows, Akst phoned his wife and then heard Al sobbing in the next room: "You've got someone to come home to. Who've I got? Not a soul in the world cares whether I live or die." In many ways the tour had been too much for his 58-year old frame and two days later he collapsed in an hotel lobby stricken with malaria.

In 1944 Jolson joined Columbia Pictures as a producer, and mulled over the proposed idea of filming his own life story. After recovering from his attack of malaria, he felt the urge to do some more singing and promptly embarked on yet another tour, but this time he concentrated on State-side hospitals and home-based training camps. One day in an army hospital at Hot Springs, Arkansas, he was asked for his autograph by a girl X-ray technician named Erle Galbraith with whom he struck up a warm friendship and later married.

January 1945 found Jolson in hospital undergoing an operation which necessitated the removal of two ribs and part of his left lung, causing him to sing four tones lower than before. Hearing the news of the operation, and expecting him to die, Associated Press actually issued a biographical obituary.

Columbia Pictures, more keen than ever to film the Jolson life story, prodded Al into agreement. At first he had visions of portraying himself but after taking an objective look at his sixty-year old face in a mirror, he said: "I don't want it. *Get* somebody." Whereupon Columbia's Harry Cohn signed rising young actor Larry Parks to play the part with Jolson's own singing voice on the sound-track – although, apparently, Al himself couldn't resist appearing on screen in long shot during some parts of the film. The result was a box office block-buster and succeeded in re-kindling Jolson's popularity as a big time recording artist. His records zoomed into the best-sellers, many of them were bought by teenage bobby-soxers who were under the impression that Jolson looked like Larry Parks. Over the past twenty or more years *The Jolson Story* has been re-issued again and again and is now listed amongst the biggest money-making movies of all time.

A 1949 sequel *Jolson Sings Again* also turned out to be a box-office winner and again his record sales were stimulated. Apart from his recordings of the songs featured in the two films, he also made records with such popular acts as The Andrews Sisters and The Mills Brothers.

Al and his wife Erle adopted a baby girl in 1949 whom they named Alicia. The child was later found to be mentally retarded. In December of 1949, Al and his wife travelled to Honolulu, Hawaii, where he gave a Christmas concert for 12,000 GIs. During the last month of his life Jolson worked tirelessly making thousands of more GIs happy with a final wartime tour of Japan and Korea in September 1950 – in which he gave 42 shows.

Back once more to the United States, and then on the evening of October 23rd at approximately 10.30 pm Al Jolson was fatally stricken with a coronary occlusion. He was 65 years old.

For the next two days, the world's newspapers carried glowing tributes to his talent and radio stations played his records night and day. 20,000 people attended his funeral in Hollywood on October 26th and Abel Green reported in *Variety* that it was 'the largest funeral gathering in Hollywood history.'

As a singer Jolson must loom large in the overall history of popular music. But while he has had scores of imitators, none of them have ever amounted to much in terms of true greatness. Jolson's own vocal greatness was part and parcel of his unique personality and gregarious character. When he died the singing style died with him. As a stylistic force he did very little to advance popular music, but as a singing *entertainer* he was the veritable fountainhead of inspiration for every performer who fancied his chances on the boards.

So what's to be made of this legendary barnstorming character called Jolson. Was he the greatest entertainer who ever lived? Or was he the most embarrassing ham of all time? Considering both questions with all their attendant polarities and conjectural ramblings, bearing in mind the colourful life he led and the vital effect he had on audiences, I would say that both definitions are correct.

At a well-attended Memorial Service for Al Jolson which took place at the Temple Rodelph Sholom in New York on October 29th, 1950, Eddie Cantor, who wrote and delivered the eulogy, observed "Jolson again turned them away."

Everything with Al was two and a half times larger than life. Even his last words were typical of him:

"Hell, Truman had only one hour with MacArthur – I had two."

## RECOMMENDED RECORDINGS

**THE JOLSON STORY – His Greatest Hits** (MCA): This might almost be regarded as the definitive album of Jolson. Certainly it contains most of the songs through which the general public identify him. Al is in excellent form here and with fourteen titles of the calibre of *April Showers, My Mammy, Sonny Boy* and *California, Here I Come*, it really does constitute a perfect basic representation of Jolson's work.

**AL JOLSON OVERSEAS** (Brunswick); This LP was issued as a tribute to Jolson's untiring efforts in entertaining the troops of the US armed forces in all parts of the world. Its release was requested by servicemen and ex-servicemen including General Douglas MacArthur. The titles, which were all recorded with the Lou Bring orchestra between 1947 and 1949, include *Whispering, Margie, Chinatown, My Chinatown, Peg O' My Heart* and *At Sundown*.

**THE IMMORTAL AL JOLSON** (Brunswick); Another fine selection of titles with Jolson in good voice. This album was one of several that were compiled from broadcasts from the late '40s. I have not yet had the opportunity to hear the other LPs, but if they measure up to the standard of these selections they can be safely recommended. Songs here include *Alexander's Ragtime Band, Rockabye Your Baby With A Dixie Melody, Best Things In Life Are Free* and Jolson's own composition *Nearest Thing To Heaven*. Accompaniments are directed by Lou Bring and the sound quality is very good indeed.

*No question about it, the happiest times in*
*my recording career were the days I worked*
*with Louis Armstrong. Just being in the same*
*room with this fellow when he's coming on*
*is a complete joy and inspiration – and I*
*really think some of it rubbed off on me . . .*

Bing Crosby

# Louis Armstrong

The importance of the late Louis Armstrong as a singer is often questioned in spite of the fact that his was one of the most individual voices that this century has ever known. But, to be fair, let us at least entertain some of this conjecture. For one thing it could be claimed that any stature Armstrong may have possessed as a singer was really subservient to his greater reputation as a jazz trumpeter – he was arguably the most influential exponent of the instrument in all of jazz history – and for another his actual singing voice, academically at least, left something to be desired (if you happen to be a John MacCormack fan, that is). But none of these arguments matter in the least, for on personality alone Louis was always most persuasive in his role of popular vocalist. This fact is well supported by such hugely successful recordings as *Gone Fishin'* (with Bing Crosby), *What A Wonderful World* and, of course, his multi-million selling version of *Hello Dolly*. And as a stylistic innovator he influenced countless popular singers with his fruity, gravelly voice and elegant phrasing.

As a jazz figure, Louis Armstrong became a legend in his own lifetime and as an international entertainer he was dubbed 'America's greatest ambassador.' As though in preparation for this he even managed to be born on the right day, July 4th (American Independence Day) in 1900.

Born in New Orleans, Louisiana, in under-privileged surroundings, Armstrong grew up with the twentieth century. Jazz was in its infancy at the same time he was, and as he grew up he became fascinated and affected by the early New Orleans jazz as it flowed out of the nearby brothels and bordellos, surfacing occasionally from its iniquitous honky-tonk surroundings to be heard at funerals, street parades and celebrations. It was during one of these celebrations that young 12 years old Louis was arrested for firing off a pistol. How he came to be in possession of such a firearm is something even Armstrong himself seemed unable to recall with any accuracy. What is certain, however, is that he was sent to a New Orleans home for waifs. And there he was given a cornet to play in the institution's band.

Some years later, in 1917, he joined Kid Ory's jazz band replacing his idol and good friend Joe 'King' Oliver who had left for Chicago. In 1918 the youthful Louis began playing on the famous Mississippi riverboats and as word of his exceptional playing ability got around, his fame began to spread as far as Chicago. In 1922 he accepted an invitation from Joe Oliver to join his celebrated Creole Jazz Band in Chicago. It was at this time that Louis made his first recordings with Oliver's band for the historic Gennett label. Included in these sessions were the original recordings of such jazz classics as *Dippermouth Blues* and *Canal Street Blues*.

Throughout the twenties, Armstrong's soaring reputation as an outstanding jazz soloist began to assume international proportions. His technical facility on the cornet was both the delight and envy of other musicians. The emotional quality and basic simplicity of his solos had no parallel in the jazz world, especially when he played the blues. He made many recordings, sometimes as an accompanist to such famous blues singers as Ma Rainey and the magnificent Bessie Smith, but most notably with groups under his own leadership (Louis Armstrong's Hot Five or Hot Seven). These particular sessions which took place between 1925 and 1928 are rightly regarded as classics of their kind.

During this highly creative period, Louis began to spread his musical talent a little further by switching from cornet to trumpet and singing the occasional vocal chorus on some of his recordings. On one such session, in February 1926, while singing a song called *Heebie Jeebies* the lyric sheet was said to have dropped off the music stand. In his recorded musical autobiography (a four-LP boxed set on the Brunswick label) Louis recalls in his own words what happened:

"This session was something special. After singing the regular words I just dropped the music and sang along in my own style – and they tell me that's how scat singing was born."

Armstrong has been responsible for many innovations in jazz and popular music. While it is not absolutely certain that he was the first singer to employ wordless phrases or "scat singing," it seems reasonable to assume that the *Heebie Jeebies* session was the first commercial, albeit accidental, exposure of the style.

With the emergence of Armstrong the singer came the enjoyable appearance of Armstrong the entertainer. By the mid-thirties his singing, not surprisingly, was finding favour with record buyers outside of the jazz world and in 1936 Bing Crosby, himself a staunch jazz supporter and Armstrong enthusiast, asked that Louis be given a part in the film *Pennies From Heaven*. Bing also saw to it that Armstrong was given some dialogue scenes as well as the chance to play trumpet and sing. A year or so later Louis appeared in another film, *Goin' Places*, which starred Dick Powell. It was in this film that he introduced a likeable novelty song which later became a big standard, *Jeepers Creepers*. These and other film appearances helped to establish Armstrong's jovial personality with the public at large. With his voice and face fitting so well together it is not hard to understand why his singing soon became more and more an essential part of his work as an entertainer.

As both a vocal entertainer and trumpeter, old Satchmo (an affectionate abbreviation of his old nickname 'Satchelmouth') was always an extremely hard worker. His doctors and friends were forever urging him to ease up and take life a little steadier. But his answer was always the same 'If I ain't got music, I ain't got nothin' and without my horn I'm dead.'

In 1959 when he suffered a severe attack of pneumonia his condition was so critical that no one believed that he could possibly rally. To everyone's surprise he recovered not only his health but also his reputation as the world's greatest jazz trumpeter. In the early sixties he played with a renewed vigour and with an enthusiastic freshness that certainly belied his age.

As a singer his popularity with mass audiences had never flagged right through the forties, fifties, and sixties. Even at the start of the seventies, when the advancing years were obviously getting the better of him and he was obliged to give up the trumpet, the Armstrong voice and personality remained as solidly entertaining as ever. He was seen on the screen adding his own special brand of magic to the Barbra Streisand musical *Hello Dolly* and he was heard on the soundtrack of the James Bond thriller *On Her Majesty's Secret Service* singing the film's love theme *All The Time In The World*.

If ever a performer belonged to his public it was Daniel Louis 'Satchmo' Armstrong. When he died on July 6th, 1971 – just two days after his seventy-first birthday – the tributes flooded in from all corners of the world and, naturally, from all areas of the music business. The world of jazz had lost its most revered citizen certainly, but popular music had also lost one of its most original and best-loved voices.

### RECOMMENDED RECORDINGS

Because of his legendary reputation as a trumpeter naturally not all of Louis Armstrong's vast recorded output features him as a singer, but for lovers of his vocal work the following LPs can be firmly recommended.

**LOUIS ARMSTRONG PLAYS W. C. HANDY** (CBS Realm); An excellent LP for jazz enthusiasts, this features Armstrong's All Stars in a well played selection of W. C. Handy's best known works (*St Louis Blues, Beale Street Blues*, etc) enriched by typically phrased and highly enjoyable vocals.

**HELLO DOLLY** (London): His biggest hit leads the way into a good programme of semi-Dixieland pieces and bouncy ballads.

**BING AND LOUIS** (Music For Pleasure): The Armstrong voice and trumpet are nicely presented in this wonderfully entertaining set of duets with Bing Crosby. The accent here is mainly on the personalities of the two artists with lots of skilfully delivered cross talk and humorous asides, but the singing carries plenty of weight too.

**THE SINGING STYLE OF LOUIS ARMSTRONG** (Verve VSP series): This two-disc package is culled from a series of albums which Armstrong recorded for jazz impresario Norman Granz between 1957 and 1960. The emphasis here is on such excellent standard material as *There's No You, Blues In The Night* and Rodgers' and Hart's *Have You Met Miss Jones?* It is often apparent that the Armstrong voice is not physically suited to such difficult and sophisticated material. But what he lacks in vocal stamina he makes up for in personality and musicianship. Accompaniments vary between a large orchestra arranged and conducted by Russ Garcia and a quartet led by pianist Oscar Peterson. A major highlight of this set is a beautifully paced rendering of the Cole Porter classic *Let's Do It* which is done in slow tempo complete with opening verse and all four choruses. Apart from hearing Armstrong's singing at its best and most subtle, this performance – all eight and a half minutes of it – affords the listener the extreme pleasure of revelling in some rare and vintage Porter lyrics which have been neglected in other recordings of this song.

**ELLA AND LOUIS** (Music For Pleasure): The same recording of *Let's Do It* pops up again in this collection extracted from a series of sessions recorded for Norman Granz's Verve label in 1957 some of which teamed Armstrong with Ella Fitzgerald. Superb though this album is there is a far more comprehensive survey of these sessions available on a Verve two-disc set bearing the same title:

**ELLA AND LOUIS** (Verve VSP series): This magnificent package collates on two records all the duets which Louis recorded with Ella Fitzgerald in 1956 and 1957 accompanied by pianist Oscar Peterson leading an excellent rhythm section. There are numerous highlights in this memorable release and particularly outstanding is *Stompin' At the Savoy*, which was recorded during a rehearsal catching both artists at their spontaneous and creative best.

**THE BEAUTIFUL AMERICANS** – **Louis Armstrong and Duke Ellington** (Roulette): This 1972 reissue of two LPs recorded in the early '60s is a particularly fine example of Armstrong's distinctive vocal work. All the songs are from the famous Ellington stable and the Duke himself provides sympathetic keyboard accompaniments to Louis' brilliant vocals. Two very interesting and contrasting samples of Armstrong singing are: *I Got It Bad And That Ain't Good*. (The difficult jump of a ninth in the first bar is usually off-putting to limited singers. Louis, of course, cheats a little at this point but his substituting phrase is still in keeping with the song's mood and the performance as a whole is quite moving) and *I'm Beginning To See The Light*, an outstanding rhythmic performance, particularly the last vocal chorus where Louis applies staggered phrases, skilfully editing the lyrics ("*I'm Beginning . . .*"). His trumpet work throughout this double album is also worthy of his legendary reputation.

Louis Armstrong is also featured to good effect on the soundtrack recording of the film 'High Society' (Capitol). Here he shares vocal honours with Bing Crosby and Frank Sinatra. He can be heard singing on only two tracks, *High Society Calypso*, and, in duet with Crosby, *Now You Has Jazz*. His trumpet is heard accompanying Crosby in two other songs *Little One* and *Samantha*.

> *He has one of the most amazing talents*
> *for making hard work look easy.*
> Danny Kaye

# Bing Crosby

It becomes difficult to evaluate Bing Crosby's contribution to popular music without reeling off a whole string of incredible statistics. For instance, his 1942 recording of *White Christmas* became far and away the most commercially successful record of all time. Up to 1965 it had sold more than twenty five million copies. His total disc sales to 1964 were estimated at a staggering figure of two hundred and fifty million (and it is worth remembering that the majority of these sales were achieved before the days of full scale commercial plugging and high-pressure personality selling). Since Crosby first entered a recording studio in 1926 he has recorded over 2,600 titles.

Statistically speaking, Bing Crosby must be the most successful popular singer of all time. His is one of the great success stories of the twentieth century. The problem here is to separate the singer from the statistics and to put the Crosby talent into its true perspective. To glean information from the singer himself does not help much for during a press interview, Crosby himself once remarked: "My talent is so thin it's almost transparent." And in his celebrated autobiography, typically entitled, *Call Me Lucky*, he explained his success:

> "Every man who sees one of my movies or who listens to my records or who hears me on the radio, believes firmly that he sings as well as I do, especially when he's in the bathroom shower. It's no trick for him to believe this because I have none of the mannerisms of a trained singer and I have very little voice."

Be that as it may, it would probably be more to the point to say that in films and on records Crosby has always projected a warm and friendly personality that the average man-in-the-street likes to identify himself with. But to enjoy sustained popularity for something like forty years there has to be more to Crosby's success than the ability to parade the nicer side of his nature before the public or to sing with the simple ease of a man taking a bath.

*Above:* Al Jolson as the world remembers him best of all—with black face—pictured in a scene from the 1936 film *The Singing Kid*...
/Vitagraph Inc

*Left:*...and as he was, without the make-up...
/MCA Records

*Below:* The Al Jolson Memorial Shrine, designed by sculptor Paul Williams, is sited in Hillside Memorial Park near Inglewood, California—the ultimate accolade to an extraordinary artist. The genuflecting Jolson is a composition of 100 professional photographs chosen by Mrs Jolson. The bronze statue is three-quarter life-size, and is surrounded by an open circular colonnade of Grecian motif constructed of white marble.

*Above:* The warm, irrepressible personality of the universally
beloved Louis Armstrong is captured perfectly in this shot from
the 1954 film *The Glenn Miller Story* in which he made a stunning
guest appearance. Apart from his supremacy as a trumpet
player, the late, great 'Satchmo' was one of the most distinctive
of all vocalists—and a pioneer stylist in popular singing.
*/Universal International*

*Right:* Perhaps the most successful solo singer of them all, Bing
Crosby still holds the world record for collective disc sales (the
present total is somewhere around the 300 million mark). The
'Old Groaner' is his usual amiable self in this shot from the 1958
film *Say One For Me./20th Century Fox*

Bing, in his first major
Hollywood movie *The Big
Broadcast* (1932). With him in
this scene is jazz guitar great,
Eddie Lang. Lang was a
regular accompanist to Crosby,
both on records and
broadcasts. In fact, Bing
personally insisted that Lang's
name was written into all of his
professional commitments.
Photos of the two together are
something of a rarity./*Paramount*

During his days as a college
student, Bing Crosby
commenced his musical career
as a drummer. Here, in this
offscreen shot—taken on the set
of the 1956 musical *High Society*
—Bing gets together with Louis
Armstrong for an impromptu
'blow'.

Well, did you EVER...! It's Bing and 'one of the newer fellows'.
Here, Crosby and his long-time friend and rival Frank Sinatra
clown it up during an unforgettable duet sequence from *High
Society*. It was the first time in their long careers that the two had
actually co-starred in a major film./*MGM*

*Above:* Ella Fitzgerald learned her vocal art with the vibrant Chick Webb orchestra in the '30s. Here, a youthful Ella is pictured making an outdoor broadcast for Radio Station WNEW, New York./*Melody Maker*

*Above right:* Ella, in one of her rare screen appearances, is seen in a lighter moment from the 1960 film *Let No Man Write My Epitaph,* in which she played a narcotics addict./*Columbia Pictures*

*Right:* A happy Ella Fitzgerald, pictured during a mid-'60s recording session at London's EMI Studios, Abbey Road.
/*EMI Records Ltd*

A popular twosome in Hollywood musicals emanating from the MGM company was that of Judy Garland and Mickey Rooney. No need to say which particular film *this* shot comes from...!/MGM

17-years-old Judy, pictured above in her most celebrated role from the early years. Co-starring with Judy in the 1939 *The Wizard of Oz* were (left to right): Bert Lahr, Jack Haley and Ray Bolger. For her efforts in *The Wizard of Oz*, Judy Garland received a special Academy Award 'for her outstanding performance as a screen juvenile'./MGM

Judy and musical friends in her
big comeback film, *A Star is
Born* (1954). In the scene
pictured above, Judy posed
wistfully as she sings *The Man
That Got Away*—possibly *the*
musical highlight from the
picture which gained for the
legendary star an Academy
Award nomination./*Warner Bros*

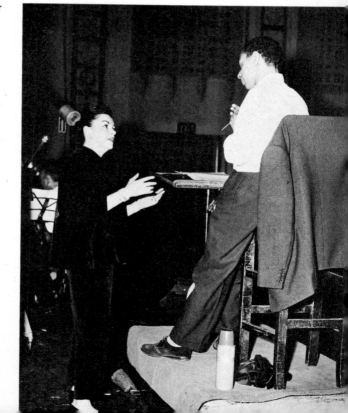

Exchanging musical viewpoints
during a London recording
session are Judy Garland and
British Musical Director/
Arranger Geoff Love.

Spotlight on a star: Judy entertaining on stage in her own
inimitable way.../*United Artists Corporation Ltd*

On stage at New York's Paramount Theatre—a happy-looking
Frank Sinatra, together with the orchestra of trombonist Tommy
Dorsey (pictured far left), with whom he spent two years as
vocalist (1940–2)./*Courtesy Fred Wadsworth*

Sailor-suited Frank Sinatra and Gene Kelly trip the light fantastic during a sequence when both sang *I begged Her,* from the 1944 MGM musical, *Anchors Aweigh./MGM*

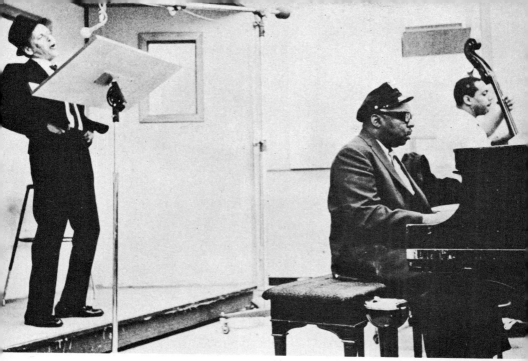

*Above left:* Sinatra, in melancholy mood, as a cynical songwriter, seems unconsoled by the attractive presence of Doris Day, in this shot from the 1954 film *Young at Heart.* Amongst the many fine songs Sinatra sang in this film were classics like *One For My Baby, Just One Of Those Things,* and *Someone to Watch Over Me.*
/Warner Bros

*Left:* A typical shot of Frank Sinatra, caught in mid-song at a 1960's recording session in Hollywood./Reprise Records

*Above:* Recording together for the first time: two musical giants, Frank Sinatra and Count Basie, make swinging music in an October, 1962, session. Basie's then bass player, Buddy Catlett, is pictured far right.
/Reprise Records

*Right:* The Guv'nor sings...
/Reprise Records

"Danny Thomas, who stars with Peggy Lee in 'The Jazz Singer,' isn't Thomas any more: he's an up-to-date Jolson copy"

*Above:* A friendly word in the ear from Al Jolson to Peggy Lee during a February, 1949 Kraft Music Hall broadcast.

*Above right:* Peggy Lee, with co-star Danny Thomas, in the 1953 remake of Jolson's *The Jazz Singer.*/*Warner Bros*

*Right:* Between 'takes' at a recording session. The musical director puts the orchestra through its paces while Peggy, cigarette in one hand and music sheet in the other, sings along. /*Courtesy of David Cavanaugh, Capitol Records, Hollywood, Calif*

The famous King Cole Trio at a CBS radio broadcast of the
'40s. *Left to right:* Oscar Moore (guitar), Nat King Cole (piano
and vocals) and Johnny Miller (bass).

Nat Cole, the stand-up singer and ballad stylist *par excellence,* in action.

Cole at the keyboard during a Capitol recording session. */Courtesy of David Cavanaugh, Capitol Records, Hollywood, Calif*

Harry Lillis Crosby was born on May 2nd, 1904 (or 1901, depending on your source of reference) in Tacoma, Washington, the fourth of the seven children of Harry and Kate Crosby. In 1906 the family moved to another Washington township, Spokane, where young Harry attended Webster School. It was around the age of seven that he stopped being known as Harry Crosby and became Bing. Being a devoted reader of a comic strip feature called the Bing-ville Bugle, his classmates took to nicknaming him 'Bingo from Bingville'. This name was later abbreviated and he was always known thereafter as Bing.

The Crosby family were by no means rich. It often became necessary for the boys to work at odd jobs out of school hours and Bing enjoyed a somewhat checkered career in part-time employment. It covered such diverse activities as an early morning paper round, working in a logging camp, apple picking, assistant bookkeeper and junior assistant in the prop department of a theatre. "It was there," recalls Crosby, "that the first priming coat of show business rubbed off on me."

His initial theatrical experiences were the elocution contests in which he took part at school, delivering such sterling classics as Robert W. Service's 'The Shooting of Dan McGrew' and 'Spartacus to the Gladiators'. He also appeared in many school plays. His real interest, however, was in the popular tunes of the day – following his father's purchase of an old wind-up gramophone:

" . . . everybody in Spokane knew when I was coming because they could hear me singing or whistling. I suppose that was because of having a dad who was always bringing a new tune into the house on sheet music or on record – I had a constant succession of them in my head. And I had to whistle or sing to get them out.

My mother once took me to a singing 'professor' for a couple of lessons, and the professor took my popular stuff away from me and told me to practice breathing and tone production in a certain way. As a result, I lost interest in singing for a long, long time."

In 1920, Crosby entered Gonzaga University as a law student and it was here that his interest in singing was rekindled. With a friend, Al Rinker, he formed a group called The Juicy Seven which later became The Musicaladers. Al played piano while Bing played drums and sang. They were, as Bing remembers: " . . . ragged but novel . . . the other musicians could read music, but they could not play the stuff the way we played it. Young folks liked us and two or three nights a week we got dates to play at high school dances and private parties."

As his legal studies progressed, Crosby became less happy about the handling of affidavits and the typing of briefs. This state of mind was nurtured by the knowledge that he could make more money out of singing and playing drums, so he and Al Rinker decided to take a chance on a musical future. Their decision, not unnaturally, met with much parental opposition but Al's sister, Mildred

Rinker – whose professional name was Mildred Bailey – was already a most successful and influential singer and she offered to help the boys by giving them some useful contacts.

The next few years were full of ups and downs, but the boys managed to keep working. As a singer, Bing was absorbing all sorts of influences from vaudeville routines to tricky jazz phrasing. His biggest idol was Al Jolson, but possibly his most useful influences were Louis Armstrong, Mildred Bailey and jazz guitarist, Eddie Lang, with whom he worked while singing with the Paul Whiteman orchestra as part of a vocal trio popularly known as The Rhythm Boys. Bing and Al were previously working as a duo until Whiteman teamed them up with a hot piano player named Harry Barris. One of the first hits they had on record was a song called *Mississippi Mud*, which was written by Barris.

The Rhythm Boys, with their snappy brand of song presentation, soon became one of the major attractions of each Paul Whiteman concert or club date. Crosby's solo vocals were also attracting attention both on stage and on record. In due time, he began making records under his own name and one of these – *I Surrender Dear* – was heard by William S. Paley, head of CBS Broadcasting network, while on an ocean liner trip to Europe in 1931. Paley was impressed by the voice and unusual style, asked for the singer's name, and wired instructions to the CBS Artists Bureau to locate and sign Crosby for a series.

Meanwhile Bing had been making a minor impression in films, having done a string of short comedies for Mack Sennett. He went to New York in response to CBS and in September of 1931 he began a fifteen-minute evening series, five times a week which went out through the entire CBS network. After six gruelling years of learning his craft, Bing Crosby became an 'overnight sensation'. He was booked into New York's Paramount Theatre. Hollywood, offered film contracts and, of course, his records were now in great demand. Among the many fine songs he recorded at this time were *Out Of Nowhere*, *Sweet And Lovely*, *Wrap Your Troubles In Dreams* and *Stardust*.

His film songs, too, were of a similar high standard – *Easy To Remember*, *June In January*, *Love Is Just Around The Corner*, *Temptation*, *I Wished On The Moon* and *Pennies From Heaven*. Throughout the thirties and forties his screen career soared despite, certainly not because of, the quality of his films. However, the famous series of 'Road' films in which he was teamed most effectively with Bob Hope and Dorothy Lamour are an exception. So is *Going My Way*, a sentimental-cum-religious movie which was distinguished by an Academy Award-winning performance by Crosby in 1944. This film also contained the Oscar-winning song of that year, *Swinging On A Star*.

The Crosby style of singing does not sit awfully well with listeners of the '70s, but throughout the late '20s, '30s, '40s and even well into the '50s no other singer – with the possible exception of Frank Sinatra – ever had such a wide, far-reaching influence as did Crosby. Before Bing came along, square phrasing and the over-precise diction of pompous tenors and the like dominated the music scene. Bing changed all that by applying a more relaxed approach to the words and a more creative method of phrasing. Even today, the basic elements of Crosby's singing style can be heard in singers like Andy Williams, Tony Bennett, Dean Martin and Sinatra.

On record, Crosby is a somewhat inconsistent performer. His recording career is full of peaks and dips. Certainly no one could ever call him a perfectionist, yet somehow he always manages to emerge, even from his trashiest recordings, as a musically capable singer. From the evidence on many of his recordings, Crosby does not appear to be a very conscientious worker. He pays little attention to the emotional content of lyrics and tackles high notes (even in his hey-day anything above D in the stave was decidedly shaky) like a man crossing a flimsy bridge unperturbed by the knowledge that it may collapse at any moment. But somehow with Crosby it never does. With characteristic wit, Bing once described himself as 'a journeyman sea-level baritone'.

On the credit side, however, Crosby's vocal assets are – or at least were – considerable. On a good day, his tone was quite breathtaking and his uncanny sense of phrasing – even nearing 70 – is something his imitators seem unable to copy. This is particularly evident at a fast or swinging tempo when his voice articulates with all the flexibility and punchy warmth of a well played string bass. One of the best examples of this can be found on the so-called soundtrack LP of the 1956 film *High Society* in which he duets most effectively with the late Louis Armstrong in a highly entertaining piece of nonsense called *Now You Has Jazz*.

In summing up Bing Crosby as a popular singer, those awesome statistics notwithstanding, he emerges creditably as a talented practitioner of his craft – and with enough personality for three men. Someone once described Bing's rise to fame from his humble beginnings to multi-million dollar opulence as nothing short of inspirational.

"This idea sounds strictly out of the popper to me," wrote Crosby in his autobiography. "In America we like to tell our youngsters that the way to succeed is by hard work and self-sacrifice. If you read my story, it'll be obvious to you – it's obvious to me – that I haven't worked very hard.

The things I've done are the things I wanted to do. Doing them was no great sacrifice. And I've been heavily paid for having fun while I did them. Singing or movie acting has never been drudgery for me. So I don't know that my story contains an inspirational point of view. However, it is certainly shot full of another American commodity – luck."

Luck, yes, but I have a strong feeling that skill and talent also had something to do with it.

RECOMMENDED RECORDINGS

**BING CROSBY IN HOLLYWOOD – 1930–1934** (CBS two-disc pack): A wonderfully historic collection of Crosby's early film songs. It traces his development over the four-year period from his vocal group work with Paul Whiteman's Rhythm Boys in the 1930 film, *The King Of Jazz*, through his early solo appearances in *The Big Broadcast* (1932) to his playing of romantic leads in *We're Not Dressing* and *She Loves Me Not* (1934). This set also demonstrates how much better Crosby was by comparison with other singers of the day. Included in the *King Of Jazz* segment of this album are two non-Crosby tracks, one of which – *It Happened In Monterey* – contains an unbelievably bad vocal by Johnny Fulton that was typical of the period. Compare this with Crosby's version of *Dinah* (track one, side two); the difference is staggering. Just think of the effect it must have had in those days.

**THE BING CROSBY STORY – Volume One: The Early Jazz Years, 1928–1932** (CBS 2-disc Pack): Like the early Hollywood set, this is another revealing testament to Crosby's individuality during the late twenties and early thirties. Also like the other set it is chronologically programmed, starting with tracks he recorded as part of The Rhythm Boys (as singer and drummer) then covering his first solo records under his own name (*My Kinda Love* and *Till We Meet*) in 1929. The rest of the collection takes the listener through some good and not so good performances and culminates in some very effective and historically interesting items of 1932. These include two fairly contrasting takes of *St Louis Blues* (with Duke Ellington's orchestra) and a lively version of *Sweet Georgia Brown*.

Considering the age of these recordings the sound re-mastering is excellent.

**BING – A Musical Autobiography** (5 LPs in a box with booklet. Originally recorded for American Decca. Issued here on Brunswick): The value of this expansive set is indeed considerable since it has a spoken commentary by Crosby in which he recalls his eventful career as a singer. Accompanied for the most part by the Buddy Cole Trio, Crosby offers brief but pleasant versions of many of his early hits for the first half of this set. The second half is given over to the original recordings with Bing in the entertaining role of disc jockey as he introduces each recording with an anecdote or a few well-chosen words. Some of his commentary, though, contains slight historical inaccuracies which many connoisseurs have since pointed out to him. As a recorded document, however, it is well worth owning.

**BING SINGS WHILST BREGMAN SWINGS** (Originally released in 1956 on the Verve label, it was recently reissued on *Music For Pleasure* minus two tracks): This is arguably Crosby's best LP from his later period. His phrasing is excellent and the songs are all well selected. The only shortcomings are the somewhat ham-fisted orchestrations of Buddy Bregman and the odd moment or two when the sound balancing goes awry. Despite the confusion around him Bing emerges with cool distinction and delivers good readings of *The Blue Room, Have You Met Miss Jones* and *September In The Rain.*

**FANCY MEETING YOU HERE** (RCA): Teaming Bing effectively with Rosemary Clooney, the marvellous Billy May orchestra and a bunch of fine songs about various countries, this album delightfully explores the 'travel' theme used in so many other LPs. Miss Clooney is a perfect foil for Bing's vocal personality and both singers appear to enjoy themselves immensely. (NB This LP has now been reissued – minus two tracks – on the RCA International label under the new title *Rendezvous.*)

**AROUND THE WORLD IN DIXIELAND** (Capitol-World Record Club): This second album with Rosemary Clooney is far less sophisticated than the RCA LP, but it is enjoyable nevertheless. The 'travel' theme has been retained, but this time everything is tied to a two-beat Dixieland feel. The result is reminiscent of Bing's pre-war duets with Connee Boswell. Miss Clooney, though she is no Boswell, responds happily to Crosby's bouncy phrasing and Billy May's tongue-in-cheek backings raise a smile or two. More of a personality record really, but good fun for those with catholic tastes.

**BING AND LOUIS** (Music For Pleasure): Crosby is quoted as saying the happiest times in his recording career were the days he worked with Louis Armstrong. It certainly seems to be the case with this LP. The crisp showmanship of both artists and the obvious enjoyment that went into the making of this record reveals itself on practically every song.

**HIGH SOCIETY** (Capitol): Bing shares the vocal honours, on this album selection from the 1956 film, with Frank Sinatra and Louis Armstrong. Highlights for Crosby include *I Love You Samantha, Little One, Well, Did You Ever* (with Sinatra) and *Now You Has Jazz* (with Armstrong). The film's big hit song, *True Love* – sung by Crosby and Grace Kelly – is really a bore, though.

**BING 'N' BASIE** (Daybreak): A superb, albeit surprising, album from Crosby. Superb, because he is in fine voice and because both the songs and the excellent Count Basie accompaniments suit him to a tee. Surprising, because it was recorded in February and March 1972 – just a few weeks before his seventy-first birthday. It proves that when he chooses to be conscientious about his singing, he can still show his rivals a thing or two about song interpretation, so shrewdly does Bing deliver his phrases, carefully pacing each sustained note, that the ravages of time are barely noticeable. As always he sings with great rhythmic buoyancy and, of course, charm. Armchair listening at its best.

*In Ella's singing the glides and jumps*
*are as graceful as a dance by Astaire . . .*
*Let the young ones listen. Ella is rare!*
Harold Arlen

# Ella Fitzgerald

If someone was given the difficult task of compiling a short list of, say, the six best popular singers of all time, there would certainly be something radically wrong if the list didn't include Ella Fitzgerald. On a purely interpretative level, the diligent connoisseurs could possibly find a dozen reasons why Miss Fitzgerald should not be included on the list, but no amount of microscopic analysis can obscure the fact that Ella Fitzgerald is a singer of true greatness, an artist whose musical assets far outweigh her stylistic shortcomings.

One of the main points that distinguishes her from other vocal giants is that she has never made any great attempt to mould herself into a show business personality. She remains – after thirty-five years in the business – purely and simply a singer. True, there have been two or three film appearances (and in one of these, *Let No Man Write My Epitaph*, she even made a half-hearted attempt at playing the part of a drug addict) but they were merely organised excuses for her to sing for film audiences. As Ella herself once said: "The only thing better than singing is more singing."

She rarely gives press interviews and on the occasions when she has, the results have not been terribly interesting. Not that she is an unintelligent person: she is just not particularly talkative. Singing is what she likes to do and singing is what she does best of all. Fellow singers and musicians with whom she has worked all readily attest to this fact. "Singing is her whole life," said guitarist Barney Kessell. "I remember when we were on tour in Europe with *Jazz At The Philharmonic*, she and I would get together and have little jam sessions in restaurants and on buses. She would make up lyrics and sing in the style of other singers and do everything possible with her voice. There is just no limit to her imagination or interest in singing."

Born on April 25th, 1918 in Newport News, Virginia, Ella started on the road to stardom quite early in life when, at the age of fourteen, she drew lots with a couple of her friends to see who should go in for a big amateur talent contest at Harlem's Apollo Theatre. Young Ella drew the shortest straw and entered the competition . . . as a dancer (she was more interested at first in dancing than singing, and was considered by her teenage friends to be a champion dancer). But on the night of the contest she nervously changed her mind about dancing and decided to sing. With virtually no rehearsal, she sang a now forgotten Hoagy Carmichael song called *Judy*. To her surprise she won not only the $25 prize money but three encores as well.

Bandleader Benny Carter was at the Apollo and was impressed enough to bring her to the attention of famous critic, John Hammond. Together they arranged for Ella to meet Fletcher Henderson, the talented arranger and bandleader. "I guess I didn't make too much of an impression," recalls Ella, "because Fletcher said he'd get in touch with me later, but nothing ever happened."

Undeterred, Ella continued entering various amateur contests and news of her healthy singing ability spread downtown to the CBS broadcasting offices where someone spoke of putting her on a show with one of the top singers of the day, Arthur Tracy the Street Singer, of *Marta* fame. Ella successfully auditioned, a contract was prepared and she was said to be in line for a buildup similar to that of Connee Boswell's – this offer was especially impressive as far as Ella was concerned, for Connee Boswell, best known then as principal singer in the Boswell Sisters vocal trio, happened to be Ella's favourite singer and original influence. But at this point the dream went awry when Ella's mother died suddenly, leaving her with no one legally responsible for signing documents on her behalf.

Shortly after her mother's death, Ella was living with her aunt. One night at an amateur show, Ella sang *Lost In A Fog*. The pianist was unfamiliar with the song as a result of which Ella really did get lost musically. She was booed off the stage by the impatient audience for the only time in her life; at all her other amateur appearances she had won prizes. In tears, she ran home to her aunt who told her: "Keep trying. Those people who booed you will come back some day and appreciate you." Those words were probably uttered more in consolation than in earnest, but in view of Ella's subsequent success, the comment was a monumental understatement.

Ella's elusive and long-delayed professional debut finally arrived in the shape of a week's engagement at the Harlem Opera House, for a fee of $50. Because she was still under age she had to regretfully turn down a full-time offer to join the orchestra of Tiny Bradshaw, who was part of that week's show. Seeking to be of some help to the desperate teenager, Bradshaw and the chorus girls held a quick collection to buy Ella a suitable gown. The following week, when the famous Chick Webb orchestra was appearing at the theatre, an audition was organised in front of a reluctant Webb who felt he had been tricked into giving up some of his precious time to listen to this gawky teenager. He was convinced that one vocalist with his band was enough; he already had a somewhat uninspired male singer on his payroll. Accompanied only by the band's guitarist, Ella stood awkwardly in Webb's dressing room and sang the only three songs she knew – songs she had learned from listening to Connee Boswell's broadcasts. Though still not convinced that he needed another singer, Webb grudgingly agreed that the youngster had talent and offered to use her on a one night stand at Yale University. The audience reaction on that date was so encouraging that a week later Ella opened with the Chick Webb orchestra at Harlem's Savoy Ballroom, the world famous 'Home of Happy Feet'.

Because of her age, Ella was still ineligible for full-time work without proper consent from a legal guardian. By this time Chick Webb, who proved to be a kindly person at heart, took Ella under his wing and went through the process of having himself appointed as her legal guardian. He took her into his home and both he and his wife accepted her as a member of the household.

Before he finally launched Ella as a full-time singer with his band in 1935, he went through almost a year of preparatory planning. He taught her how to project and talk to an audience. Every night Ella would sit patiently off-stage in scores of different dance halls and concert theatres until she had absorbed every musical move of the men with whom she was to work. Sometimes in the early evenings, Webb would lead Ella onto a deserted stage or bandstand and show her how she should make a correct appearance. He showed her what to do with her hands and the best way to make an exit when she had finished her songs. He taught her how to make the best use of her flexible vocal range – almost three octaves – and how to effectively apply her considerable sense of rhythm to the best advantage.

On June 12th, 1935, Ella made her first recordings with the band for the American Decca label. The titles were *Love And Kisses* and *Are You Here To Stay*. Two fairly indifferent little songs, they formed the beginning of one of the most durable recording careers in the history of popular music. But a somewhat more important recording session for Ella and the Chick Webb band took place on May 2nd, 1938. The song recorded was a special adaptation, by Ella in collaboration with Al Feldman, of the old nursery rhyme, *A-Tisket, A-Tasket*. It became the biggest record ever made by the Webb band and it firmly established Ella as a top singer in her own right.

When Chick Webb died of tuberculosis on June 16th, 1939, Ella took over the leadership of the band for a while. But she realised it was not an easy gap to fill. Webb had been no ordinary bandleader; he had surmounted the handicaps of colour prejudice and his own physical deformity (although he was a hunchback, he became one of the most skilfully exciting drummers in all of jazz). In 1940 Ella disbanded the orchestra and set out on a solo career. Throughout the '40s she made several successful recordings for American Decca, such as *Into Each Life Some Rain Must Fall* and *My Happiness*. In addition to her increasing popularity in cabaret and concerts, she worked frequently for jazz impresario Norman Granz, and appeared on his annual tours with *Jazz At The Philharmonic*. These tours, in which Granz presented the biggest names in jazz on one bill, took Ella to Europe and Japan and did much to increase her international following. Many of her recordings during the '40s were hampered by low-class repertoire and uninspired accompaniments, although she was nearly always capable of giving a compelling performance no matter what the conditions. This situation was rectified when, in 1955, her 20-year affiliation with Decca ended and she started to record for Norman Granz on his newly-formed Verve label. Granz also became her personal manager and under his astute guidance her career blossomed on a much broader and more profitable scale. Her first film appearance in *Pete Kelley's Blues* supplemented her already favourable reputation as a first-class singer in late 1955.

Norman Granz wisely decided that she ought to record material that was worthy of her musical talents and he initiated the famous 'Songbook' series of LPs in which Ella recorded the works of the most consistently talented composers in popular music. The expansive – and expensive – series was commenced in 1956 with a two-LP tribute to the works of Cole Porter. This was followed by further two-disc albums devoted to Rodgers and Hart, Irving Berlin and Harold Arlen. Duke Ellington was honoured and co-featured with Ella in a four-disc tribute, while the George and Ira Gershwin Songbook consumed no fewer than five LPs. Later items in the series were devoted to Jerome Kern and Johnny Mercer. Granz certainly kept Ella busy in the recording studios for, in addition to the Songbook sessions, she also recorded five LPs with Louis Armstrong (two of these were devoted to a special interpretation of Gershwin's *Porgy And Bess*), one with the Count Basie orchestra and numerous albums with such top arrangers as Nelson Riddle, Marty Paich and Frank de Vol.

During 1957, Ella set several precedents, appearing at the celebrated Copacabana night club in New York and presenting her own concert at the Hollywood Bowl. In April, 1958 she held a special concert at New York's Carnegie Hall in company with Duke Ellington to launch and celebrate the release of the four-LP set, *Ella Sings The Duke Ellington Songbook*. Her European tours became – and still are – a firm annual event.

Although Ella is generally regarded as a jazz singer, her appeal cuts across many different areas of taste. The fact that she has sold more than 25 million records would seem to suggest that she is more of a pop singer than a jazz singer. Certainly, she has been involved in a fair number of recording sessions aimed at a more esoteric market, but her finest – and indeed her most musical – work has been in the more popular context of the Songbook albums. It is these albums which bring to the fore all her musical virtues of tone and phrasing etc. To a somewhat lesser extent, these recordings also bring her stylistic shortcomings into focus. For example, on hearing such tracks as *Manhattan* (Rodgers and Hart Songbook), where she breathes in the middle of a word, or *Change Partners* (Irving Berlin Songbook), in which she sings a set of lyrics which were obviously intended to be sung by a male singer, to say nothing of the even more incongruous *Top Hat, White Tie and Tails*, it becomes obvious that Ella could hardly be called a thoughtful lyric interpreter. Musically immaculate, she is. Dramatically inspired, she is not – except on certain occasions when the song happens to jell with her own cosy personality. Then the results can be quite breathtaking.

Dotted throughout the Songbooks are numerous examples of Ella at her best: *How About Me, Get Thee Behind Me, Satan* and *You're Laughing At Me* from the Irving Berlin Songbook; *Easy To Love, Let's Do It, Ev'ry Time We*

*Say Goodbye* and, surprisingly, *Love For Sale* from the Cole Porter Songbook; *Sophisticated Lady* and *I Let A Song Go Out Of My Heart* from the Ellington Songbook; and from the Gershwin Songbook such beauties as *By Strauss, For You, For Me, Forever More, Isn't It A Pity, Embraceable You* and *Funny Face*. So in spite of their shortcomings, the Songbooks offer the best representation of the work of Ella Fitzgerald, undoubtedly one of the best half dozen singers in the wild and sprawling world of popular music.

RECOMMENDED RECORDINGS
**THE SONGBOOKS** – *Cole Porter* (2-discs), *Rodgers and Hart* (2-discs) – these two collections show Ella in good voice, but are slightly marred by inconsistent orchestrations from Buddy Bregman. *Irving Berlin* (2-discs) – fine accompaniments from Paul Weston. *Harold Arlen* (2-discs) – with flashy arrangements from Billy May, featuring numerous jazz solos. *Duke Ellington* (4-discs) – backed, not over successfully, by the Ellington band plus various excellent small groups; this set also features a four-part instrumental tribute from Duke to Ella. *George and Ira Gershwin* (5-discs) – arranged and conducted by Nelson Riddle. *Jerome Kern* (1-disc) and *Johnny Mercer* (1-disc) both accompanied by Riddle. The Kern set is perhaps the least effective vocally, but the songs are good.

**ELLA SWINGS LIGHTLY** (Verve): A beautifully sung collection of rhythmic standards and novelties (16 songs in all). Ella is in splendidly buoyant form with excellent small band backings from Marty Paich.

**HELLO LOVE** (Verve): An expertly produced album of favourite ballads – *So Rare, Stairway To The Stars*, etc – warmly performed by Ella with nice support from Frank de Vol.

**ELLA AND BASIE** (Verve): Bright and bouncy package of well-liked songs with Ella in happy voice with the Count Basie band playing some nicely constructed Quincy Jones arrangements. Highspots include *On The Sunny Side Of The Street, Dream A Little Dream Of Me* and the Basie favourite *Shiny Stockings* which comes complete with Ella's own lyrics.

**WHISPER NOT** (Verve): Ella with Marty Paich arrangements singing a nicely varied bunch of standards such as *Sweet Georgia Brown* and *Thanks For The Memory*.

**ELLA AND LOUIS** (Verve VSP two-disc pack): A vastly entertaining set of duets in which some well-known songs come in for some fairly off-beat treatments. Louis Armstrong clowns around in a good-natured manner while Ella invests each song with her lovely tone and warm phrasing – except for a brief impersonation of Armstrong at the end of *Tenderly* and a riotously impromptu *Stompin' At The Savoy*, where she displays a very different and raucously exciting side to her vocal identity.

**ELLA: SONGS IN A MELLOW MOOD** (Brunswick): Accompanied only by Ellis Larkins (piano), Ella delivers beautiful versions of songs like *You Leave Me Breathless*, *Stardust* and *Please Be Kind*. One of the most subtle albums ever recorded by Ella, this was made in 1954. Four years previously she made another album with Ellis Larkins called:

**ELLA SINGS GERSHWIN** (Brunswick): Like the Songbooks series, this shows Ella somewhere near her best. It demonstrates what a sensitive artist she can be when she tries. The simple combination of just voice and piano is well nigh perfect.

**ELLA** (Reprise): A good example of Ella in a contemporary pop setting, showing how well she triumphs over trivia (*Savoy Truffle* etc) and shallow arrangements. Also she makes an excellent job of Randy Newman's *Yellow Man*.

> *She was the most unusual voice in*
> *the first half of this century.*
> E. Y. Harburg

# Judy Garland

Without doubt the most difficult thing to define in show business and/or pop music is star quality. What it is that separates the star performer from the merely talented professional has been a constant source of fascination, particularly to journalists and even sociologists who happily spend professional time and energy analysing and magnifying the faults and virtues of star personalities in an effort to discover the source of their popularity and its effect on audiences. But no one has yet come up with a satisfactory definition.

Real star quality, and that means the rare ability to become a legend in one's own lifetime, is perhaps totally indefinable: for when the public takes a performer to its heart, it is more often than not because of that performer's personal imperfections rather than for any professional expertise. This is especially true in the case of the late Judy Garland. By no means a perfect singer or actress, she was certainly a perfect example of an artist who possessed star quality in abundance.

Whatever the diverse qualities necessary for long standing stardom, Judy Garland had them all: she was a fine actress, a talented comedienne, a good dancer and a compelling singer. On top of these professsional assets she had a curiously unique personality which enabled her to express emotion in a totally individual manner. Her warm and slightly nervous appearance combined perfectly with her pleasing vocal tone and occasionally shaky delivery. When she sang she invariably drew the full meaning out of a lyric. This was mainly due to her slight imperfections which made her sound more human than her contemporaries.

Miss Garland became one of the legendary figures of musical show business. But unlike such other legends – Crosby, Astaire, Sinatra, Jolson, etc. – the Garland legend seemed to sneak up on us. So quickly has time passed that it's hard to realise that more than thirty years have elapsed since she first sang *Over The Rainbow* in the film *The Wizard Of Oz*. Since it first appeared on the world's screen in 1939, 'Wizard' – often regarded as the greatest of all children's films – has been constantly re-issued. This tended to make people think of it as a more recent film and of Miss Garland as a much younger performer. Even in the film itself she was not permitted to show her true age. The part she played was meant to be that of a twelve-year old girl. She was, in fact, seventeen when the film was made and MGM's wardrobe department supplied her with specially tailored dresses designed to flatten her breasts. But when she sang *Over The Rainbow* the startling maturity of her tone and phrasing suggested, aurally speaking, a woman in her twenties. To quote one of her famous songs, Judy Garland really was an 'in-between'. Nevertheless, the heartwarming effect of *Over The Rainbow* and her sensitive performance of it is a rare delight that remains undiminished across three decades of changing fashions.

And this brings to mind another point that made Miss Garland such a unique artist. Whenever she sang in a film it became an oddly memorable event. The film somehow stayed in the memory simply because she happened to sing in it. For instance, that charming 1944 musical *Meet Me In St Louis* is easily recalled not so much for its plot or characters but for two really outstanding Garland vocals – *The Boy Next Door* and *The Trolley Song*. Another film of slightly later vintage was *Easter Parade* and this stands out because of her celebrated duet with co-star Fred Astaire, *We're A Couple Of Swells*.

Born Frances Gumm on June 10th, 1922 in the town of Grand Rapids, Minnesota, she was the youngest of three daughters of vaudeville entertainers Frank and Ethel Gumm. From the age of three she toured with her sisters in a junior vaudeville act. At the age of twelve she was given a screen test by MGM films who immediately signed her to a contract. Her first film was a short one called *One Sunday Afternoon* and the cast also included Deanna Durbin. This was in 1935 when she changed her name on the advice of George Jessel, the celebrated comedian/actor/director.

After making a string of feature films – several with popular co-star, Mickey

Rooney – she won a special Academy Award for her excellent work in *The Wizard Of Oz*. Throughout the '40s Judy's star continued to glow as bright as any in the Hollywood firmament. No one, at that time, considered her to be a legend but she was extremely popular with audiences all over the world. Stardom, with all its attendant pressures both private and professional, continued until 1950 when Judy was forced to withdraw from the filming of *Annie Get Your Gun* due to a nervous collapse. Personal friction with MGM resulted in the termination of her contract and it looked as though her career had come to an unhappy end.

True to the old show business tradition of 'the show must go on', she recovered her health and in 1951 made her historic debut at the London Palladium. Following the tremendous success of this engagement she returned to America and promptly repeated her triumph in New York. The appealing warmth of her earlier years was now combined with a new and completely affecting magnetism. Audiences loved, and were fascinated by, the new Garland. Naturally, the press in rediscovering her had a field day; and just as naturally, Hollywood again became interested in the Garland talent. This time she signed with Warner Brothers to play the lead in a musical re-make (with original songs by Harold Arlen and Ira Gershwin) of a 1930's Janet Gaynor – Fredric March screen drama called *A Star Is Born*. On its release it was hailed unanimously as one of the major screen events of 1954 and her recording of the film's hit song, *The Man That Got Away*, reputedly sold over a million copies. She was unquestionably back on top again. With almost twenty years' experience as a film and recording artist, Judy Garland in 1954 was universally acclaimed as a genuine super star.

It has been in the years since 1954, and that triumphant comeback, that Judy Garland has become a show business legend. The singer's emotion-charged image was as much due to her troubled, and much-publicised, private life as to her on-stage professionalism. In fact, her every public performance carried an impact similar to a Sunday newspaper true-life confession. Her songs were shrewdly selected for their dramatic and emotional impact. Every phrase, every gesture was readily accepted as a true reflection of her own private problems and emotional condition. In her later years this approach, although frequently quite moving and touching, bordered on the maudlin and sometimes became more of an embarrassment than an entertainment.

Sometimes even her audiences rebelled. A typical case in point was her appearance, during the last year of her life, at London's Talk of the Town, She had developed a disconcerting habit of turning up late for her cabaret spot, sometimes she was so late that the audience and management felt sure that she had no intention of appearing at all. On one particular evening when she turned up late she was met with derisive shouts and jeering from the audience who threw cigarette packets at her and generally refused to let her start her act. But in spite of incidents like this, Judy Garland somehow always managed to retain her general popularity as one of the world's most beloved entertainers.

When she died, in a London flat in 1969, it came as a great shock to the entertainment world even though it was fairly common knowledge that she had been a sick woman for some time. Naturally, all sorts of theories were put forward as to the cause of her death and certain newspapers even hinted at suicide. In fact, all angles were exploited to try and present her death as some kind of ludicrous grand finale to The Judy Garland Story complete with fade-out and end titles. But there was really nothing spectacular or melodramatic about her death. Quite simply, she was a frail and sick little woman of 47 – perhaps relying a little too heavily on sleeping tablets and other such aids – who passed away under sad and rather insignificant circumstances. A far cry indeed from the tinsel and glitter of the Hollywood that launched her into the world's spotlights.

At her funeral, which took place in New York, actor/dancer Ray Bolger – who co-starred with her in *The Wizard Of Oz* – referred to her as '. . . . a little girl who never grew up'. A perceptive description indeed. Just to watch one of her films or to listen to one of her recordings makes one realise that growing old and being a venerable old lady would never really have suited her anyway.

## RECOMMENDED RECORDINGS

**OVER THE RAINBOW** (Music For Pleasure): A pleasantly nostalgic collection of songs from her MGM film period.

**A STAR IS BORN** (Hallmark – CBS): A worthwhile souvenir of one of Garland's best films. The original songs by Harold Arlen and Ira Gershwin – with the exception of *The Man That Got Away* – fall somewhat below the standard expected from such distinguished craftsmen, but the Garland personality comes to the rescue and every track, except the tedious *Someone At Last*, is a winner. The two main highspots, though, are the brilliant *The Man That Got Away* and the lengthy, semi-biographical *Born In A Trunk* which is cleverly punctuated by such fine oldies as *I'll Get By*, *My Melancholy Baby* and *Swanee*.

**YOU'LL NEVER WALK ALONE** (World Record Club): Formerly known as *The Garland Touch* (Capitol), this is splendidly representative of Garland's later (early '60s) period but without too many of the physical shortcomings that often marred otherwise good performances. The song selection is above average and a little more varied than usual.

**JUDY GARLAND AT CARNEGIE HALL** (Capitol): This two-record album – which incidentally sold over a million copies – gives some clear idea of the impact that Garland had on audiences. Recorded in 1961, this set presents her in fairly good voice singing and chatting her way through a typical evening with Garland. Many of her admirers regard this as her finest recorded work, but for the ardent connoisseur of popular singing it probably falls slightly short of the singer's best efforts musically. Faults apart, though, this set certainly captures to perfection the true essence of the Garland legend. And it is very entertaining.

**THE HOLLYWOOD YEARS** (Polydor/MGM): As far as Judy Garland's early years (1937 to 1950) are concerned, this attractively-produced two-LP set of her most famous film songs is probably the ultimate bargain. All the big ones are here – *Over The Rainbow*, *The Trolley Song*, *The Boy Next Door* and that oh-so-nostalgic 'Dear Mr Gable' routine based on *You Made Me Love You*. The album comes complete with a lavishly illustrated booklet with shots from all the films involved plus details of casts, production credits and composers. An excellent production that would have been even more enjoyable had the songs been programmed in chronological sequence rather than strung together in haphazard fashion as they are. A small criticism perhaps but a valid one in this case.

> *Frank Sinatra is the kind of singer*
> *who comes along once in a lifetime –*
> *but why did it have to be* my *lifetime?*
> Bing Crosby

# Frank Sinatra

"For me, in recent years, the world has been neatly divided into two groups of people: those who dig Sinatra and those who do not. There is, on the subject of singing, an impenetrable curtain between them."

So wrote celebrated American jazz critic, Ralph J. Gleason. His point about the world being divided into two groups of people is a remarkably apt one where Frank Sinatra is concerned, for while Sinatra remains after more than thirty years the most consistently popular of all popular singers he appears to have just as many detractors as admirers. The sound of that unique voice and the mercurial quality of his nature stamp him, for better or worse (depending on which group you belong to), as the most positive personality in all of popular music. For many people he epitomises – in song – the twentieth century common man, and while this is a lofty mantle to hang on a popular singer, there are times when Sinatra's potency with a set of good lyrics almost justifies it.

It is possibly this same potency which inspires such positive dislike of his work amongst the anti-Sinatra element.

Today, despite his recent retirement from show business, Sinatra's power in the entertainment world is unequalled. Apart from his eminence as a singer, he has managed to achieve success – complete success, too – as a screen actor, film producer, hotel owner, television impresario, record company director and musical conductor. Singing, however, seems to be the activity he enjoys (or rather enjoyed) best. Basically, it remains the source of his power, and the magnetic aura that surrounds Sinatra begins and ends with that unique singing sound and style.

As a singer of the more musicianly type of popular song, Sinatra presents his credentials with a firm accent on good taste (this taste lapses on occasions, but such lapses are usually short-lived). He possesses just about all the qualities one could wish for in a popular singer; his voice ranges over two octaves, he has a good feeling for tempo, his breath control is exceptional, his tone – though a little too hard for some tastes – is well rounded and full of expression. Best of all, his stunning delivery of lyrics carries an uncanny impact which is achieved without resorting to strident note-bending or clumsy hysterics. Whether one cares for Sinatra's singing or not, it is patently obvious that he possesses an abundance of talent.

The story of how he discovered and developed that talent is a long and interesting one. Like most success stories, it is dotted with setbacks, disappointments and a liberal quota of frustration. It began in the dockyard city of Hoboken, New Jersey, a sort of American equivalent of Liverpool. Francis Albert Sinatra, the only child of Martin and Dolly Sinatra, was born on December 12th, 1915. The scars of that birth, due to a clumsy forceps delivery which almost cost him his left ear, are still visible today. Sinatra's publicists have always depicted him as 'a slum kid who made it'. While it is true that he was born in a low income area, his parents were not typically working class. The family moved house several times and their subsequent addresses suggested a certain amount of social progress. His father was Sicilian and his mother came from Genoa. Both had blue eyes and were often taken for Irish, which was something of an advantage in those days when the Irish element was strongly registering in local politics, the police force and boxing.

Since she was enthusiastically involved in local politics as a Democratic ward leader, Dolly Sinatra often left young Frank in the care of his grandmother who lived in a nearby apartment or with an aunt or sometimes with a Jewish neighbour. His father, when he wasn't busy working as a boilermaker in a local shipyard, sometimes fought locally as a bantamweight boxer under the Irish alias of Marty O'Brien. With some financial help from his mother-in-law, Martin Sinatra eventually bought a tavern which, with his wife's rising power as a political worker, elevated the family's status another notch or two.

These non-musical influences to which Frank was exposed during his early life (politics and boxing) played a certain part in his later activities. For example in 1960 he used his talent and influence to campaign for President John F. Kennedy. Also at several points in his career he has taken a financial interest in numerous prizefighters, one of whom was the famous heavyweight contender Tami Mauriello.

Throughout his childhood years, Frank showed little interest in singing apart from an occasional half-hearted chorus or two of the latest pop songs with his pals under a corner lamp post. On leaving school (he was not a particularly outstanding pupil), he worked for a while as a truck loader and copy boy on a local newspaper. His intention of becoming a singer was developed almost unconsciously. One night in 1933 he took his girl friend, Nancy Barbato – who was later to become his first wife – to see Bing Crosby at a Jersey City vaudeville theatre. A lot of radio singers made no impression on him at all until he heard Bing Crosby. Crosby was different, he had something the others lacked. It was this personal quality of Crosby's that aroused Sinatra's interest in the more expressive side of popular singing. Sinatra himself recalled the effect that Crosby's performance had on him. "He performed on stage with a guitarist named Eddie Lang. And I watched him . . . he had such great ease that I thought, if he can do it that easily, I don't know why I can't. That was one of the big turning points of my life."

The next two years were spent entering talent contests and generally singing wherever and whenever he could; clubs, dances, cafes, etc. His parents were a little disturbed that he should want to embark on a 'sissy career like singing'. While his mother never gave up trying to get him to take further education and choose a more sensible career, she did buy him an elaborate portable amplifier complete with microphone and loudspeaker. The ownership of a PA system gave him a slight edge over other struggling singers but even so his progress was far from smooth. He spent a year or so as part of a vocal/instrumental group called The Hoboken Four who were featured on the Major Bowes Amateur Hour contest. The Bowes show was a kind of 1930s equivalent of the Hughie Green TV series 'Opportunity Knocks' and from all accounts it was equally as banal.

Following his stint with the Hoboken Four, Frank landed a job as MC and vocalist at a place in Englewood, New Jersey, called The Rustic Cabin. Even in those early days Frank handled his own affairs with the same critical aggressiveness that later characterised his legendary comeback in 1953. He was keenly aware of the value that radio had been to Bing Crosby's success, so he wasted no time in offering his services to programme directors of the Jersey and New York radio stations. He even agreed to sing for no fee and under these conditions he was accepted by WNEW, a local station. Whenever there was an unfilled air slot, Frank was there – music in hand – to fill it. Pretty soon his voice was heard on practically every wavelength at all hours of the day and night. Since it was costing them nothing, WNEW felt they were getting the best of the bargain. But Frank Sinatra knew differently and he was soon to be proved right.

It was mid-June 1939 and trumpeter Harry James was in New York with his four months old band, looking now for a suitable male singer. After hearing Sinatra's voice on the radio, he quickly contacted the singer and offered him the job. Frank Sinatra signed a contract to sing with the James band that same month of June. On July 13th, 1939 he made his first ever professional recordings. Accompanied by the James band he sang *From The Bottom Of My Heart* and *Melancholy Mood*. There was nothing exceptional about the session. No one could have dreamed just where it would lead. No one, that is, except Frank.

According to James "Frank got along beautifully with all the guys. He fitted right into the band." He had been with the band only six months, during which time he had recorded ten titles including the excellent *All Or Nothing At All*, when he was heard by Tommy Dorsey. Dorsey, who was possibly the most popular bandleader in America at that time, was on the lookout for a good male singer and Sinatra had just the qualities he was seeking. The only problem was his existing contract with Harry James.

Frank's relationship with Harry James was really more like a friendship than a business tie-up. Such a warm association made it easy for the bandleader to realise what it meant to Sinatra when Dorsey offered him a job. Harry simply offered Frank a warm handshake and grinned 'Get out of here'.

He stayed with the Dorsey band for two years and eight months. It gave him a great deal of international exposure, not to mention a higher income. But it meant something more. The wealth of musical talent in that orchestra from Tommy Dorsey on down – this included arrangers like Sy Oliver and Axel Stordahl, singers like Jo Stafford and The Pied Pipers and great instrumentalists like drummer Buddy Rich, pianist Joe Bushkin and the legendary trumpeter Bunny Berigan – provided Frank with a musical and stylistic education he could not have received in any other band. The most valuable single influence in the band as far as Sinatra was concerned was Tommy Dorsey himself. He spent hours watching and listening to Dorsey's individual style of trombone playing. It was on this smooth legato approach to phrasing that he modelled his own singing style.

At a time when every male singer in the business was copying Bing Crosby's *portamento* approach, Sinatra went in a completely new direction, firstly by absorbing the musical influences around him and secondly by applying a new emphasis to lyric interpretation. If it was a sad lyric, he would make an effort to sound forlorn, and it if was a happy piece, he would endeavour to sound elated. His singing soon took on a more personalised quality, which was quickly seized on by the younger audiences, especially the females. Sinatra remained with Dorsey for more than two and a half years during which time he cut over ninety records as band vocalist, many of which were hits simply because he happened to be singing on them.

One thing was obvious, Sinatra was becoming too popular to remain a dance band singer. His increasing popularity caused some tension between Dorsey and himself and late in 1942 Sinatra was obliged to buy himself out of his contract with the band. Although he was bitter about the expense involved in this move, he never minimised his musical debt to Dorsey and the benefits derived from working with his band.

Basking in the attendant publicity of his debut as a solo singer, Sinatra made a shrewd move by putting his career in the hands of George Evans, a clever and publicity-conscious operator who saw to it that the seeds of Sinatra's star potential were properly nurtured and developed. Sinatra-fever had already hit the young female population of America. This was wartime and most of the nation's young men were posted abroad, so Sinatra was a vocal substitute for the boy friend who wasn't there. At least that's how Evans saw the situation and it clicked! Sinatra himself volunteered for Army service but was rejected because of a perforated eardrum.

He made many fine recordings during these years, mostly in company with the talented Axel Stordahl whose unusually constructed orchestrations did much to give these recordings an individual quality. Frank's films at this time were less impressive (not to put too fine a point on it, they were downright feeble) and no one would ever have imagined that he would later develop into a screen actor of considerable power. Of course, artistic considerations were hardly the order of the day at this particular point in Sinatra's career. High pressure publicity and slick sensationalism were the main ingredients in George Evans' *modus operandi*.

All kinds of freakish stories found their way into the press telling of the fantastic effect that Sinatra was having on female fans. Because one girl was reported to have fainted during one of the singer's performances, it was rumoured that Evans paid a number of teenage girls to repeat the procedure for the benefit of the press. But whether the incredible antics of Sinatra's many fans were real or induced, there is no denying the genuineness of the mass hysteria that took place at New York's Paramount Theatre in October 1944, for not even a canny operator like George Evans could have organised an event of such a spectacular nature.

News reports referred to it as 'The Columbus Day Riot at the Paramount' and a riot it certainly was. The press could not have been guilty of overstatement even if they had tried. The bare facts were colourful enough. Over 10,000 fans formed a queue, six deep, that ran west along 43rd Street, trailed down Eighth Avenue and then wound east up 44th Street. As if that were not enough an additional 20,000 teenagers, according to police reports, jammed Times Square stopping not only the mechanised traffic but pedestrians too. The theatre's ticket booth was smashed, as were several shop windows. Passers-by were trampled and girls fainted (some genuinely). New York had never known anything like it before and has certainly never witnessed anything to compare with it since.

Events such as this proved beyond question just how powerful was Sinatra's popularity. But then, as now, he often used his power and influence in many strange and generous ways. One such incident occurred while he was appearing at the Paramount in 1945. Alec Wilder, the gifted composer/arranger, brought to his dressing room a recording of two compositions he had written for oboist Mitchell Miller and the Columbia Symphony Orchestra. Frank was so impressed he asked if Wilder had any other such pieces and was delighted to learn that the composer was indeed a prolific writer. "We'll make a complete album of your music," Frank told Wilder. "And I'd like to conduct it." Wilder was taken aback "But you can't read music," he told Sinatra. "That's alright," said Frank. "I'll find a way to do it. What's more, using my name on the record will help your music."

Alec Wilder relates the story this way: "Frank got straight on the 'phone to Manie Sachs of Columbia Records and told him of his intentions. I swear I could hear Manie's chair going over backwards. The first session took place on December 5th and Mr Sachs had a real conductor standing by just in case things went wrong, but somehow they didn't. On entering the studio, Frank turned to the violins and said 'I need your help because I want to help this music.' His scores looked kind of crazy. It would read 'cellos enter' then four measures later 'violas enter' and so on. A lot of people to this day think he didn't do it. But I was there and he did do it. I don't know how he did it, except by possibly following the soloists. He did a fantastic job and the music was beautifully rendered."

Sinatra's popularity continued unabated through the next four years or so. He made many excellent records and several bad films – with two exceptions; *Anchors Aweigh* in which he co-starred with Gene Kelly and Kathryn Grayson, and a short film on racial intolerance called *The House I Live In*. For his appearance in this last film he received a special Academy Award.

In 1949 his popular image started to slip. His record sales were poor and to make matters worse he was having trouble with the newly appointed A & R manager at Columbia Records, Mitch Miller. Although a fine musician, former oboe player Miller was bent on putting commerce before art – which was probably the whole point of his job. Sinatra's records weren't selling and Miller was determined to do something about it. He kept sending "commercial" songs for Sinatra's consideration and Sinatra kept sending them back. Due to his innate good taste, Sinatra found himself unable to convincingly sing songs in which he didn't believe. One of the songs he rejected was *My Heart Cries For You*, which soon after turned out to be a million seller for Guy Mitchell, at that time one of Mitch Miller's hottest artists.

From early 1950 to 1953 Sinatra's career underwent a frustrating succession of ups and downs – mostly downs. The 'ups' were represented by a new radio series he had been given called *Light Up Time*, in which he had complete freedom to choose the kind of songs he liked; and after scoring a huge success in a guest appearance on The Bob Hope Show, he was given his own TV series. On record, he even managed to see eye to eye with Miller on at least one occasion and the result was a set of excellent sessions – in April 1950, in which Frank delivered lively versions of such fine songs as *You Do Something To Me*, *The Continental*, *My Blue Heaven* and *When You're Smiling* with some quite inspired arrangements from the underrated George Siravo. But the 'downs' presented themselves in greater profusion. He developed throat trouble and was forced to quit singing for a while. His TV series ran into difficulties, he appeared at New York's Copacabana and flopped miserably; MGM terminated his film contract. He divorced Nancy and, in the midst of much unfavourable publicity, embarked on his turbulent courtship with Ava Gardner.

All these unpleasant factors and frustrations took their toll on his voice. His celebrated ability to sustain notes and long phrases was failing, he was having difficulty in reaching certain notes and it was obvious that he wasn't singing quite as immaculately in tune as before. Nevertheless, it is worth observing that while his singing fell below par technically during this unstable period, his singing revealed emotional depths that were only hinted at in previous recordings. He was delivering his lyrics with far more conviction and the vocal weakness somehow increased his emotional strength.

A particularly telling episode from this period occurred on March 27th 1951 when Frank recorded a song in which he also shared composing credits, *I'm A Fool To Want You*. Ben Barton, a close friends of Sinatra's as well as being head of his publishing company, recalls the session: "It was terribly emotional, Frank was really worked up. He did the song in one take; then he just turned around and walked out of the studio, and that was it." Noted American music journalist, George T. Simon referred to the track as "the most emotional side of Frank I have ever heard."

Very different indeed was Sinatra's outlook – and voice – on a June 3rd, 1952 session which resulted in no less than five tracks, the best known of which is the exuberant *Birth Of The Blues*. The voice seemed to have more authority and certainly greater physical power than on previous sessions. His high notes had a strong ringing quality that was particularly apparent on *Birth*. One of the other songs, a happy piece of trivia called *Bim Bam Baby*, showed a keen rhythmic buoyancy in the singer's phrasing that had not been heard since the Siravo sessions of two years previously. His Fats Waller-like comment at the end of *Baby* showed a more snappy personality. Despite the fact that his Columbia contract was on its last legs, the Sinatra voice was coming back to life again.

Three months later, on September 17th, Sinatra recorded his last song for Columbia. Its title was particularly apt; *Why Try To Change Me Now?* Although the sales of *Birth Of The Blues* reached encouraging figures, Columbia made no effort to continue with Sinatra as a recording artist. He left the label at the end of 1952 owing the rather startling sum of $110,000 in unearned advances (the

LPs which were later made up from his Columbia singles easily consumed these advances and, these days, continue to earn Sinatra royalties of over $50,000 per year).

Finding a new record company proved to be a major problem. After being turned down by several leading labels, including RCA, Sinatra was eventually accepted by Capitol Records. His initial session for this label took place on April 2nd, 1953. At first it was an uneasy liaison; the company offered no cash advances of any kind, and all arranging, copying and musical costs were to be borne by Sinatra himself. Furthermore the contract was for only one year. So in April of 1953, Frank Sinatra was hardly the hottest property in show business. Ironically the reigning singers at that time were Frankie Laine, Guy Mitchell and Johnnie Ray, all of whom were recording on Frank's old label, Columbia, under the proud and smiling supervision of Mitch Miller.

As he started to pick up the pieces of his broken recording career, Sinatra also seized at a remote opportunity to revive his sagging image as a screen actor. He had just read the famous James Jones novel *From Here To Eternity* and noticed with interest that Columbia Pictures were preparing to film it. He wasted no time in approaching the company with a view to playing the part of Private Maggio. He was told that the part had already gone to another actor, but he insisted on testing for it anyway. He got the part (which he was delighted to play for a very low salary) and it earned him the Academy Award for the Best Supporting Actor of 1953. That was the start of the most phenomenal comeback in the history of show business.

His Capitol recordings started to attract full scale attention. The new Sinatra had more confidence and everyone could feel it. The voice was not only stronger, it was also becoming deeper (for proof of this, hear the quality of his low notes in the 1955 recordings of *What Is This Thing Called Love?* and *Deep In A Dream*). The style was more mature and the personality more invigorating. People who had previously sneered at the skinny singer from Hoboken were swiftly changing their minds. No other singer, it seemed, was able to project emotion with quite the same unforced skill as Sinatra. And today, almost twenty years later, he is still the undisputed master. His ability to capture the total implication of a song's lyric line and turn it into a moving experience seems to come as naturally to him as breathing. Although it should be noted that his 1954 ballad version of *Day In, Day Out* was the smooth result of no less than thirty one takes. An exceptional instance of Sinatra the perfectionist at work!

From 1953 to 1961, Frank Sinatra recorded well over 250 titles for the Capitol catalogue. Connoisseurs of the singer's work generally agree that this was the most creative and consistently satisfying period of his entire recording career. The standard of his accompaniments was remarkably high (foremost amongst his musical directors were Billy May, Gordon Jenkins and – most consistently – Nelson Riddle), his songs for the most part were tastefully chosen and many of the albums he recorded, such as *Songs For Young Lovers*, *In The Wee Small Hours* and *Songs For Swingin' Lovers*, have become cherished classics of popular singing.

In December 1960, several months before his Capitol contract was due to expire, Sinatra recorded the first titles for his own independent record label, Reprise. Some people felt that Frank was making a mistake in leaving the security of the Capitol label to form his own company but they reckoned without his natural flair for organisation and business know-how. Reprise went from strength to strength – with top names like Sinatra, Dean Martin, Sammy Davis, Jr, Duke Ellington and Bing Crosby it could hardly have done otherwise. In 1963, Sinatra sold the label at a handsome profit to Warner Brothers Records, a deal which also brought him into business partnership with Jack L. Warner and resulted in his occupying a substantial position on the board of Warner Brothers Pictures.

As a singer, Sinatra has been a consistent winner of many international jazz polls. This kind of success probably mystifies Frank since he has never claimed to be a jazz singer. However, it is no secret that he has a definite admiration for the work of jazz musicians (and many jazz musicians – Miles Davis and Duke Ellington among them – have unhesitatingly named him as their favourite singer). Such players as Harry 'Sweets' Edison, Red Norvo, Buddy Collete and Milt Bernhart are typical of the musicians with whom he has chosen to record. But jazz singer or not, Frank certainly sings with a solid rhythmic thrust that is guaranteed to get the foot tapping, although his rhythmic singing does not seem quite so impressive on his latter day recordings as it was in the mid-'50s. This probably stems from the fact that he had been using heavier rhythm sections of late which tended to extract a good deal of the subtlety from his phrasing. Compare, for instance, his heavy handed delivery of *Some Enchanted Evening* (1967) with his marvellously propulsive phrasing in *All Of Me* (1954). The difference is astonishing!

Of his work on the Reprise label, the earlier albums offer the more musically rewarding examples of his work, probably because his choice of songs was more astute in those days, also his selection of arrangers was more idiomatically correct. To be honest, his later insistence on singing only new material of a pop-orientated nature did result in some rather strange choices and, in some cases, even stranger interpretations.

Take for instance his 1970 album *Watertown*, which was written especially for him. Both the tunes and the arrangements were mundane enough, but the lyrics were pretentiously mawkish and dramatically inept – some passages in fact made no real sense at all. Not that his entire contemporary output has been poor, far from it. Indeed, there are some performances such as *Didn't We*, *Watch What Happens*, *By The Time I Get To Phoenix* and the hauntingly beautiful *Cycles* which stand comparison with his best work on the Capitol label.

Some of his records and TV appearances over the last few years suggested that the famous voice was showing signs of fatigue, thus creating the impression that Frank was past his best. Anyone, of course, can have off-days and Sinatra is no exception. But his two charity performances at London's Royal Festival Hall in May 1970 proved beyond question that his voice was as great as ever and lacking none of the magical technique and vocal stamina for which he has always been renowned. Probably because of his lofty position in show business, Frank Sinatra has perhaps become a creature of inspiration. It's perfectly obvious that he no longer needs to sing for money, so if the inspiration was lacking on certain recording sessions of recent years (and this certainly does not apply to all of his sessions) it was not at all lacking on those two memorable May evenings when he skilfully reinforced his reputation as the world's most distinctive and most durable singer of popular songs. And a subsequent set of concerts in November of the same year were almost, if not quite, up to the same high standard.

But just a few months later in June 1971, he felt an inspiration of a different kind and decided to quit singing and everything else connected with being a performer. Amongst the welter of tributes that appeared in the world's press, Benny Green, the jazz critic of *The Observer*, captured the essence of Sinatra's influence on popular music and what his retirement really meant in aesthetic terms, when he wrote: "What few people, apart from musicians, have never seemed to grasp is that he is not simply the best popular singer of his generation, a latter-day Jolson or Crosby, but the culminating point in an evolutionary process which has refined the art of interpreting words set to music. Nor is there even the remotest possibility that he will have a successor. Sinatra was the result of a fusing of a set of historical circumstances which can never be repeated."

But just to hark back to Ralph J. Gleason's theory about the world being split into two groups where Sinatra's singing is concerned. There are now two further groups; those who believe he will stay in retirement and those who think he will come back. Indeed, there was a rumour that Sinatra had entered a recording studio in Los Angeles on January 19th, 1972 and cut three titles with the Nelson Riddle orchestra. Yet when Riddle visited London in February he claimed to have had no knowledge of any such session taking place.

Whether or not Sinatra ever comes back into the vocal spotlight it's a pretty safe bet that the Frank Sinatra story is far from finished.

## RECOMMENDED RECORDINGS

**THE DORSEY-SINATRA SESSIONS** (RCA 6-LP boxed set): This beautifully produced and superbly documented six-record package – covering every single commercial recording that the young Frank Sinatra made over the two years and eight months he spent as vocalist with the Tommy Dorsey orchestra – is a veritable collector's dream-come-true. Never before has the record fan been presented with so complete a picture of a young artist's development. It has often been said that the most important and crucial stage in Sinatra's early career was the period with Dorsey. Here, in one modestly priced superpackage is the full musical story of that period. It permits the listener to study Sinatra's progress literally session by session. The whole album was the brainchild of producer Alan Dell who diligently gathered all the information together by working in conjunction with Sinatra collectors both in Britain and America, after which he approached RCA Records in London. The company reacted with enormous enthusiasm to his project and the result is one of the most fascinating, nostalgic and instructive albums ever produced. No less than eighty-three vintage vocals from the young Sinatra.

**FRANK SINATRA'S GREATEST HITS: The Early Years** (CBS): This is a useful two-disc package covering highspots from his association with American Columbia. An even more expansive account of the same period is presented in the three-disc set, 'The Essential Sinatra' (CBS). This is an intriguing 48-track survey of the singer's development from his first-ever recording session with the Harry James Orchestra in 1939 to his final session for American Columbia in 1952 prior to signing with Capitol.

The very first long-playing records Sinatra ever made were on Capitol – 10 inch, of course, in those days. These were 'Songs For Young Lovers' (1953) and 'Swing Easy' (1954). Both albums find him in superb voice with tasteful small band accompaniments directed by Nelson Riddle. Both of these beautifully produced programmes were reissued some years later on one 12 inch 16-song LP under the title 'Swing Easy' and 'Songs For Young Lovers' (Capitol).

**IN THE WEE SMALL HOURS** (Capitol): Technically this is possibly Sinatra's finest ballad album with beatifully rendered versions of such choice material as Alec Wilder's *I'll Be Around*, Porter's *What Is This Thing Called Love*, Ellington's *Mood Indigo* and Jimmy Van Heusen's *Deep In A Dream*. The sheer excellence of this 1955 set makes one wonder why it has been unavailable for so many years.

**SONGS FOR SWINGIN' LOVERS** (Capitol): Sinatra's biggest-selling LP and the one which contributed more than any other to the Sinatra image as we know it today. This immensely enjoyable collection of wonderful songs (in which Nelson Riddle developed and established his now famous orchestral sound) set the pattern for the celebrated Sinatra/Riddle partnership.

**COME FLY WITH ME** (Capitol): Teamed on this occasion with Billy May's colourful orchestrations, Sinatra applies his vocal skill to an attractive collection of songs dealing with the 'travel' theme, i.e. *London By Night*, *Brazil*, *Autumn In New York*, *April In Paris*, etc.

**ONLY THE LONELY** (Capitol): Nelson Riddle names this as his personal favourite of all the albums he recorded with Sinatra. Certainly, it is an outstanding example of the singer's artistry on sad ballads and Riddle's accompaniments have a majestic elegance that fit the mood of the album perfectly.

**NO ONE CARES** (Capitol/World Record Club): Another superior collection of sad songs and one of the best albums to team Sinatra with Gordon Jenkins. The latter's arrangement for *I Can't Get Started* is quite breathtaking and inspires Sinatra to deliver one of his finest individual performances. Though the bleak mood of unrelieved sadness is not to everyone's taste the extreme beauty of other songs like *Just Friends, I'll Never Smile Again* and especially *Here's That Rainy Day* reveal the Sinatra voice at its most potent.

**THE SINATRA TOUCH** (Capitol/World Record Club): This well programmed package of six LPs in a box offers a treasure chest of Sinatra's halcyon years on the Capitol label from 1952 to 1961. The choice of material for the most part is wonderfully satisfying. Most of Sinatra's best-loved hits from this worthy period are included (*Young At Heart, The Tender Trap, Learnin' The Blues, Three Coins In The Fountain, Witchcraft,* etc) together with shrewdly chosen tracks from some of his best LPs. With a total of 60 songs covering many of the highspots – and a couple of low spots too – from the cherished Capitol years, this set cannot be recommended too highly.

**RING-A-DING DING** (Reprise): The first album that Sinatra recorded for his own Reprise label is of more than just historical interest. It's a vigorously performed set of rhythmic standards arranged by Johnny Mandel. The standout track is a nicely re-vitalized treatment of Cole Porter's *In The Still Of The Night*.

**I REMEMBER TOMMY** (Reprise): Sinatra's 1961 tribute to his old boss, the late Tommy Dorsey. Apart from the fine vocals, this album is especially interesting for the way in which Sy Oliver cleverly up-dated the old arrangements (many of which were written by him back in the '40s) without losing the essence of their original charm and appeal.

**SINATRA AND STRINGS** (Reprise): This exceptionally fine LP of well-loved standards (*I Hadn't Anyone Till You, Come Rain Or Come Shine,* etc) marked the first occasion that Sinatra worked with arranger Don Costa. Not surprisingly this rewarding partnership was to be repeated many times over the ensuing years.

**THE SEPTEMBER OF MY YEARS** (Reprise): An album with a most original theme, that of a man in middle age looking back reflectively over his past life and loves. Gordon Jenkins' arrangements – Mahler-inspired in places – are superb and Sinatra's approach to the lyrics is masterful. The only track that does not quite ring true is *September Song*, which suffers from a slightly jerky treatment. There are plenty of gems though in such pieces as *It Was A Very Good Year*, *The Man In The Looking Glass* and the title song.

**A MAN AND HIS MUSIC** (Reprise): A two-LP pack, this was issued in 1965 to coincide with Sinatra's fiftieth birthday. It presents him narrating – from a very shallow script – a potted version of his career as a recording artist. In spite of its faults it does manage, through clever editing, to cram a lot of good music into just two records.

**A MAN ALONE** (Reprise): The first time in his career that Sinatra had devoted a whole LP to the songs of one composer, in this case Rod McKuen. Although the singer sounds tired in places, he certainly delivers the songs (some excellent, some only average) with warmth and conviction. The occasional passages of poetry are also interesting, if not totally effective. Don Costa provides the arrangements.

**MY WAY** (Reprise): Accompanied once more by Don Costa, this album features his biggest hit in recent years, *My Way*. There are many Sinatra enthusiasts who dislike this song intensely, but it must be admitted that Sinatra's skilled reading of the rather clumsy lyric has captured the public's imagination in no uncertain terms. Basically this is quite a satisfying LP with Sinatra in good voice with reasonably good songs. In fact, it is one of the best examples of the latter-day Sinatra.

**SINATRA AND COMPANY** (Reprise): This has been officially announced as the last LP in the Sinatra recording career (not counting possible future reissues). It's rather an odd programme, with the first side devoted to seven songs composed and accompanied by Antonio Carlos Jobim (salvaged from a previously unreleased album) and the second side compiled of recent pop songs – *I Will Drink The Wine*, *Leaving On A Jet Plane*, *Close To You* etc. Unexpectedly the album does hold up as good listening (with side one taking the honours in the long run), but it seems a rather strange way to climax such a distinguished and significant career.

*If you don't feel a thrill when Peggy*
*Lee sings, you're dead, Jack.*
Leonard Feather

# Peggy Lee

There is a well-worn theory, seemingly shared by most people in the music business who are over the age of 30, that in order to become a fully accomplished popular singer you must first get some experience singing with a dance band. Unlike many theories this does have some substance when one considers that Frank Sinatra, Ella Fitzgerald, Bing Crosby, Sarah Vaughan, Perry Como and Doris Day, to name but a few, all started out as band vocalists. So did Peggy Lee.

Miss Lee, who is arguably the most respected female singer in the profession, once outlined the advantages – and some of the shortcomings too – of working as a band vocalist for Benny Goodman:

"Band singing," she said in an interview with America's *Metronome* magazine, "taught us the importance of interplay with musicians. We had to work close to the arrangement. Even if the interpretation of a particular song wasn't exactly what we wanted, we had to make the best of it. I can remember some songs I sang with Benny when I felt they should have been treated just the opposite way he'd had them arranged. So, like all band singers, I learned to do the best with what they gave me.

I will say this: I learned more about music from the men I worked with in bands than I've learned anywhere else. They taught me discipline and the value of rehearsing and how to train."

Peggy Lee is a perfect example of what a popular singer can achieve as a result of working with a dance band during one's formative years. Of course, her natural musicality and instinctive good taste also have something to do with her overall success. For, unlike so many popular singers Miss Lee's rise to prominence was no overnight affair nor was it due to a runaway top twenty hit. Rather it is the result of dedicated effort and artistic development.

The road to international success was an arduous but not an unenthusiastic one. She was born Norma Dolores Egstrom in Jamestown, North Dakota, on May 26th, 1922. During her childhood years she showed a strong interest in singing which was initially expressed in her work with various choirs in the community. As a teenager she sang with bands in local clubs, often with great success. At the age of 18, with her heart now set on a full time singing career, she persuaded her father, a railway worker, to lend her his company pass so that she could leave North Dakota to seek a singing career in California.

Breaking into music proved to be much more difficult than she imagined. If there was one thing California didn't need, it was another girl singer – the employment agencies were full of them. "During those early years," she recalls, "things were so bad they were funny." The odd club date came along and the occasional one night stand and, in desperation, she even took a job as a carnival spieler. These were the bad years but things slowly began to improve. She had changed her name to Peggy Lee and people found it an easier name to remember. Then, as word got around that audiences were reacting favourably to her voice, the work started to come in a little more regularly. But still the big time was quite a way off.

It was in the spring of 1941, while working in a vocal group in Chicago, that she was heard by Mrs Benny Goodman who was sufficiently impressed by her singing to recommend her for a job with the Goodman band. Benny himself was pleased with the way she handled a song. From July of 1941, Peggy found herself on a regular payroll as vocalist with Benny Goodman, at that time the biggest name in swing music. In September of that same year she entered a recording studio to make her first professional recording as part of the Goodman band. The song was Irving Berlin's *How Deep Is The Ocean* and Peggy sang it competently in the routine style of any band singer of the period. She made numerous other recordings with the Goodman band, but it was not until July of the following year, when she recorded her first big hit *Why Don't You Do Right*, that she revealed the individuality of style that was later to bring her such lasting fame.

With a hit record to her credit and the tempting prospect of a profitable solo career in the offing, Peggy Lee exercised her female prerogative in March, 1943, changed her mind about singing for a living and married Goodman's guitarist, Dave Barbour.

Concentrating on being Mrs Barbour, she remained in retirement for several years except for the occasional recording date. These sessions sometimes included her own compositions, with her husband as co-composer and accompanist. The most notable of these were *It's A Good Day*, *I Don't Know Enough About You* and – one of the biggest hits of 1948 – *Manana*. This last recording, which earned Peggy her first gold disc, held the number one chart spot in the USA for nine successive weeks and went on to become a major seller in many other parts of the world.

Following the success of *Manana*, offers for her services came in thick and fast. Her recordings were in great demand and the best nightclubs were bidding for her unique brand of vocal entertainment. A profitable solo career was, once again, hers for the asking. This time, however, the rewards were far greater. She was now an international attraction. Naturally, she accepted. What performer wouldn't?

The next few years saw her talent developing in various directions. Apart from her continued output of fine recordings such as *Don't Smoke In Bed* and her spectacular mambo-inspired version of Rodgers and Hart's *Lover* (which brought her a second gold disc for over a million sales), she made her film debut in 1950 in the Crosby film *Mr Music*. By this time she had already changed record companies, moving from Capitol to American Decca (which meant that her records were issued in Britain on the Brunswick label). Her marriage, however, was not going well and in 1952 it ended in divorce, as did her three subsequent marriages in later years.

In the early '50s she formed a songwriting partnership with famous Hollywood composer, Victor Young. This resulted in many fine songs, one of the most beautiful of which was *Where Can I Go Without You*. Shortly before his sudden death in 1956, Young told a reporter: "Peggy Lee is more than just a singer. Her talent should be shouted from the rooftops."

Her talent, while not exactly shouted from the rooftops, was certainly well showcased on records during the early '50s. At this time the record companies were developing the market for the long-playing record and one of Peggy Lee's early ventures into this medium was a brilliant album – which many experts consider to be her best ever recording – called *Black Coffee*. Accompanied by a quartet only, she performed with great feeling and sympathy for the excellent material which included such gems as *Easy Living*, *I Didn't Know What Time It Was* and *A Woman Alone With The Blues*. Musicians, and critics too, have compared her work in this particular album to that of the late Billie Holiday, who was always one of Peggy's own favourite artists. The comparison is only partly justified in as much as Miss Lee sings with the same soulful approach to the lyrics, and in this respect the comparison is a compliment. But on the whole Peggy emerges as a completely distinctive singer ... as always.

As a songwriter during the '50s she supplied songs for two very successful children's films – Walt Disney's *Lady And The Tramp* and *Tom Thumb*. As an actress she gave an inspired performance in the 1955 film *Pete Kelly's Blues*, for which she received an Academy Award nomination. Considering the amount of prestige she gained from that film, it makes one wonder why she never made any more films.

In 1957 she left the Decca label and went back to her old label Capitol, but not before she put one more big hit in the Decca catalogue – the plaintively beautiful *Mr Wonderful*, one of the best tunes of 1956. The production chiefs at Capitol wasted no time in getting Peggy into the studios and the ensuing recordings made everyone happy. They were all triumphs on artistic as well as commercial levels. On the one hand, she recorded superb albums such as *The Man I Love* and *Things Are Swingin'* and on the other she delivered some excellent pop singles. The most noteworthy of these was *Fever*, which earned Peggy her third gold disc. Even today, some twelve years later, it sounds remarkably modern. No wonder it is often regarded as one of the most unusual pop records of all time.

In the '70s Peggy Lee's position in popular music shows little sign of diminishing. Just what is the secret of her sustaining success, not only within the profession but with the public at large? She never debases her talent by singing down to the technically limited standards of most of today's pop scene, yet she still somehow manages to remain a part of it. The answer would seem to lie in the fact that with Peggy Lee the performance is everything. Because she has such extraordinarily good taste there is no difference between Peggy Lee singing an exquisite ballad like Duke Ellington's *All Too Soon* and Peggy Lee singing a commercial triviality like *A Hard Day's Night*. The net result in both cases is still great singing.

Hers is not a big voice; it has physical flaws which would probably make her the despair of a legitimate singing teacher. Yet it is a measure of her artistry that she is able to turn those flaws to endearing advantage with unquestionable musicianship (she plays piano and has a solid knowledge of harmonies and intervals) and complete dedication to giving a lyric its proper emphasis. Since her musical ability is always obvious she never seeks to baffle her audience with pretentious displays of technique.

Musically, she is the vocal equivalent of Count Basie's economical piano style; she will never use three notes when two will do and she'll say more artistically with those two notes than many singers can with twenty. This, in essence, is the keynote of her longstanding reputation: she prefers her singing to go straight to the heart of her listeners rather than turn each performance into a series of vocal somersaults. This, in fact, is something she shares with the other great singers who started out as dance band vocalists and all of whom have enjoyed enduring success in what is, perhaps, the most transient business of all: pop singing.

## RECOMMENDED RECORDINGS

**BLACK COFFEE** (Ace of Hearts): For anyone remotely interested in the subtle art of lyric interpretation, this LP is required listening. Originally issued in this country in the early '50s on the Brunswick label as a 10in LP, it was reissued some years later (about 1962) as a 12in album with four extra tracks from some other session. It may be difficult to obtain these days, but it's well worth searching for.

**SEA SHELLS** (Ace of Hearts): Very much off the beaten track, this album is an infectiously charming collection of folky material and Chinese love poems. Miss Lee is accompanied only by the harp of Stella Castalucci. Best known track is the haunting children's song, *I Don't Want To Play In Your Yard*. The only slack moments in the album are when Miss Lee recites the poems, yet even these tracks carry a small degree of interest.

**THE MAN I LOVE** (Capitol): With fine – but sometimes over-lush – arrangements by Nelson Riddle and orchestra conducted by Frank Sinatra, this is an excellent album of Peggy Lee's ballad work. The repertoire is very strong and includes her celebrated version of Jerome Kern's *The Folks Who Live On The Hill*.

**MINK JAZZ** (Capitol/World Record Club): Possibly her best album in recent years, Peggy Lee is on top form here. Her artistry is revealed in a nicely contrasted choice of good songs in various tempi. The small band accompaniments, featuring superb trumpet solos by Jack Sheldon, couldn't be more appropriate to Miss Lee's supple style.

**THINGS ARE SWINGIN'** (Capitol/World Record Club): With beautifully punchy arrangements from Jack Marshall, this refreshing album ranks with Miss Lee's best work. As with most of her work on LP the songs are consistently good – *I'm Beginning To See The Light, Riding High, Life Is For Living*, etc – and the recording quality is exceptional. Seldom does one hear such a fine balance of voice and orchestra.

**BIG SPENDER** (Capitol): A well rendered selection of pop novelties and standards demonstrating Peggy Lee's mastery of various idioms in the popular field. While the material in this album is not consistent, the standard of the vocal performances certainly is.

**IF YOU GO** (Capitol/World Record Club): Peggy Lee's special way with a sad ballad is given full emphasis in this first-rate LP. Quincy Jones provides arrangements that help Miss Lee to give the songs (*Smile, As Time Goes By, I'm Gonna Laugh You Out Of My Life*, etc) that extra something.

**I LIKE MEN** (Capitol/World Record Club): This can be enjoyed for the slightly cheeky way that Peggy deals with the album theme – Men! Jack Marshall's orchestrations give good support and the LP is full of colour and variety.

**BEAUTY AND THE BEAT** (Capitol): A big seller for many years, this LP is a good souvenir of a 1959 concert in Miami, Florida, that teamed Miss Lee with the popular George Shearing and his quintet. Highlights include *You Came A Long Way From St Louis* and *All Too Soon*.

**THE BEST OF PEGGY LEE** (Capitol): With 16 of her best known songs from the Capitol catalogue, this album is full of good music and is an excellent bargain.

*Popular music in America has many*
*influences, as is very natural in a*
*nation made up of such originally*
*disparate influences. Nat was the*
*first big success – in the vocal field*
*and in the small instrumental field –*
*who was based on jazz. Today more and*
*more performers are leaning on the jazz*
*side for what they do. Nat did it first*
*and he did it best, for my taste.*

Ralph J. Gleason

# Nat 'King' Cole

One theory that readers will find liberally distributed throughout this book is that jazz-influenced singers usually make the best popular singers, artistically speaking. The late Nat 'King' Cole was a shining example of this. He started his professional career as a jazz pianist, and an extremely influential one too.

Early admirers of this fine singer recall with pleasure the days of the King Cole Trio when Nat's reputation as a singer was subservient to his sparkling piano playing. It is worth noting that famed jazz pianist Oscar Peterson has said on more than one occasion that Cole was his first influence and Peterson's playing, even today, offers fragmentary reminders of how pianist Cole used to sound. Unlike most jazz-grounded vocalists, Nat Cole achieved enormous public acceptance. This is because he was able to effectively combine his considerable musical ability with an appealingly smooth delivery and a gentle infectious charm. But the rhythmic and harmonic strength gained from his jazz background could often be detected even in his most widely popular records.

Nathaniel Coles – he abbreviated his surname when he entered show business – was born on March 17th, 1919 in Montgomery, Alabama. The son of an ordained minister, Nat was raised in Chicago where he studied piano as a child. His link with jazz soon established itself, firstly via his enthusiasm for the recordings of pianist Earl Hines and later through his own work with various local jazz groups. At the age of 19 he made his recording debut in a small band led by his brother, bassist Eddie Cole.

Soon after this Nat formed his own band and left Chicago to tour with a vaudeville revue called *Shuffle Along*. When the show terminated he found himself in Los Angeles where he worked for a while as a solo pianist in various night clubs, then in 1939 he formed the celebrated King Cole Trio with Oscar Moore on guitar and Wesley Prince on bass. Legend has it that Nat never even thought of himself as a vocalist until one night an insistent customer, who had been drinking rather more than was good for him, kept requesting a vocal version of *Sweet Lorraine*. Not wishing to invite trouble Nat, who happened to have a lyric sheet on the piano, obliged by singing one chorus of the song.

The response was so encouraging that it was agreed to include vocals as part of the group's act. Between 1940 and 1941 they recorded for Decca after which they were featured on two obscure labels. It was in 1943 that Nat signed a recording contract with a new company called Capitol Records and in November of that year the trio recorded one of his compositions, a rhythmic novelty called *Straighten Up And Fly Right*. It proved to be the group's first big hit.

During the next three to four years Cole's career underwent a subtle change. Though still instrumentally active, he progressed almost imperceptibly from pianist/singer to singer/pianist. Even so, this did not prevent him from winning, as a pianist, the Esquire Gold Award (1946), Esquire Silver Award (1947) and the Metronome Jazz Poll (1947). The trio also won the Small Combo Award in Downbeat (1944–'47) and Metronome (1945–'48).

As a recording unit the trio made several discs during these early years that have since become minor classics – *Route 66*, *It's Only A Paper Moon* and the memorable *Sweet Lorraine*. In the 1940 Decca version of this tune (the trio also recorded it for Capitol) guitarist Moore ended the performance on a ninth chord with a flattened fifth. A startling departure in those days, it has since become a cliche practice.

In August, 1946 Cole recorded for the first time with a string section. The number was the highly successful *The Christmas Song*, a charming tune which had been presented to Nat by its composer, singer Mel Torme. This recording paved the way to greater things and did much to establish Cole as one of America's foremost ballad singers, although a recording session held in December of that same year provided a pleasantly ironic touch to this particular point in his career.

Having just been voted top pianist of 1946 by the readers of *Metronome* magazine, he was loaned out to Columbia Records to take part in a recording of unusual significance. In company with other poll-winning jazz players of that year such as Buddy Rich, Johnny Hodges and Charlie Shavers, pianist Cole formed part of the *Metronome All-Stars*. This distinguished group had been engaged to accompany the singer of that year, Frank Sinatra, on a special commemorative recording. The song Sinatra sang was *Sweet Lorraine*.

Back on the Capitol label, Nat 'King' Cole's reputation as a singer continued to flourish and as the demand for his vocal recordings increased he was obliged to discontinue the King Cole Trio. His piano work soon became a thing of the past. By 1949 he was recording almost exclusively with big orchestral accompaniments. Success followed success as Nat applied his smooth vocal style to such winning songs as *Mona Lisa* and *Too Young* (with the Les Baxter orchestra), *Orange Coloured Sky* (with Stan Kenton and his orchestra), *Walkin' My Baby*

*Back Home* (with the Billy May orchestra) and *Unforgettable* (with orchestra arranged and conducted by a talented new arranger named Nelson Riddle, who was soon to become world famous through his work with Frank Sinatra).

Throughout the '50s Nat 'King' Cole became solidly established as a top-flight international entertainer playing all the best locations and making concert tours of Australia, Cuba, South America and Great Britain. He also made singing and acting appearances in numerous films including *Small Town Girl*, *The Blue Gardenia* and *St Louis Blues*. In the last he played the leading part as blues composer, W. C. Handy. He also played himself in a technicoloured two-reeler called *The Nat King Cole Story*. In 1956–'57 he was the first Negro artist to have his own series on network TV; but he later abandoned the show because of the agencies' failure to find a national sponsor.

By 1962, Nat's disc sales were totalled at over 52 million and at the time of his death – from lung cancer on February 15th, 1965 – his record sales were in the region of 7 million copies per year. In the years since his death his popularity has shown little sign of dwindling. His recordings are still heavily featured on radio programmes and his albums still appear in the best seller lists. Cole's warm voice and suave sentimental approach may seem strangely at odds with the hectic times in which we now live but his enduring appeal probably lies in the fact that he provides the perfect antidote to the noisy present – the peaceful past!

If, as some of the younger listeners claim, Nat 'King' Cole sounds stylistically *passé*, there is absolutely no denying that musically he was far ahead of most of today's crop of hit paraders. Nat was never one to boast of his own ability but in the early '60s he became a little disturbed at the lack of quality in popular music. His remarks were characteristic of his professional outlook:

"There's more frustration now in the business than ever before. We know the overall quality is lower and so the incentive has been killed for some really good writers and performers. It's a terrible shame, isn't it, when you're told you can't do something because 'it's too good', and when so many people judge you not by whether you're good or bad but whether you're there in the first place. The big thing seems to be get there as fast as you can. Never anything about quality or whether it's going to last."

## RECOMMENDED RECORDINGS
**FOREVER YOURS** (Capitol/World Record Club): An expansive (but not too expensive) boxed set of six discs covering just about every aspect of Nat's talent from his piano-and-vocal work with the trio (*Sweet Lorraine*, *Route 66*, etc) through fine standards such as *Stardust* to well-known Cole hits like *Unforgettable* and *Mona Lisa*. The standard of repertoire is pretty high through most, if not all, of the 60 tracks. But the standard of Nat's performances never varies – he was a total professional and this deluxe package constitutes a worthwhile tribute to his talent.

**NAT KING COLE SINGS WITH THE KING COLE TRIO** (Music For Pleasure): This LP gives us the opportunity to hear voice and piano in a crisp jazz setting. Four of the tracks are taken from early trio sessions on Capitol, probably from the late '40s, while the remaining eight selections have been lifted from a marvellous 1956 re-union album called *After Midnight*. In the latter sessions the trio was re-formed with John Collins (guitar) and Charlie Harris (bass) plus Lee Young (drums). This tight little unit was augmented with some notable guest soloists including Juan Tizol (trombone) and Willie Smith (alto sax). The standard of singing, playing and material was of an exceptionally h h order.

**LOVE IS THE THING** (Capitol): Possibly Cole's most popular album, this features him with the lush string-laden arrangements of Gordon Jenkins and singing such mellow favourites as *When I Fall In Love, Stay As Sweet As You Are* and *At Last*. The net result is soft, restful listening but there are one or two moments when Jenkins lays on the saccharine a little too strongly and this can be nauseating to the cynical listener. But a person would have to be totally insensitive not to appreciate the sheer artistry of both singer and arranger in their splendid treatment of Hoagy Carmichael's *Stardust*.

**WHERE DID EVERYONE GO** (Capitol/World Record Club): This could well be considered as Nat's best ballad LP. It has more depth than *Love Is The Thing*. His way with a lyric was sometimes needlessly transparent, not so on this LP. The Cole voice never sounded so dramatic – listen to his subtle lyric nuances to be heard in the title song. The whole thing gets a bit gloomy in places – thanks to Gordon Jenkins, whose orchestrations occasionally go off the deep end – but the album as a whole is a beautiful piece of work from both singer and arranger.

**JUST ONE OF THOSE THINGS** (Capitol): Here's an album that should be included in any short-list of Cole LPs. Although Nat's reputation was established with soft caressing ballad performances, this LP is a solid reminder of his excellence as a rhythmic singer. The orchestrations (for brass, reeds and assorted percussion, etc) show off the full measure of arranger Billy May's talent. Not all the tracks are wildly swinging for there are one or two fine ballad selections. There is a masterful interpretation of *These Foolish Things* which starts in fine *colla voce* style then builds elegantly over one of the best arrangements May has ever conceived.

**COLE ESPANOLE** (Capitol): Nat Cole was one of the very few artists who recorded successfully in other languages. This skilfully rendered album which consists of Spanish love songs must be considered a huge success by any standards.

**NAT KING COLE AT THE SANDS** (Capitol): The only 'on-stage' recording of Cole, this was recorded in 1960 before a specially invited audience but was not issued until after the singer's death. Despite slight shortcomings, most of which have to do with the accompanying orchestra, this is well worth adding to one's collection. Why it was kept 'on ice' for so long is something of a mystery for, apart from a slight slip in the lyrics of an otherwise magnificent version of *Surrey With The Fringe On Top*, the whole LP shows Nat in wonderful voice.

**WILD IS LOVE** (Capitol, later issued on World Record Club): Cole described this album as 'the biggest thrill of my recording career'. With original songs by Ray Rasch and Dotty Wayne, the LP was conceived as a complete love story with Nat singing the songs and speaking the narrative. Not 100% successful it was nevertheless a gallant attempt at utilising the LP medium to try something different. Some of the songs – *A Beautiful Evening, Tell Her In The Morning, A Beggar For the Blues* and the title tune – are quite good and Nelson Riddle's fine orchestrations help to sustain interest, but it is really Nat Cole who commands the attention and makes the album worth buying.

**THE BEST OF NAT KING COLE** (Capitol): For a handy reference to most of the singer's biggest hits – and some of his most musicianly performances too – the casual record buyer could hardly do better than this well-programmed album. Because of his supreme musicality Nat Cole seemed able to invest any song with an element of greatness. A fact proved by all the tracks on this album.

*What was she like? Very easy to work with – never a problem!*

Les Brown

# Doris Day

The great girl singers have come in a variety of shapes, sizes and styles, and record collectors over the past 30 years have had an amazing selection of talents to choose from. Ella Fitzgerald with her wonderful phrasing. Sarah Vaughan's near-instrumental melodic improvisations, Jo Stafford and her academic perfection, the warmth and unpretentiousness of Dinah Shore and Rosemary Clooney, Eydie Gorme and her sheer professional skill, the heart-rending emotionalism of Judy Garland and Barbra Streisand. These and many others widened the fields of feminine vocalism to an extent undreamed of in the '30s.

It was in 1948 that Doris Day hit record buyers and film fans with a new element. Charm! Singing ability, yes, but it was her personal charm allied to a delightful unspoiled vivacity that, for a few years at least, entitled her to the World's Sweetheart throne vacated many years previously by Mary Pickford. You could even say she *was* the Mary Pickford of the '40s and '50s: the nice girl nothing bad could ever happen to, the blonde whose appeal to masculine instincts was the antithesis of that of the Grables and Monroes. (Well, may be Alice Faye had aroused the same instincts, but hers was a more mature, almost sophisticated appeal compared to that of Doris Day.)

Yet but for a near-fatal accident in her teens the world might never have heard of singer/actress Doris Day. Doris Kappelhoff the *premiere danseuse* maybe, but a singer, no. Even though her father was a trained musician and vocal coach in Cincinnati, Ohio, where she was born on April 3rd, 1924, Doris's one ambition and over-riding interest was dancing, and at the age of twelve she was on tour with a revue masterminded by film and stage choreographer Fanchon. But when a car in which she was travelling between dates lost an argument with an express train on a level-crossing, and Doris was hauled out of the wreckage, her leg was so severely broken that it was more than a year before she could walk, let alone dance.

Still fired by show business ambitions she now diverted her energy to trying to make it as a singer. So it was that 16-year-old Doris made her bow on a sustaining programme on Cincinnati's local radio station. (In lay terms this means she wasn't paid, but many singers used this means to gain exposure and hope that someone influential might be listening.) In Doris's case the influential listener was one Barney Rapp, a bandleader whose 'New Englanders' were one of Cleveland's musical landmarks, and who gave the youngster her first professional date at his club. The fee was all of 25 dollars, but its significance was less financial than a recognition of the fact that Doris Kappelhoff had faded out of the picture and Doris Day was on her way to stardom. It was Rapp who decided, not unnaturally, that Kappelhoff wasn't a great stage name, and changed it. There is a legend that he took the name from Doris's favourite song *Day By Day*, but as all this happened in 1940 and the song wasn't written till 1945 the story is presumably apocryphal.

This being the era of big bands, Doris Day, like so many others, set out to get a good grounding in band work. She played odd dates with Fred Waring's Pennsylvanians and was appearing at New York's Strand Theatre with the Bob Crosby band when Les Brown offered her the star vocal spot with his up-and-coming band. Shortly after, George T. Simon reviewed the band's engagement at Glen Island Casino in *Metronome* and said the following of the new singer:

". . . Doris Day, who for combined looks and voice has no apparent equal. She's pretty and fresh-looking, handles herself with unusual grace, and what's most important of all, sings with much natural feeling and in tune."

All this and still only sweet sixteen. But not too young for romance, and the Day career came to a halt a year later when Doris married trombonist Al Jordan and retired to domesticity. But with Jordan permanently on the road with Jimmy Dorsey's band the marriage broke up and she returned to Brown a few years later, just in time to notch up her first big record seller. This was *Sentimental Journey*, on which she was featured vocalist, and which later became Brown's signing-off theme. This and other band vocals like *'T ain't Me* and *Take Me In Your Arms* show her to have been a dependable singer indeed, although necessarily limited in terms of self-expression by the demands of dancing tempos and the need to subordinate her talent to that of the band.

This hit gave her the impetus to go solo, and she was appearing at the Little Club in New York when approached by Warner Brothers to do a screen test. Her first interview with brilliant director Michael Curtiz was something of a disaster, as her second marriage into the world of musicians, this time saxist George Wiedler, had also come unstuck and Doris was in a low state. But Curtiz recognised her talent and starred her in her first film *Romance On The High Seas* (retitled *It's Magic* in this country). Despite personal problems her debut was astonishing, revealing a gay, fresh personality, a supremely natural way of handling her lines, and a marvellous way with a song, be it the romantic *It's You Or No-one* or the jaunty novelty *Put 'Em In A Box*, which she sang with the Page Cavanagh Trio. In case the point hasn't been made, she was a natural! Someone in authority at Warners on seeing the film is supposed to have said 'Don't ever teach this kid to act!' One of the perks of this film was the gold disc she picked up for her recording of *It's Magic* (she had had her first one the previous year for *Confess/Love Somebody*, a pair of amiable duets with the late Buddy Clark).

From then on both Columbia Records and Warner Brothers kept her busy, and she turned out 15 Warner musicals in the next six years. All of them were pleasant but few memorable; their selling points were Doris Day's entertaining musical routines with people like Dennis Morgan, Jack Carson and (especially) Gordon Macrae. Obviously the bothersome leg of her teens had mended, as she proved a more than adequate partner for such expert dancers as Gene Nelson and Ray Bolger. Just when it seemed her screen musicals were getting in a rut Warner's handed her the plum role of *Calamity Jane*, a rumbustuous Western with Howard Keel. Even if it's ever forgotten as a film, which seems unlikely, it *will* be remembered as the source of her best-ever record, the song always associated with her – *Secret Love*. From then on she was more selective in her choice of musicals. One good choice was *Young at Heart* in which she and Frank Sinatra made nice music together. She had no male vocal competition in *Love Me Or Leave Me*, made on loan-out to MGM and in this biography of

'20s singer Ruth Etting she sang the entire score herself. This rather more dramatic portrayal showed the way Doris Day was to go in the next few years. There was one last fling with one of the best musicals of all, *The Pajama Game*, and although she returned in 1962 with *Jumbo* Doris Day was now, for better or for worse, an actress.

She got right away from type, playing terrified wives in *Julie*, *Midnight Lace* and *The Man Who Knew Too Much*, and although the latter gave her one song to sing (*Que Sera Sera*, another Hit Parade topper) audiences and critics alike were getting a little weary of her tear-stained face in movie after movie. Comedies like *Tunnel Of Love*, *It Happened To Jane* and *Please Don't Eat The Daisies* were better, and even if Doris had now forsaken musicals she generally managed to get a title song going to maintain her disc status.

Her albums for American Columbia (issued here on Philips) all did well, but even the most faithful must have noticed a deterioration in her singing. The dewy innocence of her early days had given way to a more brash approach to up-tempo numbers and a positive sloppiness of diction in ballads. In fact, it was sometimes difficult to distinguish her increasingly coy mannerisms from those of Alma Cogan, who had always emulated the Day style to a certain extent. Albums such as *Day By Night* and *Hooray for Hollywood*, chockful of good songs, suffered most in this respect and although *Bright & Shiny* and *I Have Dreamed* were above her current average it was still a case of 'things ain't what they used to be'.

Screenwise she achieved her most commercial impact in the '60s with a series of Ross Hunter comedies for Universal, but it was becoming increasingly difficult to accept a 40-year-old Doris Day as the chased but chaste maiden. Maybe her buoyant, natural approach of 15 years previously would have been wrong for these particular scripts, but the blatant over-acting in which she now indulged only succeeded in alienating at least one long term and fervent admirer.

Then suddenly, musically at least, she seemed to find herself again and maturity sat well on her in *Latin For Lovers*, a delightful CBS album of bossa novas. Doris had moved with the times, and in the right direction. But with the comparatively recent death of her husband, producer Marty Melcher, with whom she had found the happiness denied her in those immature musicians' marriages, Doris Day seems to have suspended, or at any rate relaxed, her professional activities.

In any event, she has been less involved in music in latter years, and we must assume she has no desire (certainly she has no need financially) to battle through the rat race to resume her former position in the world of records. But the dozens of likeable and often beautifully conceived 78s with which she brightened the scene in the '40s, and the thirty or more albums which enhanced the catalogues in the '50s and '60s, plus the TV re-runs of her old movies, lend more than a little validity to any claim she may have to be listed among the great popular singers.

RECOMMENDED RECORDINGS

**CALAMITY JANE/THE PAJAMA GAME** (CBS): One normal price LP containing the (almost) complete soundtracks of what are probably her two greatest screen musicals. Doris never sang better and as a bonus there are the lusty vocal talents of Howard Keel and John Raitt (though incredibly Raitt's *Hey There*, the big ballad of the mid-'50s, is omitted from the 'Pajama' score).

**LOVE ME OR LEAVE ME/YOUNG AT HEART** (CBS): Another single disc with double value. The soundtrack recording of the Etting biopic has 14 oldies, impeccably sung and swung. The half-dozen from *Young At Heart* are studio jobs; though they didn't become standards (although *You My Love* deserved to) the original compositions are worth remembering, plus the interpolated *Just One Of Those Things*.

**THE MAGIC OF DORIS DAY** (Hallmark): **GREAT MOVIE HITS** (Hallmark): So closely were her two careers interlinked it's hardly surprising that Doris Day's best albums reflect her film work. These two have many of her film hits, *Magic Of* concentrating on those early days with Warners and *Moonlight Bay*, *Tea For Two*, *I'll See You In My Dreams* etc. It also includes one of the warmest performances ever of Alec Wilder's great standard *I'll Be Around*. *Hits* recalls her later title songs like *Do Not Disturb*, *Pillow Talk*, *Send Me No Flowers*. *Magic* has one or two duplications from the *Calamity Jane* and *Love Me Or Leave Me* albums but at 79p who cares?

**LATIN FOR LOVERS** (CBS): The latter-day Doris reminds us what a good singer she can still be when she tries. Marvellous material including the best of Antonio Carlos Jobim – *Quiet Nights*, *Meditation*, *How Insensitive*, *Desafinado* – along with superior pops like *Our Day Will Come* and *Dansero*. Evocative string backings avoid the fulsome approach that could have swamped the delicacy of the idiom.

**SENTIMENTAL JOURNEY** (CBS): A reminiscent look at some of the great songs of the war years – also Doris Day's formative years; she must have sung many of these on the road with Les Brown. She does very well by *The More I See You*, *At Last*, *I'll Never Smile Again*, *It Could Happen To You*, *Serenade In Blue*, the title tune and many others of similar quality. This is one of these albums that quite convinces one that 'they don't write songs like that any more'.

AJ

*Mel is a constant pleasure to work with.*
*Some singers don't really know the*
*difference between a good arrangement*
*and a bad one . . . He not only appreciates*
*your work; he himself contributes more*
*to the planning of a vocal record than*
*just about any other singer you can name.*

Johnny Mandel

# Mel Torme

The pop music business is probably the only industry in the world that continually rejects material because it is 'too good to sell'. This strange attitude implies either a rigid determination not to improve the musical and artistic standards within the industry or simply a low regard for the public mentality.

This is not to imply that unpopularity or incompatibility with commercial requirements are the basic requisites of a great artist; take the case of Frank Sinatra, for instance, who has usually been able to make the kind of solidly musical records he wanted to within a completely commercial framework, or Peggy Lee, who seems to have worked on the principle of making one or two records to please other people in order to obtain the artistic freedom to make one record to please herself. Take the case, in fact, of all the singers in this book. The one thing they seem to have in common is that by pleasing themselves they have somehow ended up pleasing the general public, though not always the connoisseur. The exception to this rule is Mel Torme.

Torme is the only singer whose career is dealt with in this part of the book who does not possess a gold disc, which means that he has never made a record which sold a million copies. He is, in fact, the epitome of the type of artist who is, in the words of the industry, 'too good to sell'. But his exceptional singing skill, impeccable taste and the remarkable musical consistency of his recordings over the past twenty or so years constitute more than enough good reasons for his inclusion in this book. He is, quite undeniably, one of the very great popular singers.

Not that success has eluded Torme; on the contrary his records have occasionally enjoyed a measure of hit parade exposure and he is continually listed as one of the highest paid night club performers in the USA. As a composer, he was reponsible for that charming and perennially popular seasonal opus, *The Christmas Song*. One of the very few non-nauseating Christmas ballads, it was originally recorded by Nat 'King' Cole in 1946 and has since been recorded by just about every other major singer: Crosby, Sinatra, Bennett, Johnny Mathis, Jack Jones, etc. Annual royalties from this song alone have probably given Torme a reasonable income each year. He has other talents too: pianist, drummer, arranger, scriptwriter and actor. But it is as a singer that Torme has made his biggest impression – quite often with the general public, but always with the connoisseur.

Melvin Howard Torme was born in Chicago on September 13th, 1925. An avid radio listener from virtual infancy, he would sing along with all the well-known broadcasting bands of the '20s. It might be true to say that Torme could sing almost before he could talk. His father, pleasantly startled by the uncanny accuracy of his son's vocal pitch, took the youngster to meet Joe Sanders of the famous Coon-Sanders Orchestra. As a result of this meeting Mel Torme gave his first professional performance – two choruses of *You're Driving Me Crazy* with the accompaniment of the Coon-Sanders Orchestra at the Blackhawk Restaurant in Chicago. At the time of this momentous debut, Torme was just four years old.

By the time he had reached his sixth birthday, Mel was well on his way to becoming a seasoned entertainer. To supplement his singing ability he took up drums and later taught himself to play piano. At the age of eight, he graduated into radio 'soap operas' (a term used to describe a typical long-running radio drama or comedy series, because they were usually sponsored by soap manufacturers). In high school, Torme turned songwriter and at the age of fifteen wrote his first hit song called *Lament To Love*, which was later recorded by the Harry James Orchestra with Dick Haymes handling the vocal.

On leaving high school, Mel's musical talents were noticed by veteran drummer and bandleader-cum-agent, Ben Pollack, who took Torme under his wing. One of Pollack's projects at that time was to organize a band to be fronted by Chico Marx (of the Marx Brothers). Pollack arranged for the 17-year-old Torme to join the band as singer, vocal arranger and substitute drummer. He remained with the band until it broke up and the following year (1943), Mel made his film debut in *Higher And Higher* (a picture that also marked the first solo film appearance of Frank Sinatra).

The next phase of Torme's career proved to be one of subtle musical development when he formed his celebrated vocal group, The Mel-Tones, which emerged as a stimulating forerunner of excellent units like The Hi-Los and the Four-Freshmen. Torme had been introduced, through Ben Pollack, to a group of five Los Angeles City College students who sang mostly for fun. What interested Torme was that they sang extremely well. Their own arranger and bass singer was about to be drafted in to the Army, so the four remaining members of the group were happy to join forces with Torme who just happened to be a vocal group arranger without a vocal group. After working for a while as The Skylarks, it was generally agreed that The Mel-Tones would be a better and more appropriate name.

Artistic recognition for the Mel-Tones was quickly achieved throughout the profession because of their superior musicianship. The public at large, however, were a little harder to convince. While the group were unable to rely on the income from their records for a good living, they were constantly in demand on radio shows and film soundtracks. Bandleader Artie Shaw was impressed enough to offer some choice work to the group which included the recording of a batch of Cole Porter songs. One of these – *What Is This Thing Called Love* – proved to be a good seller and even went on to be regarded as something of a pop classic. The Mel-Tones were also notably featured on Bing Crosby's recording of *Day By Day*. The group broke up in 1945 when Torme was called up for Army service. After his discharge, a year later, the Mel-Tones re-formed for a while but they were still too imaginative for the public taste and commercial response was not strong enough. Regretfully, Torme disbanded the group.

In November, 1946, he put his affairs in the hands of manager Carlos Gastel, who successfully launched him on a solo singing career which to this day has not been interrupted, although it has been bolstered on occasions by Mel's activities as a composer, actor and writer.

As a composer he formed a creative partnership with ex-drummer Robert Wells, the fruits of which can be found in such excellent songs as *Born To Be Blue*, *Willow Road*, *The Christmas Song* and the delightful *County Fair*, which was written for the 1947 Walt Disney feature film *So Dear To My Heart*. The latter composition, which was a remarkably successful attempt at extending the popular song form into a complete and varied narrative depicting all the fun and activities of a typical county fair, was obviously the precursor to an even more ambitious work which Torme later wrote by himself, *The California Suite*.

He spent six months composing the music and lyrics for this 30-minute suite dedicated to his adopted home state and, on its completion, it was recorded by Capitol with Torme singing the leading part opposite a girl calling herself Susan Melton (a *nom de plume* for none other than Peggy Lee). Eight years later, when Torme was recording for the American Bethlehem label, a second version of the *California Suite* was recorded. Artistically, there is very little to choose between the two versions, but the second one is technically better from an orchestral and recording point of view and, of course, the older Torme certainly sings with far more authority. The first version, however, carries perhaps a little more charm in the overall interpretation.

Among the films in which Torme appeared in the late '40s were *Good News* – with June Allyson – and MGM's all-star tribute to the work of Rodgers and Hart, *Words And Music*. In this last film, Torme was prominently featured singing *Blue Moon*, a song which subsequently became one of his biggest hits on record.

In December, 1954, while appearing in cabaret at Hollywood's Crescendo night club, his performances were recorded by jazz impresario Gene Norman and the tapes resulted in an album called *Mel Torme At The Crescendo*. In March, 1956, when the LP was released in Britain on the old Vogue-Coral label, Alan

Dell – one of this country's more tasteful disc jockeys – played one of the tracks over the air. The song was Rodgers and Hart's *Mountain Greenery* and Torme's distinctive treatment of it brought forth a totally unexpected flood of mail from excited listeners eager to hear more of this man Torme. For some years previously, he had been known to the American public as the 'Velvet Fog' because of the smooth misty texture of his voice. The term was quickly taken up by British disc jockeys. It was not long before the whole of Britain became Torme-conscious and *Mountain Greenery* (which had been quickly issued as a single) shot into the hit parade.

It was not, as many people believed, his first record to be issued in Great Britain. Torme had been scoring minor successes in the British market for some years through his fine work on the Capitol label with discs such as *Four Winds And The Seven Seas*, *Again* and *Blue Moon*. But *Mountain Greenery* was definitely his first British chart entry. When news of its success reached him in California he was delighted, but somewhat puzzled since he had no great recollection of having recorded the song.

When he made his first visit to this country in July, 1956, the press and music critics – some of whom had openly doubted his ability to hold an audience because of his extreme vocal subtlety – found themselves eulogising along with the general public over his supreme professionalism and magnetic showmanship. The most amazing point about Torme's triumph was that it occurred at the height of the rock 'n' roll era when tasteless out-of-tune caterwauling was the 'in' thing. This rare enthusiasm for a true professional gave the very solid impression that the pop industry had at last come to its senses. But, unfortunately, as soon as Torme left to return to the States it was back to 'business as usual'.

In the years since 1956, Torme has been a fairly regular visitor to Britain. He still commands a reasonably healthy following and his shows are always successful. The sheer technical brilliance of Torme's singing has always made him something of a loner in the pop field. He has devoted himself with unworldly dedication to creating the finest musical impressions of the very best songs. This was especially apparent in the middle-to-late 1950s, when he made a number of really exciting and subtle LPs with arranger/conductor Marty Paich that fully revealed his exceptional vocal talents. But it is this remote quality, this hermetic perfection, which has resulted in Torme being criticised as an unemotional singer. But what is emotion? To some people, it is the tortured lung-bursting belting of Tom Jones or it could be the honest cracked-up wailing of Ray Charles or maybe the darkly brooding tones of Sinatra at his most melancholy. Torme belongs in none of these categories. But his cool college-boy voice certainly does carry its own level of emotion.

To take a specific example. Compare Torme's interpretation of *When The World Was Young* (from the Atlantic LP, *Mel Torme At The Red Hill*) with Frank Sinatra's version (from the Capitol LP, *Point Of No Return*). Sinatra certainly sounds much lonelier than Torme. In fact he sounds like he has just encountered his fiftieth successive taste of unrequited love. It's a convincing study of submissive loneliness. Torme's voice, on the other hand, has a more innocent quality and suggests a completely different environment. He sounds like a newcomer to loneliness, as though this was his *first* case of heartbreak. The sadness is there, but it's a muted sadness not as immediately communicative as Sinatra's approach perhaps, but stylishly effective in its own way and so beautifully rendered.

On the cabaret floor Torme has one of the most dynamic and entertaining acts imaginable. His singing voice (which, on record, tends to sound small) is unbelievably powerful and he has a rare gift for alternating between wild jazz, with high comedy overtones (his vocal impression of Miles Davis's trumpet playing is particularly funny – and clever), to softly intoned ballad interpretations without losing an ounce of authority or communication on either level.

As a rhythmic singer, Mel Torme has absolutely no peers. His ability to swing, to generate excitement, in any tempo makes him the most unrestricted stylist in the popular field. This was well demonstrated in 1962 when he employed his rhythmic prowess to excellent commercial effect with his hit recording of the rhythm-and-blues number *Comin' Home, Baby*. In fact, he must be the only white singer to score a substantial hit in the R & B world without using a pseudo-Negro accent. In analysing the reasons for Torme's lack of large-scale mass acceptance, American journalist and lyricist Gene Lees observed that Torme would occasionally strike a hit formula but instead of following it up with more of the same, his next recording would be of a completely different nature. Consequently, the average record buyers find it difficult to follow his activities. True to his form, Torme did not continue to cash in on the success of *Comin' Home, Baby*. His subsequent recordings were of a far more sophisticated character. In 1965 when Torme was in London, I asked him about this continued rejection of a commercial formula. His reply was typical of his reputation: "Well, first of all the word formula turns me off. The very word formula indicates that one is going about music in a precise manner and this leaves no room for any creative instincts . . . I never make an album with the intention of it being a hit. I try to the best of my ability to make it a good musical album. If it happens to sell too, great! Now that may be an unrealistic attitude for a singer to take . . . but, in deep frankness, that's the way I feel." Another subject on which I tackled Torme was his notorious dislike of cheap and artless pop music. I asked him if he saw any likelihood of an improvement in hit parade trends. "It's difficult to say. Just when it seems to be improving, something horrendous musically comes along and shatters my faith. I think that it improves in very, very slow waves . . . it improves minimally. But I think that, more than ever, we're in a crassly commercial market where the bulk of the show business idiom is dedicated to my old favourite saying – Prosperity and not Posterity. Everything has become purely that – a cold-blooded cash business. Whatever sells, whatever makes the most money – it doesn't matter whether it's creative, amateurish, professional, sloppy, horrible, beautiful – as long as it makes money."

Though one can sense a certain underlying bitterness in Torme's words, jumping onto someone else's bandwagon is something that he can never be accused of – and on the occasions when he does manage to get into the hit parade, he doesn't even jump onto his *own* bandwagon. But, as Gene Lees wrote in *Down Beat* magazine:

> "Those who like him – and a great many musicians and singers rate him their favourite male vocalist – aren't much interested in the proper defini-tion of him. They just dig the way he sings: in a style that can be soft and subtle, or hard and belting, as the lyrics may demand; with a clear under-standing of words and their meaning; with precise near-perfect time; with a control of pitch that is almost uncanny."

Torme has always managed to remain very much his own man. With his artistic attitude it is perhaps not surprising that he has never earned a gold record, but as pop music continues to dash headlong into an uncertain future, the wonderfully skilful recordings of Mel Torme will surely become more golden as the years go by.

## RECOMMENDED RECORDINGS

**MEL TORME SWINGS** (Verve VSP series): This double pack comprises two LPs from the early '60s. The first, a collection of show tunes, was originally titled *Torme Swings Shubert Alley*. This is utterly brilliant in every respect and perfectly highlights the joint musical ingenuity of Torme and musical director Marty Paich. The second record, a vocal tribute to two great bandleaders, was issued in 1962 as *I Dig The Duke, I Dig The Count*, and is not nearly so successful. It suffers from poor sound balancing and some slightly heavy orchestrations by Johnny Mandel. Also Torme's choice of keys seems to have robbed his voice of its full tonal potential (an odd move for *him* to make). Nevertheless, there are some good tracks even on this LP. Buy this package for the first disc and you'll be able to live with (or without?) the second.

**SUNDAY IN NEW YORK** (Atlantic): All the components one could wish for in a first-class vocal LP are here; great singing, fine arrangements (by Johnny Williams, Dick Hazard and Shorty Rogers) and top-class songs. The LP is beautifully produced, with the appealing title song setting the mood for a nicely contrasting set of tunes about New York.

**LULU'S BACK IN TOWN** (Atlantic Special): A reissue of the first LP to feature Torme with the celebrated Marty Paich Dektette. The standard of Torme's musicianship is well showcased here and so is his biting sense of humour (lend an ear to his treatment of Rodgers and Hart's *I Like To Recognise The Tune*). Although this set was recorded in 1956 neither the arrangements nor the singing seem to have dated, and this compelling freshness makes such wonderful tracks as *When the Sun Comes Out*, *The Blues* (a marvellous excerpt from Duke Ellington's *Black, Brown and Beige* suite) and *The Carioca* even more valuable to an interesting record collection.

**MEL TORME AT THE RED HILL** (Atlantic): Although slightly pretentious in places, this is a stimulating sample of Torme showing off his incredible technique as a scat vocalist. His improvisations on *Love For Sale* (which also reveals his ability as a pianist) and *Anything Goes* are quite magnificent. But a little of this expertise, no matter how brilliant (and they don't come any better than Torme) goes a long way. Fortunately, this album contains some sensitive ballad treatments of songs like *Nevertheless*, *When The World Was Young*, *Fly Me To the Moon* and *Early Autumn*.

**SWINGING ON THE MOON** (World Record Club): Torme is in top form in this very listenable album of moon songs – *Blue Moon*, *I Wished On The Moon*, *Moonlight In Vermont*, etc – and is also responsible for writing a thoroughly imaginative title song which gets the album off to a grand start. Good arrangements, too, from Russ Garcia.

**RIGHT NOW** (CBS): Like all great artists, Torme has the talents to rise above poor or indifferent material. On this LP of 'current' pops of the mid-'60s, he does just that. Not all the material is bad though. Amongst the better songs are Burt Bacharach's *Walk On By* and Simon and Garfunkel's *Homeward Bound*. Of particularly interest to Torme fans is his more musical re-make of his 1963 hit *Comin' Home, Baby*.

**RAINDROPS KEEP FALLING ON MY HEAD** (Capitol): A shining example of the 1970 contemporary Torme, this LP reveals his ability to move with the times. He is one of the very few singers of his generation who seems to grasp the meaning of today's pop music without losing his own stylistic identity. The majority of the fourteen tracks on this album offer full proof of this point although he could have made a more sensitive attempt at Lennon and McCartney's *She's Leaving Home* which is taken at too brisk a tempo or *You Made Me So Very Happy*, which suffers from a dreadful arrangement. Torme's own composition *Into Something* shows that he can also write effectively in the contemporary idiom. For two beautifully contrasting tracks, listen to his unique approach to the Blood, Sweat & Tears hit *Spinning Wheel* and compare it with his high-powered version of Donovan's *Sunshine Superman*.

The on-screen Doris Day sings with piano accompaniment from
Oscar Levant (in her debut film *It's Magic*—US title *Romance On
the High Seas*)and...with famous songwriter Hoagy Carmichael
(a scene from *Young Man of Music*)./Warner Bros

*Above:* A radiant Doris Day in a scene from the 1954 film *Young at Heart.*/*Warner Bros*

*Below:* The young Mel Torme. A publicity shot from the '40s.
/*Melody Maker*

*Right:* Torme at a social gathering with Marilyn Monroe, Sammy Davis Jnr and friend.

The mature Mel Torme making a 1965 guest appearance on a
BBC-TV variety show./*BBC*

The incomparable Sarah Vaughan on one of her many visits to Great Britain./*Courtesy Arthur Jackson*

A friendly smile from Tony Bennett.

Bennett on stage. Every performance is an object lesson in audience communication.

In the recording studio Tony Bennett prefers to sing in front of
the orchestra rather than work from an enclosed vocal booth as
most other singers do today. 'Just put me out front next to the
piano', he says to the engineers. 'That way everything'll feel more
like a real performance'. In the background bass player Arthur
Watts and Tony's regular accompanist, John Bunch./Harry Prosser

While recording, Tony Bennett works on a purely intuitive level
preferring to emphasise the *emotional* rather than the *technical*
aspects of a song./Harry Prosser

Ethel Waters, a superb vocalist and possibly the first of the great
Negro entertainers.

*Left:* The last of the red hot mamas. The irrepressible Sophie Tucker of course.

*Below left:* The first of the romantic crooners—or at least the first to earn a gold disc award—Gene Austin. This, of course, is a latter day portrait. Mr Austin died in January, 1972, this picture was probably taken a year earlier./*RCA Records*

*Below:* Another latter day study of perhaps the most celebrated crooner of the pre-Crosby period, Rudy Vallee./*Warner Bros*

*Right:* 'One of the really great ladies of the singing business' is how Bing Crosby described Connie Boswell, and the great Ella Fitzgerald was said to have modelled her style on Connie's unique vocal approach

Best wishes from

Connie Boswell

The handsome Russ Columbo—
seen here in the 1933 film
*Broadway Through a Keyhole.*
The attentive young lady is
Constance Cummings. Columbo,
a much respected singer in his
day, was regarded as the only
really serious rival to Bing
Crosby. Unfortunately he died
before anyone was able to
properly assess his talent on a
scale comparable to Crosby's.
The year after this film was made
Columbo was killed accidentally
while cleaning a gun./*United Artists*

Remember *The Very Thought of
You, Goodnight Sweetheart* and
*By the Fireside?* These were just
three of the songs so closely
associated with the late Al
Bowlly. Today, more than three
decades after his death in a
London air raid, his recordings
are still being bought by avid
collectors. Appreciation of his
singing has almost reached
cult-like proportions. In his
hey-day, South African-born
Bowlly was undoubtedly Britain's
most important contributor.

The peerless Fred Astaire introduced more great songs to the standard popular repertoire than any other performer in the history of show business. Although his enduring fame has rested mainly on his dancing ability, he has come to be recognized over the years as an important and certainly unique vocalist.

Dick Powell—pictured here in *On The Avenue* with co-star Madeleine Carroll—enlivened a whole string of Hollywood musicals in the '30s. Though never a particularly inspired stylist, Powell was certainly one of the most successful song salesmen of his era. Amongst the fine standards originally popularised by him are *I Only Have Eyes For You, I Get Along Without You Very Well* and, from the above 1937 film, *I've Got My Love to Keep Me Warm.*
*/20th Century Fox*

Alice Faye sings, Al Jolson listens. A scene from the 1939 film *Rose of Washington Square.* The delectable Miss Faye, who once worked as vocalist with Rudy Vallee's band, sang in a natural and unaffected style well in keeping with her attractive screen image. She was responsible for the original popularity of such excellent songs as *This Year's Kisses* (1937) and *You'll Never Know* (1943) to mention but two./*20th Century Fox*

*Above left:* 'A total professional' is how someone once described Jo Stafford. Jo's early professional experience as a staple member of Tommy Dorsey's fine vocal group The Pied Pipers has always stood her in good stead musically—while subsequent million sellers like *You Belong to Me, Shrimp Boats* and *Make Love to Me* proved her commercial value as a solo performer.

*Above right:* Dinah Shore on stage at the London Palladium, 1949. Dinah was perhaps America's most popular female vocalist of the '40s. Today, she is still a top attraction on US television... and singing just as well as ever.

The lovely young Lena Horne and Eddie 'Rochester' Anderson vocally agree that *Life's Full of Consequences.* A memorable duet sequence from the 1943 musical film *Cabin in the Sky.* /MGM

Lena Horne as she is today. Still one of the world's most exciting singers—both vocally and visually./Ember Records

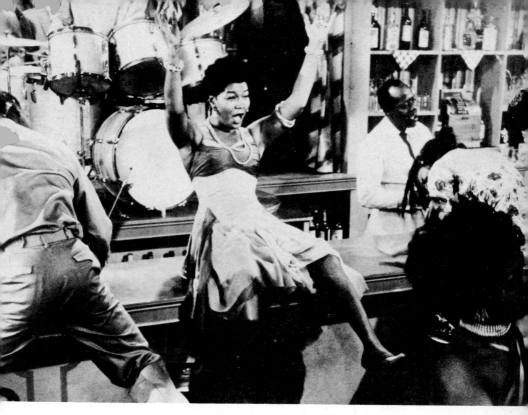

*Beat Out That Rhythm on a Drum* sings Pearl Bailey in this lively scene from that exciting 1954 film musical *Carmen Jones*. For many years the gifted Miss Bailey has hovered close to real greatness as a jazz vocalist, but her pre-eminence as a comedienne and raconteur somehow got in the way. But for the connoisseur—or anyone who takes the time to listen—the singing of 'Pearlie Mae' is always a rewarding experience.

Margaret Whiting, daughter of the famous song-writer Richard Whiting, was responsible for the original popularity of that beautiful standard *Moonlight in Vermont* which she turned into a million seller in 1944. She was also the first female vocalist to set up her own music publishing company, promoting many famous songs written by her father who died in 1938. Her warm and musicianly voice made her queen of America's juke boxes between 1945 and 1950.

*Above left :* Durability is the most enviable quality a singer can possess. After three decades at the top, Vera Lynn—the 'Forces Sweetheart'—has firmly established her staying power and even today it shows no signs of weakening.

*Above right :* The exuberant Kay Starr, easily America's most dynamic female singer of the '50s, Kay's vocal career goes back many years. She sang with the Glenn Miller orchestra at the age of 16, and by her early twenties she was a most accomplished jazz singer. Commercial success came in 1952 with her world-wide hit *Wheel of Fortune*, which proved to be the first of many such triumphs. She was, however, a far more subtle singer than her hit records suggested. But that's show business for you!

*Sassy irritated me for a long while . . .*
*She was groping around, searching for*
*a style, for a musical identity. She*
*finally found it . . . just straight singing*
*with very little of that wandering around*
*in the upper stratosphere . . . Sassy is*
*so good now that when I listen to her I*
*want to cut my wrists with a dull razor.*

Frank Sinatra

# Sarah Vaughan

Probably the most difficult task in the field of jazz, from the point of view of acceptance, is that undertaken by the vocalist. According to the so-called pundits, jazz is an idiom reserved almost exclusively for instrumentalists. The constant argument that there is no such thing as a jazz vocalist is in itself ridiculous since the earliest forms of jazz were nothing but vocal. But things being the way they are, one of the few ways for a singer to make an impression with the 'hip' faculty is by adopting – or trying to adopt – an instrumental approach, ignoring the meaning of lyrics and concentrating almost solely on sound for its own sake.

This is the contemporary approach – slick, cold and clinical. It may explain why the last ten years have failed to produce any artists of the calibre of Sarah Vaughan and it may also explain why Sarah has shown the good sense to concentrate on making records of a more popular nature. Not that her taste is infallible, but the quality of her musicianship and the sheer beauty of her tone place her undeniably among the great singers. The fact that she has successfully wandered from the esoteric confines of the jazz field into the fickle world of pop music, while still maintaining her musical worth, qualifies her for inclusion.

It must be added that as a jazz vocalist Sarah will never be as significant as Billie Holiday. Nor are her record sales likely to be as great as Ella Fitzgerald's. But Miss Vaughan has influenced more vocalists than the other two put together. And like them, she is immediately identifiable and completely original.

Blessed with a strong mellow voice of almost operatic dimensions (three octaves, give or take a couple of notes), endowed with a gift for pitch that must make other singers green with envy plus an impeccable sense of time, 'Sassy', as she is sometimes called, has the lot. Indeed, in the technical department she is beyond reproach. These very qualities, which have always endeared her to fellow singers and musicians, were skilfully applied to such hit parade items as *Broken Hearted Melody* and *Passing Strangers* (with Billy Eckstine).

Sarah Lois Vaughan was born March 27th, 1924 in Newark, New Jersey. Her father was a carpenter, her mother a laundress. Like so many other singers, Sarah started as a member of the local church choir. At the age of seven she took piano lessons, which later led to an interest in the organ, at which she became fairly proficient. As her interest in music developed, she found an ear for jazz. In 1943 she won an amateur singing contest at Harlem's Apollo Theatre and was heard by Billy Eckstine, then vocalist with the Earl Hines band. On Eckstine's advice she was signed by Hines as singer and second pianist.

A year later she joined a new band formed by Eckstine, a band that was to become one of the most celebrated units in jazz history. Eckstine, who played valve trombone then, took an occasional vocal. But mainly it was Sarah who did the singing. The band was well received and much has been written about it since. There remains, alas, very little recorded evidence to support its reputation. Such recordings that the band did make were so poorly balanced that they were deemed unsuitable for release. Sarah's own recorded efforts at this time proved much more fruitful. Her first solo recording session, which was organised by noted jazz critic Leonard Feather, took place on December 31st, 1944, and these were certainly of a releasable standard.

After leaving the Eckstine band in 1945, Sarah worked for a couple of months with the John Kirby group at New York's Copacabana club. Shortly after this she began to make a favourable impression as a solo performer. In 1947 she married trumpeter George Treadwell, who devoted himself to successfully building her into a star attraction (he even continued to assist her career after they were divorced).

By the early '50s she had gained an international reputation almost comparable to that of Ella Fitzgerald, toured Britain and France and became a major concert attraction in the USA. Over the past twenty years her popularity – despite the expected commercial ups and downs – has continued to flourish. In 1969, her twelve-year-old duet recording with Billy Eckstine of *Passing Strangers*, a perennial favourite on radio request programmes, made a surprising appearance in the British top twenty.

For all her vocal ingenuity and tonal richness, there are some aspects of Sarah Vaughan's singing style that can be quite irksome – sometimes even to her most ardent admirers. That peculiar little-girl characteristic, so winsome on her early recordings (notably her 1945 recording of *Lover Man* with Charlie Parker and Dizzy Gillespie), has become embarrassingly coy over the years. That wonderful voice is so often unnecessarily burdened with tasteless mannerisms and pointless affectations which add nothing to her artistic stature and only serve to diminish her emotional powers.

Dubbed by critics and musicians as the Divine Sarah, she often comes uncomfortably close to losing that divinity by wilfully overstepping the boundaries of good taste. She has, of course, turned out a fair proportion of remarkable and near-flawless recordings. Her warmly poignant *September Song*, which was enhanced by the fine trumpet playing of the late Clifford Brown, shows her at her best. A prime example of her singing outside of jazz is her immensely powerful straight reading of *The Lord's Prayer*. This proves what a truly exceptional singer she can be.

It is said that artists are usually bad judges of their own work. Sarah Vaughan is obviously well aware of her magnificent musical gift, but the sheer grandiloquence of her voice would register with far more authority if she could take a leaf out of Ella Fitzgerald's book, relax and be herself. The talent she has needs no artifice. It should be allowed to speak for itself. And speak it certainly did on her 1972 tour of Great Britain in which she displayed a perfect balance of taste and technique. According to trombonist/bandleader Harry Roche, who played on the tour, Sarah was "singing better than I had ever heard her before. And I have heard her lots of times before. In my opinion Sarah Vaughan could very well be the finest female singer in the business."

## RECOMMENDED RECORDINGS

**SARAH VAUGHAN featuring Clifford Brown and others** (Mercury): Quite simply, this is Sarah at her very best. The songs, for the most part, are very good and the accompaniments (apart from some out-of-tune flute playing from Herbie Mann) are pleasantly unobtrusive. Sarah's mannerisms are less evident and her attention to lyrics is quite touching. Brown's trumpet work is a thing of beauty and the general feeling is that here is one of the great vocal and instrumental records of all time simply because Sarah Vaughan and Clifford Brown are on it.

**SARAH VAUGHAN SINGS GEORGE GERSHWIN** (Mercury – 2 LPs): One of the most consistently tasteful sets ever recorded by Sarah. As is to be expected with Gershwin, the songs are first class and Hal Mooney's orchestrations are perfectly complementary to both singer and material. As for Sarah, she treats the songs with the maximum of sympathy and the minimum of fuss. Absent is the exaggerated phrasing and in its place a warm and forthright respect of the composer's intentions.

**YOU'RE MINE YOU** (Allegro/Roulette): A fine crop of songs (*Witchcraft*, *The Best Is Yet To Come*, *The Second Time Around*, etc) and good arrangements by Quincy Jones seem to spur Sarah into giving a good account of herself in spite of the odd moment or two when her attention to lyrics gives way to senseless note-bending. It's still an album worth hearing, though.

**THE EXPLOSIVE SIDE OF SARAH VAUGHAN** (Eros): This LP, which shows Sarah in fine voice (still slightly affected, in places) is worth having for some beautifully constructed arrangements from Benny Carter. The accompaniments, for the most part, inspire Sarah to phrase in a way that benefits the lyrics. The only exception is a disastrous *I Believe In You*. But the rest of the album is wonderful.

**A TIME IN MY LIFE** (Mainstream-Red Lion, USA): A monumental example of Sarah's great versatility. Here she transfers perfectly into a totally contemporary 1972 pop groove. Fine arrangements from Benny Carter and a well selected batch of 'today' songs make this a satisfying slice of Sarah's art.

> *I know that he has never ceased to respect*
> *quality in a writer, both lyrically and*
> *musically, and to insist throughout his*
> *career on singing the good song – as*
> *opposed to the topical song . . . He challenges*
> *fashion. He takes chances – and he wins.*
>                                                    Alec Wilder

# Tony Bennett

Tony Bennett is one of that small, and rapidly diminishing, group of popular singers who realise the full value of audience communication. Not just the mass communication that comes from a string of hit records (although Bennett has certainly had an impressive quota of commercial success on disc), but the genuine desire to get out in front of flesh-and-blood audiences and sing with noticeable enthusiasm night after night: to be, if you like, an *entertainer*.

Not that Bennett puts on any professional airs, on the contrary he manages to somehow communicate the impression of the ordinary man who has been talked into getting up to sing a song for his friends. There is even something slightly clumsy about his on-stage deportment, but his manner is humble, his smile is infectious and he looks as though he genuinely enjoys every minute up there in front of the band. So if Bennett's records do sell in vast quantities it is as much due to this humble quality as it is to his unique voice.

Like Crosby and Sinatra, Bennett has mastered the art of making everything he does seem pleasantly casual. That this is not as easy as it looks was made clear to me when I first met Tony Bennett at London's Mayfair Hotel in May, 1965. An appointment had been arranged for me to interview him for *Crescendo* and I was accompanied by the magazine's editor, Mr Tony Brown, who had brought his camera along in the hope of getting a photograph. Mr Brown got his photograph all right – but I didn't get my interview.

Bennett met us in the hotel's reception lounge and explained that he had received a call for an urgent rehearsal in connection with a TV show he was doing for the BBC. It was immediately necessary for him to work through a large portion of his repertoire so that the show's producer, Yvonne Littlewood, could get some idea of how many numbers could be included in the show's allotted time and to determine which songs would finally be featured. Bennett apologised for his unavailability but suggested that if we joined him at the rehearsal in the Lansdowne Room (the only available room in the hotel that had a piano) then our journey may not be completely wasted. Naturally, we accepted his invitation.

Although there was no opportunity on this occasion to interview Bennett (I had to wait until 1967 for that), I found that watching him in rehearsal – accompanied by Ralph Sharon (piano), Hal Gaylor (bass), Billy Exiner (drums) and Bobby Hackett (cornet) – presented me with a far sharper picture of Bennett the professional than could possibly have been gleaned from an interview. What follows is an edited transcript of my report which appeared in the June, 1965 issue of *Crescendo*.

Like all the best singers, Tony Bennett is never satisfied with second best and the two highly enjoyable hours spent watching (and hearing) this talented man certainly confirmed this. He picks the best songs, uses the best musicians (and works them extremely hard) and sings, with considerable intensity, to the best of his undoubted ability.

Apart from his obvious vocal qualities, Bennett has a penchant (one might almost call it an obsession) for unearthing many excellent songs, unhackneyed items which might otherwise remain in obscurity. For example, there was his opening number *Take The Moment*, an engaging little swinger with a nice chord sequence and a charming lyric. This was followed by another 'find' of equal merit called *Two By Two*. But during the warm-up, Bennett wasn't happy about the group's phrasing behind his vocal. "Hold it for a moment. You're not in the right groove. Just dig what I'm singing here. Okay? Let's go again."

During what seemed to be a satisfactory run-through, Bennett nodded his approval – but still issued instructions to drummer Exiner at the end: "Don't lay it on so heavy when you take the break after the piano solo. Make it very soft, I don't want to come in shouting on the last chorus." One more run-through and Bennett was satisfied. He was smiling.

But the real problems, not just for the musicians but for Bennett too, came in the routining for *Fly Me To The Moon*. Opening with the verse out-of-tempo, Bennett implored the group to take special notice of his choice of tempo for the chorus. Again, it was Billy Exiner who was at fault: "It's too fast, Billy." Without further comment, Bennett sailed straight into the verse again. It should be noted that Bennett is one of those singers who don't need the pianist to keep reminding them which key they're singing in. Once he gets the note in his head, it stays there regardless of interruptions. Once again, the tempo was too fast: "Dig what I'm singing, Billy, please. That goes for you too, Hal."

Three more attempts, and the problem still remained. Bennett held up his hand: "Stop." He handed cigarettes around and, after lighting up, said in a quiet voice: "I can only feel this song one way, *my* way. The tempo is going to be so slow, you won't believe it." Bass player Gaylor said: "I don't see how it can go much slower, I'm only playing one accent in the bar. Unless it moves a shade faster, my part is going to sound empty."

"Look baby," counters Bennett, "take my word for it – everything will work out fine if you can only get into my groove. Why should it be such a problem?"

"Well it is a problem," said Exiner. "It's a physical problem and we ought to stop and think about it for a moment."

"Take all the time you want," said Bennett. "Years ago when I worked with dance bands I had to sing everything in strict, square tempo." He pointed to the metronome on top of the piano. "This song here may seem wrong to you as far as my treatment is concerned, but I can tell you fellas that if I can only feel it one way. . . then that's the *right* way for *me*. So can we do it, please?"

The next attempt was only slightly closer to what Bennett wanted.

"Hold it, hold it," he said, gesturing to Bobby Hackett who had been blowing a tasteful and relaxed obligato to the singing. "I got an idea, Bobby, I want you to make like a string section. You know – a long, lyrical, sweeping sort of intro. That might get everyone in the mood."

Hackett blew a brief, but beautiful intro showing just why he has remained one of the most respected horn men in jazz.

This brought a smile from Bennett, but it didn't solve his problem. He threw up his arms in apparent resignation. "Just think about it, will you? If you get that first bar right, it'll be right all the way."

Ralph Sharon began playing the first few bars in an attempt to feel out Bennett's tempo, getting progressively slower. On the third try Bennett looked across at Sharon. "That's it," he said. "Thank you very much. Let's try again." This time the result was perfect and Bennett's smile was broader than ever. There followed a string of more familiar songs – *How About You, April In Paris* and *Anything Goes.* This last one, Bennett had decided to turn into a minor jam session with solos for everyone and a vocal only on the first and last chorus. He nodded his approval. "We'll do it that way on the concerts."

Hal Gaylor suggested a faster tempo. "I don't think it would work in a faster tempo," said Billy Exiner. "You've got to think of how the lyrics will sound."

"That's OK," said Bennett. "If you boys can get a better feeling at a faster pace, let's give it a try and see what happens."

He began to sound less dogmatic and more generous. You begin to realise that it isn't all temperament. He's an artist and a perfectionist. Probably that's why he stays at the top.

Bennett stays at the top for the same reason as any other big star, he knows what his followers want and he knows how best to give it to them. If it appears from the above report that he spends too much time on the niceties of interpretation, it's worth remembering that Bennett has been at the top now for something like twenty years. Obviously, his methods are the right ones.

Born Antonio Dominick Benedetto on August 3rd, 1926 in Long Island, New York, Tony developed an interest in singing fairly early in life. Apart from family sing-songs with his sister Mary and brother John, Tony often took part in school functions and choir work. When the first cornerstone was laid for New York's Triborough Bridge, Tony's school was asked to do a show for the ceremonies. In company with some of his chums, six-year-old Tony offered a rousing version of *Marching Along Together*.

In addition to his regular appearances in school plays and operettas, he also began to show a remarkable aptitude for painting and sketching. With the intention of becoming a commercial artist, Tony entered New York's High School of Industrial Arts. While studying, he commuted every weekend to nearby Paterson, New Jersey, to sing in local restaurants and clubs for 10 or 15 dollars a week.

His art studies and vocal activities were interrupted by Army service in 1944. He spent the next three years with the 63rd Infantry Division in Germany. In 1945 when the war ended he was transferred to Special Services, the Army's entertainment branch. With the help of a friend, Tony assembled an Army jazz band with which he toured, singing for the troops. He also worked for a while as record librarian for the Armed Forces Network in Wiesbaden.

Singing songs of the day, such as *Sentimental Journey*, *It Could Happen To You* and *I'll Be Seeing You*, and noting the favourable reaction and heartwarming applause, Bennett made up his mind once and for all to follow a singing career when he got back to civilian life. On his release he enrolled at the American Theatre Wing's professional school under the G.I. Bill. He studied drama and music theory and, at weekends, found work as a singer in night clubs and on local radio and TV shows.

His first important break came in 1950 during a one-week engagement at the Greenwich Village Inn. The show's star was Pearl Bailey. At the end of the week, Miss Bailey told the manager: "Keep that boy on. I like the way he sings." She wasn't the only one who liked the way he sang. One night soon afterwards, Bob Hope came in to see Pearl Bailey and was so impressed by the young Italian singer that he offered him a featured spot touring with the Bob Hope Show. "I think we'll lose that name Antonio Benedetto," said Hope, "from now on your name is Tony Bennett."

The exposure he received on the Hope tour enhanced his reputation considerably. When the tour ended, Tony got together with a pianist and made a demonstration disc of a song he liked, *Boulevard of Broken Dreams*, and sent it to Columbia's artist and repertoire director, Mitch Miller, who heard it and immediately signed Tony to a contract. His first session took place on April 17th, 1950 and he recorded *Boulevard of Broken Dreams* again, this time with a full orchestra. Ten days later the disc was released. It sold 500,000 copies.

Eighteen months later, Bennett received his first gold disc award for his version of *Because Of You*, which sold more than a million copies. Soon after this he was awarded a second gold disc for *Cold, Cold Heart* and then a third for *Rags to Riches*. Since then, Bennett has consolidated his position as one of the world's leading ballad singers not only through further big hits like *In The Middle Of An Island, I Wanna Be Around* and, most spectacularly, *I Left My Heart In San Francisco*, but also with a continuous stream of fine LPs, two of which – *Tony Bennett's Greatest Hits* and *I Left My Heart In San Francisco* – have also won gold awards.

In the last few years, Tony Bennett's British concert tours have become an annual event. During his 1967 visit, I finally got the opportunity to interview him. The results were published in *Perfectly Frank*, the journal of the Sinatra Music Society, an organisation of which Bennett is an honorary member. The following is an edited transcript of that interview:

I was ushered into Bennett's double suite on the 27th floor of the London Hilton. Just inside the door was a portable record player and I could hear Sinatra singing *I'm A Fool To Want You*. Next to the record player lay the sleeve of the CBS double-LP set, *Frank Sinatra's Greatest Hits – The Early Years*.

While I was waiting I looked through some of the other records that were stacked near the player. There was a tasteful cross-section of jazz, quality instrumental and vocal albums, but not one Tony Bennett disc. But what really aroused my curiosity was an LP called *The Art Of Modern Singing* by Carlo Menotti. It was not an LP in the normal sense, but a collection of scales and exercises in *bel canto*. It consisted of fundamental scales, like the C major arpeggio, to items of a more advanced nature.

"I use that record to practise my scales whenever I get some time to spare," Tony explained. "It's a great help when there's no piano around." He had answered my first question before I had even asked it, and the interview – well, friendly conversation really – had begun.

"*Throughout your recording career, you have shown a strong preference for jazz flavoured accompaniments . . . Do you consider yourself a jazz vocalist?*"

"Personally, I don't know. I never phrase any song the same way twice so maybe in that connection I could be called a jazz singer. But that doesn't mean you can write 'Tony Bennett thinks he's a jazz singer'.

It depends on a person's viewpoint. To me Harry 'Sweets' Edison represents total jazz. Now, if someone said to me that 'Sweets' is not a jazz player, I'd argue with him all day. Jazz is like art, it's a matter of viewpoint."

*"Speaking of art, we know you studied sketching and painting. Now much time do you devote to it these days?"*

"Not as much as I would like, but I always keep a sketch pad at the ready. For instance, I have a habit of sketching the view from hotel windows or apartments where I happen to be staying. Would you like to see some of them?"

Needless to say I was most interested to see this private side of Bennett's talent and I was agreeably impressed with what he showed me. Without being brilliant, his work did have a remarkable consistency about it and carried more than a faint suggestion that Bennett is a very sensitive person on a quiet scale. Here again, his love of good songs was apparent because each of the sketches was titled after a song (eg *All Alone, Shadow Of Your Smile, When Your Lover Has Gone*). In my opinion, the most impressive of all was a sketch of what looked like a back garden with a football in the foreground and a young boy in the background. Mr Bennett's title for this? *Happy Days Are Here Again . . .*

*"Who are your favourite singers?"*

"There are no surprises in my answer to that one. I like all the usual people . . . Frank, Ella, etc. I don't think we hear enough of singers like Dick Haymes, Blossom Dearie or Johnny Hartman. Oh, I must mention before I forget – I really dig Fred Astaire as a singer. That man introduced more great songs than anyone else. He's just wonderful . . . his energy is incredible."

*"Do you have any favourite composers?"*

"Again, you'll find no surprises. I like all the usual ones – Gershwin, Porter, Richard Rodgers and Larry Hart, Arlen, Mercer and the rest. If you tried to nail me down to one composer, I would probably choose Jimmy Van Heusen. His work is as good as any of the others and he is still turning out great songs today. Just look at all those wonderful songs he wrote for Crosby and Sinatra. I would like to have him write some special material for me. Alec Wilder, he's another master. Of the newer songwriters, I like Cy Coleman very much."

*"Most record companies are of the opinion that ballad singers – especially those who perform tasteful standard material – are just not commercial. Yet your records continually sell in vast quantities all over the world. How do you equate your success with the general commercial attitude of the record companies?"*

"I don't know very much about the marketing of records, I can only judge by audience reaction. I have been with CBS now for 17 years . . . Each year I make a lot of money for CBS and they tell me the company's statisticians just can't understand why I sell in such large quantities. Goddard Lieberson, the top man at CBS, says I am allowed to record whatever I want, whenever I feel like it. I think a lot of marketing men make a big mistake in trying to do the public's thinking for them. As far as my career is concerned I know I have been lucky . . . there are a lot of fine artists who have to struggle just to make a living."

Being a good singer is obviously not enough by itself to achieve the kind of success that Tony Bennett enjoys. It probably all boils down to this thing called audience communication, and Bennett has certainly sung to all kinds of audiences – from Las Vegas to London – and always with marked success. Whether he is performing in a vast concert hall or an intimate supper club his effect on an audience never varies. In London in 1966, he sang in the Royal Variety Show for the Queen, and in Washington in 1967 he sang at the White House for the President of the United States and the Prime Minister of Japan. But he seems to be just as happy to sing at the Odeon, Hammersmith, for Mr and Mrs Joe Bloggs. To the ordinary man in the street, Tony is an alright guy. And it is difficult to think of another singer who creates this kind of feeling. So it is true to say that much of Tony Bennett's longstanding success is based on his uncanny communication with audiences – all kinds of audiences.

His fantastic drawing power was perhaps best exemplified by his concert at the Royal Festival Hall in February, 1972, when it was reported that *all* tickets had been sold 45 minutes after the box office had opened.

As a craftsman, Bennett attracts the ardent admiration of many fine musicians – and rightly so, for he is musically as well as emotionally thrilling in his overall delivery. Like all the best stylists he has a tendency to improvise in most of his performances. He often takes huge liberties with the tempo, sometimes falling dangerously behind the beat and then skilfully telescoping his phrases to pull the performance neatly together again. Audiences seem to love this element of suspense which Bennett injects into his work, musicians are impressed by it – but certain critics, who tend to think rather symmetrically, regard it as a fault. As a performer, though, Bennett has always tended to go against the grain rather than with it. Where other singers indulge in mindless chatter and the telling of jokes while on stage, Bennett does nothing but sing to his audiences (and this possibly perplexes certain critics who expect every popular singer to be 'an all-round entertainer'). His cogent awareness of lyrics and his striking ability to command the listener's attention at all times are really the prime ingredients of his singing art. It was probably these very qualities that prompted Frank Sinatra, in a 1965 interview with *Life* magazine, to say:

"Tony Bennett is the best singer in the business, the best exponent of a song. He excites me when I watch him – he moves me. He's the singer who gets across what the composer has in mind, and probably a little more."

RECOMMENDED RECORDINGS

**THIS IS ALL I ASK** (CBS): This impressive album shows Bennett's love of various types of material; good show tunes like *Young And Foolish* and *On The Other Side Of The Tracks*, up-tempo items like *Moment Of Truth* and the jazzy *Tricks* (with jazz drummer Chico Hamilton); dramatic ballads like *Autumn In Rome* and the appealing title song – and even old-time vaudeville songs like *True Blue Lou* and Al Jolson's *Keep Smilin' At Trouble*. Only a man with a great love for popular music could have turned out an album like this. Consistently good listening. The arrangements are by Ralph Burns.

**FOR ONCE IN MY LIFE** (CBS): In this album, Tony has re-recorded *Keep Smilin' At Trouble* using the same Ralph Burns arrangement, but at a much slower tempo – and the result is infinitely more satisfying than his previous recordings. Other standout tracks include *Sometimes I'm Happy*, *Out Of This World* and a beautifully under-stated and warmly tender ballad reading of Gershwin's *They Can't Take That Away From Me*. The much-recorded title song is given its finest interpretation on this occasion.

**I LEFT MY HEART IN SAN FRANCISCO** (CBS): Bennett's most famous song should be reason enough to buy this album, but there are a number of other equally rewarding songs such as the delightful *Marry Young*, the rhythmic *Taking A Chance On Love* and the plaintively sympathetic *I'm Always Chasing Rainbows* to add to the listener's pleasure.

**SONGS FOR THE JET SET** (CBS): Another fine example of Bennett at his undiluted best. The opening track, *Song of the Jet* (*Samba do Aviao*) is possibly the finest individual performance he has ever recorded. Of course, a good deal of credit must go to Don Costa's electrifying arrangement for orchestra and chorus – replete with a fine tenor sax solo from Al Cohn and some imaginatively conceived stereo sound effects. But the Bennett voice is in great shape throughout. Other tracks include Duke Ellington's *Love Scene*, Jobim's *How Insensitive*, an ultra-slow ballad styling of *Fly Me To The Moon* and the always popular *If I Ruled The World*.

**TONY BENNETT SINGS HIS ALL-TIME 'HALL OF FAME' HITS** (CBS): A handy compendium of some of Bennett's most famous songs including *I Wanna Be Around*, *In San Francisco*, *The Shadow Of Your Smile* and early hits like *Because Of You* and *Rags To Riches*. Despite the familiarity of the material even hardened Bennett fans will still find the album interesting for Tony's casual narrative and particularly for his superb ballad montage incorporating *It Had To Be You* and *One For My Baby*. This track is beautifully sung against a fine sensitive piano accompaniment from John Bunch.

**GET HAPPY WITH THE LONDON PHILHARMONIC** (CBS): An exciting and well-produced souvenir of Bennett's memorable 1971 concert at London's Royal Albert Hall in aid of the LPO Appeal, this album gives some idea of Bennett's magnetic effect on a 'live' audience. Accompanied by the huge London Philharmonic Orchestra under the baton of Robert Farnon – and augmented by a smattering of London's top jazz musicians – Tony puts on a first-class show of good singing and fine songs including *Old Devil Moon, Country Girl, Tea For Two* and *Let There Be Love*. But perhaps the real vocal highspot of this album is his stunning interpretation of Antonio Carlos Jobim's *Wave*, a real masterpiece by any standards and a performance that lulled the 7,000 strong audience into a state of complete rapture. To be honest, the sound quality is not as good as on other Bennett albums, and the orchestra is not as well-balanced as it might have been. But this was perhaps understandable under the circumstances. Yet considering that Tony Bennett was using a hand mike throughout the entire proceedings the general balance on the voice is extraordinarily good, all of which reflects well on Bennett's mike technique.

Incidentally, the elegantly designed gate-fold sleeve contains some charming Tony Bennett sketches – the first to be published in this country.

**YESTERDAY I HEARD THE RAIN** (CBS): In addition to Bennett's outstanding version of the title song this album is well worth hearing for the inclusion of a hitherto unheard-of George and Ira Gershwin song called *Hi-Ho*. It was presented to the singer by Ira Gershwin himself and this is the only recording of it, and it is an absolute gem. The remaining tracks are all ideally suited to Bennett's personality with the exception of the rather oddly selected *Sweet Georgie Fame*. Basically this is a fine album though.

**LOVE SONGS** (CBS): Excellent two-LP pack of superior ballads shrewdly selected from various Bennett albums. Highlights include *I Cover The Waterfront, Penthouse Serenade* and *The Very Thought Of You*.

**WITH LOVE** (CBS): Recorded in London in late 1971, this LP is one of Tony Bennett's best efforts of recent years. The accompaniments by Robert Farnon are in the main a real delight and only on a couple of tracks – *The Riviera* and *Love* – do the scores tend to sound fussy and over-elaborate. On songs such as *Dream, Harlem Butterfly, Twilight World* and that exquisite but neglected Jerome Kern composition *Remind Me* Bennett is in top form. The choice of material throughout is tasteful and well planned. For example, listen to the sheer delicacy of Bennett's phrasing throughout *Lazy Day In Love* and compare it with the strong bravura quality of his last note and the thrilling changes he executes on the climax. This surely is a master craftsman at work.

# Part Three

# *Style and Personality*

*All styles are good except
the tiresome sort.*
    Voltaire (1694–1778)

# Sophie Tucker

Popularly known as 'the last of the red-hot mamas', Sophie Tucker was perhaps in reality the *first* of the great female pop singers. To certain purists, that may sound like a sweeping statement, for it must be admitted that Miss Tucker was not a particularly clever singer nor did she have any marked influence on other singers. On the credit side, though, her personality – and this was reflected in her singing – was magnificently infectious. She was the epitome of the show-must-go-on tradition and this was borne out by the fact that her career was effectively longer than any other in the whole history of show business. In her vocal hey-day it was audience communication that counted more than anything else, and this she certainly had. This and talent.

Born Sophia Abuza in Poland in 1885, her family moved to the USA and she spent most of her childhood in Boston until her parents opened a restaurant in Connecticut. Her aptitude for singing showed itself quite early in life when her school teacher would ask her to lead the choir singing.

She left school bent on a show business career. Ragtime music was all the craze and she changed her name to Sophie Tucker, presumably because it sounded more appropriate to the surroundings in which she worked. After some initial experience singing in cabaret and honky-tonk establishments she got her first big break from Tony Pastor – one of New York's biggest showmen – who featured her extensively for a while at his theatre. This led to her being given a part in the famous Ziegfeld Follies, on the opening night of which she was said to have stopped the show with her singing much to the chagrin of the leading lady. Offers soon poured in for her services and she swiftly became one of the most popular and successful artists on the fiercely competitive Vaudeville circuits.

With all the popularity that she was finding, Sophie Tucker soon became a prime prospect for music publishers and song pluggers, who were continually urging her to feature their material. In those days the recording business had not fully blossomed and radio plugging was unheard of, so the only way of getting a song into the public consciousness was by having it sung night after night to live audiences – and preferably by top-class artists who were constantly appearing in all the major cities. And Sophie Tucker, along with Al Jolson, Harry Richman and Norah Bayes, was one of the country's foremost hit makers in the pre-World War I era.

In those days every top artist longed to find a song that would form an integral part of their act and constitute a form of identification. In Sophie Tucker's case it was the 1910 composition *Some Of These Days*. The song had previously been featured by its composer Shelton Brooks and by the popular Hedges Brothers and Jacobson at the Majestic Theatre in Chicago, but without any noticeable success. But when Sophie introduced it into her act it became so resoundingly successful that she immediately adopted it as her own speciality and subsequently made the song world famous in the years that followed.

Another great standard which Sophie helped to promote was that famous 1914 composition by W. C. Handy, *St Louis Blues*. At first the song had been rejected not only by singers – but by publishers too (Handy, in fact, finally formed his own company and published the song himself). While *St Louis Blues* has never been closely linked with her name, Sophie Tucker certainly helped to give the song a considerable measure of popularity. In later years many recording artists latched on to the song and it is now listed as the second most recorded song of all time.

In 1919 Sophie met a young songwriter named Jack Yellen who offered to write original material for her act and this turned out to be the start of a memorable partnership. Yellen (who was later to become famous through such durable songs as *Ain't She Sweet*, *Hard Hearted Hannah* and *Happy Days Are Here Again*) wrote several good numbers for Sophie Tucker, the most notable being that other Tucker speciality *Louisville Lou*.

For some time she had been working with pianist Frank Westphal until she formed an accompanying group 'The Five Kings', which she later disbanded in favour, once again, of piano accompaniment. This spot was filled by Ted Shapiro, who remained with Sophie for the rest of her career.

With the arrival of talking pictures one would have imagined that Sophie Tucker would have carved a solid film career for herself. Certainly the opportunities were there, but her screen appearances were surprisingly infrequent. They included *Honky Tonk* (1929), *Broadway Melody of 1938*, *Sensations of 1945*, and *The Joker Is Wild* (1957).

Throughout her long career she made several trips to Britain, appearing on her fourth visit in the Royal Command Performance of 1934.

In later years her act placed less emphasis on her singing ability. Instead she concentrated on a sort of semi-spoken repartee which found its outlet in pieces like *Life Begins At Forty* and *You Can't Sew A Button On A Heart*. Of course she never neglected to give the audience a chorus or two of *Some Of These Days* and sometimes *My Yiddishe Momme*. Throughout the whole of her career she was a tireless and diligent performer and not long before her death in 1966 – in her 81st year – she played a successful and triumphant season at London's Talk Of The Town.

Sophie Tucker was not really a prolific recording artist, although she did do a fair amount of recording, some of which have been issued in LP form on such labels as Ace of Hearts, Fontana Special and CBS. But her reputation as a great singer was totally established before it became fashionable to be a successful recording artist. That's probably why she was called 'The last of the red-hot mamas'.

KB

# Ethel Waters

Ethel Waters, born on October 31st, 1900 in Chester, Pennsylvania, was the first singer with a jazz/blues background to break through into the popular music field and as such she has had a very far-reaching influence on practically everyone who followed her, most noticeably on that school of singers, such as Billie Holliday, Ella Fitzgerald and Lena Horne, whose work straddles the fence between jazz and pop.

Her childhood was spent in the roughest coloured quarter of Philadelphia but her career started when she attended a Halloween party in a local club on her 17th birthday and was called upon to sing. She was heard by a small-time vaudeville team who offered her a job in their act at the Lincoln Theatre in Baltimore. The song she chose for her debut had only been performed professionally by one other person, a female impersonator named Charles Anderson, and so a 17-year-old girl became the first woman to sing the *St Louis Blues* in public!

After some years on the lower rungs of the Negro vaudeville theatre world she started work at Edmond's Cellar in New York, a small speakeasy with a tough clientele. There she remained for several years.

In March 1921 she made her first record, thus becoming the fourth female blues singer to record. The evidence of her early records is quite startling, in that it shows her phrasing with a rhythmic freedom and attack, despite often stiff and very unswinging accompaniments, which was at least 10 years ahead of its time. To put it in a nutshell, Ethel could and did swing in the sense which that world implied in the 1930s and it was not until Louis Armstrong began to sing on records some four or five years later that any stylistic comparison can be found.

By 1925 she was sufficiently well known to be starring at the Plantation Club on Broadway. It was here that she introduced *Dinah*, which became the first international song hit to emerge from a nightclub. Her Broadway debut came in 1927 in a show called *Africana* and shortly afterwards she was headlining at the Palace Theatre, which in those days was as high as you could get in vaudeville.

The year 1929 found her making her movie bow in a film called *On With The Show*, from which came another smash hit *Am I Blue*. In 1933 she was at the Cotton Club with another new hit song, Harold Arlen's *Stormy Weather*, and in the same year she became the first Negro woman to star in a

Broadway show alongside white performers when Irving Berlin booked her to appear in his revue *As Thousands Cheer*, in which she gave the first and definitive performance of the memorable *Heat Wave*. She was now an international star (she had toured England and appeared at the Palladium in 1932) and throughout the remainder of the '30s she continued to triumph on Broadway, at Carnegie Hall, on radio and television. In 1939 she was accorded the highest praise for her straight dramatic performance in a play called *Mamba's Daughters*.

In 1940 she starred in the Broadway musical *Cabin In The Sky*, in which she introduced *Taking A Chance On Love*, and then went to Hollywood for the film version, which had Rochester and Lena Horne in support and an extra song, *Happiness Is A Thing Called Joe*. Other films and plays followed, notably *Pinky*, for which she won the supporting Academy Award in 1949 and *A Member Of The Wedding* in 1950. In later years she has worked only spasmodically and today appears to have retired into private life, apart from appearances with the evangelist Billy Graham; it seems that she is devoting her life to religion.

From 1917 to around 1923 her material was mainly blues or at least blues-based, but from that time onwards she expanded her range to cover everything from point numbers to comedy to ballads and few performers have employed such a wide range of material with such complete success. Ethel's was not the big deep-voiced blues shouting of a Bessie Smith. Her voice, though basically contralto, was smaller and very much lighter and more agile, with a sweet rounded tone and a wide range, but her greatest gifts were her rhythmic sense already mentioned and a way with a lyric which places her securely among the two or three best interpreters in the history of popular music. Ethel Waters is a great dramatic actress and this comes through when she sings a song. A classic performance such as she gave to Irving Berlin's *Suppertime*, with its sombre lyrics of lynching and heartbreak, can only be compared with the very best of Billie Holiday or Bessie Smith.

Several small labels have produced LPs from Ethel's earliest blues recordings but the work of her mature years is only represented by an American LP on CBS which covers some of the high spots between the years 1925 and 1940. A later LP taken from a live concert performance, which would seem to date from the early 1960s, is currently available on World Record Club and shows her voice in a rather frayed condition, but her sense of swing and feeling for lyrics unimpaired. In fact, despite the deficiencies of the voice as such, this is still a superb performance as Ethel re-creates some of the highlights of her career with sympathetic accompaniment from Reginald Beane at the piano.

CE

# Gene Austin

History does not always record facts in their proper perspective. For example, when one thinks of the early crooners of the '20s the name Rudy Vallee springs immediately to mind, yet in reality the most popular singer of the '20s (certainly in terms of record sales, and this must be a reasonable criterion) was Gene Austin.

The science of making and marketing records had not been developed to anything like the degree it is today. To sell a million copies of a record in the '20s really meant something. Gene Austin's place in pop history is clearly signposted by the inescapable fact that his recording of *My Blue Heaven* sold no fewer than 5 million copies, whereas not one of Vallee's recordings even reached the 1 million mark.

Austin was born in Gainesville, Texas on June 24th, 1900. As a youngster he developed a strong sense of adventure and the urge to do something about it. He promptly joined the US Army and in 1916 (he is said to have given his age as 18) he saw combat experience on a Mexican Punitive Expedition and later in World War I.

Having well and truly satisfied his early urge for action and adventure – *Boy's Own Paper*-style – he decided to get himself a reasonable education before it was too late, for by the time he got out of the army he was 'an old man of 18'. Here, the facts of Austin's life are a little hazy, but what is certain is that he attended Baltimore University and some time between 1920 and 1921 he entered show business as a singer and songwriter.

In 1923 he became a singer in a vaudeville double act and after breaking into radio – which in those days was only in the pioneering stage – he landed a recording contract with Victor Records and made many discs. With each successive release his career increased in stature and when at last he found the right song, *My Blue Heaven*, he became the first singer to truly reveal the vast potential of the recording industry. Next came *Ramona*, which was also historically important in two ways. Firstly it made Tin Pan Alley history as the first great film theme (it had been specially written for the exploitation of the silent film *Ramona*, which starred the sultry Dolores Del Rio) and secondly it was the first song to mark the beginning of a new era – the talking film. It actually pre-dated Al Jolson's *The Jazz Singer*. The assistance that the song *Ramona* received from Gene Austin's recording is incalculable. Suffice to say that had it not been for Austin's recording the song may not have been quite the durable standard it still is today, 45 years later.

As a composer, Gene Austin was perhaps best known for the standard *Lonesome Road*, which was later recorded individually by Tommy Dorsey, Muggsy Spanier and Frank Sinatra, to name but three of the many artists who have helped to perpetuate its popularity.

As a singer, Austin had quite a pleasant voice and an engagingly cheerful personality. He could never be referred to as a stylistic innovator nor even a vaguely significant vocal influence. His place in history – and for the sake of the record, let's get the facts perfectly clear – is not so much based on his musical contribution as on his results as the first great commercial pioneer. And this is as good a monument as any to the cheerful singer from Gainesville, Texas who passed away on January 24th, 1972.

KB

# Rudy Vallee

No history of popular singing would be complete without a tribute to Rudy Vallee, who was the very first idol in the days of prehistoric pop. The screaming and swooning may have happened with more attendant publicity to Sinatra and Presley in later years, but they happened first (albeit perhaps in more genteel fashion) to the tall, wavy-haired darling of the flappers in the '20s and '30s.

Born on July 28th, 1901, Hubert Prior Vallee taught himself the alto sax by playing along with Rudy Wiedoft records, eventually using what musicianship he had garnered by this dubious example to pay his way through Yale. On leaving college he formed his own band, and it was as front man for his Connecticut Yankees that Vallee became the musical equivalent of a matinee idol as he sang *Goodnight Sweetheart* and *The Stein Song* through the inevitable megaphone.

He progressed through *George White's Sandals* and various musical films but Vallee's nasal, expressionless singing meant little without the megaphone (his sax playing meant even less) and the young Bing had taken over in the affections of the public. Vallee, one of the most astute business men in music, turned to straight acting and in *The Palm Beach Story* created the prototype of the role of the smug, stodgy suitor he was to repeat with variations for the next 30 years.

But he did return to music when America entered the war, as director of the US Coast Guards Band, entertaining the US forces in all spheres. One of his musicians confided to me many years later that in private life Vallee was the same as his latter-day screen image – precise, stuffy, and mean to the nth degree, although paradoxically he would be generous to a fault if any old friends were in genuine need.

Today Rudy Vallee is well established as a character actor (especially after emerging once more as a great star at the age of 65 in stage and screen versions of *How To Succeed in Business Without Really Trying*) and only the original fans in his own age group can recall the furore of his early musical career.

No, Vallee won't be remembered all that well as a singer. Even the budget labels haven't reissued any of his old records. But he was the first in a long line of singing idols and as such has his place in musical history.

AJ

# Connee Boswell

Call her Connie or Connee (either is valid), she's still the girl referred to by Irving Berlin as the finest ballad singer in the business. That statement too is valid, even today when Miss Boswell has been inactive for many years.

The supremacy of the Boswell Sisters has been dealt with in the chapter on vocal groups; they set a standard never exceeded and rarely equalled, and when sisters Martha and Vet retired Connee carried on as a single, despite the handicap of having been crippled after an accident. She often did guest spots in films, her infirmity concealed by voluminous gowns hiding the stool on which she would perch, or else like the spot in *Kiss The Boys Goodbye* when she sang the memorable yet now seldom heard *Sand In My Shoes* sitting quite naturally at a table beside a swimming pool.

Connee Boswell *was* a fine ballad singer, yes, but never merely bland. Somehow her name is seldom introduced into those eternal discussions on who is or isn't a jazz singer, yet surely to goodness, of the world's popular singers she above all possessed and displayed an inherent jazz feeling in everything she did. Obvious enough in the swing numbers at which she excelled (like the *18th & 19th on Chestnut Street* and *Bob White* duets with Bing), the rhythmic phrasing and New Orleans intonation also showed through in the love songs. There was a quality, an attack, in her voice that with just a little more emphasis could have almost been called abrasive.

As it was Connee stayed firmly on the side of good taste and wonderful musicianship, and was a potent lyric interpreter long before the phrase became fashionably applied to such as Sinatra and Bennett. With a talent and reputation like this it's incredible to realise that to anyone under 30 this is all hearsay. There's little enough recorded evidence apart from 78's hidden away in private collections, and odd tracks appearing in anthologies of '30s recordings. There were a couple of 10in Brunswick collations in the early days of LP, a cheap label set of Irving Berlin songs which vanished from the scene a decade ago, and an equally short-lived RCA album which teamed Connee with the Original Memphis Five in a lustily swinging batch of Dixieland standards. Not much of a tribute, is it?

AJ

# Russ Columbo

Ruggerio de Rodolfo Columbo, better known under his professional name of Russ Columbo, was born in 1908 and met a tragically early death on September 2nd, 1934 when an antique pistol that he was examining went off and he was shot through the head.

Details of his early life are hard to come by. We know that he was the son of an Italian theatre musician, and indeed there was the faintest trace of an accent in his singing. He appears to have started his career as a violinist, and in that capacity he joined Gus Arnheim's Coconut Grove Orchestra, somewhere around 1929. The Arnheim band was based in Hollywood and there it had a long and successful career, which is principally remembered today for providing a springboard to fame for no fewer than three of its members: Columbo, sax player/vocalist Fred MacMurray and Bing Crosby. Columbo, in fact, was playing in the Arnheim band when Crosby joined them as vocalist after the breakup of the Rhythm Boys in 1930. When Crosby left the band Columbo took over the singing chores and soon attracted favourable attention with his good looks and smooth crooning style. His image was more overtly sexy than Bing's and this was at once his strength and his limitation.

In 1931 he left Arnheim to try for a solo career and on September 3rd of that year made his first records under his own name for Victor with a studio orchestra which included Jimmy Dorsey on clarinet. All three of the titles he recorded on that day (*I don't Know Why, Guilty, You Call It Madness*) became hits, and eventual standards. In 1932 he was following in Rudy Vallee's footsteps as a crooning bandleader leading his own orchestra at the Park Central Hotel in New York. This included Benny Goodman, Gene Krupa and Joe Sullivan, although unfortunately he never recorded with them. His Victor records continued to have backings by session musicians.

During his stay with Arnheim he had already made one or two brief appearances in films (*Wolf Song, Street Girl*, etc), but in 1933 he went back to Hollywood as a star, hoping to emulate Crosby's success. For a short while it seemed as though he might succeed, and the fan magazines carried stories about the 'Battle of the Baritones'. He was a hit in *Broadway Thru' A Keyhole* and followed this with *Moulin Rouge* playing opposite Constance Bennett. At the time of his death he was reputed to be earning $10,000 a week.

In view of the supposed rivalry with Crosby it is perhaps surprising to find, on listening to Columbo's records today, that he was very heavily Crosby-influenced in his singing style. The voice was a light baritone with a good range, rather more smoothly textured than Crosby's, and lacking some of the depth of tone. His phrasing was very much in the Crosby mould, but his songs were invariably romantic ballads and whether he would ever have been able to tackle successfully the more rhythmic type of number must remain an open question. Listening to him now one is tempted to conclude that he would have developed more along the lines of Perry Como, who, whether by coincidence or design, revived Columbo's greatest hit *Prisoner of Love* with great success in 1947. Little of his work has appeared in LP form, only the occasional track on anthology type albums and his memory today has grown dim. But he will always justify his place in the history books as the first and probably the most successful, at least in a limited field, challenger for Crosby's crown.

CE

# Fred Astaire

Most people will readily agree that Fred Astaire is to dancing what Olivier is to acting. But mention the subject of his singing and the reaction, although never unfavourable, is not one of total enthusiasm. Of course, everyone knows that Fred sings and that his voice, like his appearance and personality, is always likeable and that's about as far as it goes. Yet an Astaire film musical would be incomplete, and indeed unthinkable, without its quota of Fred's inimitable singing. Yes, inimitable is the right word to describe an Astaire vocal. His actual singing voice may be a little thin tonally but the sound is never less than pleasing; he may not be a very flexible stylist but he delivers lyrics with an overwhelming charm, the effect of which can often be quite rivetting. And this certainly makes him inimitable.

Furthermore, Fred Astaire has introduced and popularised more great songs of lasting worth than any other artist in the history of popular music. He has managed to do this by combining naturally graceful phrasing with unforced yet razor-sharp diction. His engaging personality and infectious grin do the rest. Back in the 1930s this was a service he frequently performed for composers like Irving Berlin, Cole Porter, George Gershwin, Jerome Kern and Arthur Schwartz. It could be argued, of course, that because of his association with these master songwriters he *acquired* rather than earned his reputation as the best song salesman of the century. But his potency as a song stylist really goes far beyond the fact that he was in the right place at the right time. Astaire, for all his local limitations, has a charisma that makes even a bad song sound like a masterpiece.

Born in 1900 Fred started his show business career in vaudeville at the age of five. He and his sister Adele formed a juvenile dancing act and trouped around the American variety circuits building a steadily rising reputation until their Broadway debut in 1917 in a show called *Over The Top*. From that point, the team of Fred and Adele Astaire starred in a whole procession of popular stage musicals which took them occasionally to London and culminated in 1932 with the marriage of Adele to Charles Cavendish, the second son of the Duke of Devonshire.

Fred continued his career as a solo artist and in 1932 starred in a successful Cole Porter musical *The Gay Divorcee*, which ran for 248 performances in New York and for a respectable run of 180 performances in London. His film debut was in *Dancing Lady* (1933). After this he teamed with Ginger Rogers in *Flying Down To Rio* (1933) and the famous series of classic Astaire-Rogers musicals: *The Gay Divorce* (1934), *Roberta* (1934), *Top Hat* (1935), *Follow The Fleet* (1936), *Swing Time* (1936), *Shall We Dance* (1937), *Carefree* (1938), *The Story Of Vernon And Irene Castle* (1939). When the team broke up (apart from a mildly successful comeback in *The Barkeleys of Broadway* (1949) Astaire starred and danced with numerous other partners, such as Eleanor Powell, Rita Hayworth, Paulette Goddard, Cyd Charisse, Judy Garland and Leslie Caron. Some years later Astaire was asked in a press interview who had been his favourite dancing partner. "Bing Crosby," he replied. He had starred with Bing in two films *Holiday Inn* (1942) and *Blue Skies* (1946), both of which contained a whole host of Irving Berlin tunes.

Amongst the many memorable songs introduced by Astaire over the years are *Isn't This A Lovely Day, Cheek To Cheek* (from *Top Hat*), *I'm Putting All My Eggs In One Basket* (from *Follow The Fleet*), *I Used To Be Colour Blind, Change Partners* (both from *Carefree*), *They All Laughed, Let's Call The Whole Thing Off, They Can't Take That Away From Me* (from *Shall We Dance*) and the Cole Porter classic *Night And Day* (from *The Gay Divorcee*). When Cole Porter first presented the latter song to Astaire, Fred claimed that it was beyond his vocal range (it required him to hit an E flat and Astaire rarely sang anything above D). But Porter insisted that Astaire could handle it and that furthermore it would be a big success. Fred co-operated and found to his surprise and delight that he had a better range than he had given himself credit for.

Astaire's popularity over the last 40 years has never really waned. In 1949 he gained an Academy Award 'for his unique artistry and his contribution to the techniques of motion pictures'. In recent years he has sung and danced in his own TV spectaculars (for which he also won numerous awards) and emerged in films as an effective straight actor, notably in *On The Beach* (1959) and *The Pleasure Of His Company* (1961).

Fortunately, the record companies have not neglected Astaire the singer and there are several representative samples of his work available on various labels. World Record Club, for instance, have issued the cast recordings of such fondly remembered Gershwin shows as *Funny Face* (1927) and *Lady Be Good* (1924); the latter album features Gershwin himself at the piano and an added bonus in the shape of extra songs from *The Gay Divorcee* (including *Night And Day*) and *Flying Down To Rio*.

Talking of cast recordings, there is a particularly interesting piece of gramophone history on the RCA International label's release of songs from the 1931 hit musical *The Band Wagon*. Recorded in October 1931 these sessions were part of an experimental project of Victor Records in presenting to the public for the first time recordings playing at $33\frac{1}{3}$ rpm. Unfortunately the project was not successful and was scrapped due to lack of interest. Since the tracks were not transferred to the conventional 78 rpm they became extremely rare and much-sought-after items. To hear the spoken introductions from Leo Reisman, Fred and Adele Astaire and composers Arthur Schwartz and Howard Dietz is an amusing experience which no record collector can really afford to miss.

Coming slightly more up to date there is a delightful double-LP pack on the Verve VSP label which features Astaire in company with (A) a sextet of top jazz players and (B) a big orchestra led by Buddy Bregman. The sessions (1952 and 1958 respectively) concentrated mainly on re-makes of Astaire's most famous songs plus a number of the singer's own compositions including *I'm Building Up To An Awful Letdown*, *No Time Like The Present* and *Just Like Taking Candy From A Baby*.

As a final testament to Astaire's effectiveness purely as a singer, it is worth pointing out that both Mel Torme and Tony Bennett (two people who know what they're talking about) personally rate Fred Astaire as one of the greatest of all the great singers.

KB

# Dick Powell

Dick Powell was the possessor of a breezy manner, an engaging grin and a robust tenor voice and for the best part of a decade he was Bing Crosby's only serious rival for the title 'King of the Film Crooners'. Actually, he was a crooner by casting rather than by nature. Compared to Crosby's his style was square and somehow one always felt that he should have been singing Romberg or Friml rather than Warren or Berlin.

He was born in Mountain View, Arkansas, on November 14th, 1904 and christened Richard Ewing Powell. His first singing experience was in local church choirs, originally as a boy soprano and later as a tenor. He also learned to play saxophone, clarinet and cornet during his college days. In his teens he held a variety of jobs ranging from soda jerker to grocery clerk before joining the Royal Peacock Orchestra in Louisville, Kentucky in 1925 as vocalist. A year or so later he went to Charlie Davis' Orchestra as vocalist/banjoist and it was with them that he made his recording debut for Vocalion in 1928. These records show him to have been a saloon bar tenor with a strident delivery which makes them almost unlistenable today.

1930 found Powell acting as MC at the Stanley Theatre in Pittsburgh. It was here that he was spotted by a talent scout from Warner Brothers and signed to a film contract, making his debut in 1932 in a minor role in a film called *Blessed Event*. Several unimportant parts followed until in 1933, he was put into *42nd Street*, one of the classic film musicals, with a starry cast that included Bebe Daniels, Ginger Rogers, Warner Baxter and Una Merkel; it inaugurated a series of tremendously popular Busby Berkeley directed spectaculars which continued throughout the '30s, and which more or less summed up his appeal of that time. Powell sang *I'm Young And Healthy* and the title song, also providing the romantic interest for Ruby Keeler.

Among the many numbers that Powell sang in his films one remembers *Pettin' in the Park* (with lyrics that are surprisingly *risqué* for their time), *I've Got To Sing A Torch Song* (both from *Gold Diggers Of 1933*), *Honeymoon Hotel* (from *Footlight Parade*, 1933), *I'll String Along With You* (from *Twenty Million*

*Sweet Hearts*, 1934), the outstanding *Lullaby of Broadway* (from *Gold Diggers of 1935*), and *Lulu's Back In Town* (from *Broadway Gondolier*, 1935).

1937 found him on loan-out to 20th Century Fox for a better than average film *On The Avenue*, which had an Irving Berlin score including *I've Got My Love to Keep Me Warm* and provided him with two leading ladies, Alice Faye and Madeleine Carroll.

Among the better songs that Powell sang in the latter part of his career were *You Must Have Been A Beautiful Baby* and *Hit The Road To Dreamland*, which he sang with Mary Martin in *Star Spangled Rhythm* in 1943, but by this time his popularity was waning and though he had developed into an acceptable light comedy actor his few attempts at dramatic acting (including an unbelievable Lysander in the 1938 *A Midsummer Night's Dream*) had been uniformly disastrous.

In 1944 he made his last film musical *Meet The People* co-starring with Lucille Ball and in that same year, realising that at 40 he would have soon become the world's oldest juvenile leading man, he changed his image completely to portray Raymond Chandler's private eye Philip Marlowe in RKO's *Farewell, My Lovely*, a big success. For the next few years he continued to star in tough-guy parts in minor thrillers, but after making a very popular comedy, *Susan Slept Here* opposite Debbie Reynolds, he retired from the screen in 1954.

His subsequent career as a highly successful television executive/part-time actor and film director does not really concern us here. He died of cancer on January 3rd, 1963 leaving a widow (film star June Allyson, his third wife – he had previously been married to Joan Blondell, his oft-time co-star in his Warner Brothers days and before that to Mildred Maund) and over a million dollars.

As a singer he improved throughout his career. His diction was excellent, he always sang in tune and the tendency to force top notes lessened with the years while the tone quality mellowed, though one can still never escape the impression that when Powell sang, inside him was an Allan Jones striving to get out. His weakest point was interpretation. In Powell's hands even sentimental ballads tended to sound rather jolly and the few attempts he made at rhythmic phrasing à la Crosby (eg *Lulu's Back In Town*) have dated badly. His natural successor was Doris Day's early co-star, Dennis Morgan.

An American CBS double album contains 28 of his songs from the period 1933 to 1935 and an English Ace of Hearts LP covers much of his later film career.

CE

# Alice Faye

When Al Jolson made *The Jazz Singer* back in 1927 it was the start of what became known as the 'all talking – all singing – all dancing' era in movie history and a new way of promoting popular songs was born. Already in the silent days the movies had flirted with theme songs to help promote a film and pianists in cinemas hammered out *Ramona* while Dolores del Rio emoted on the screen in dumb show. Now the audience could see and hear the new songs being performed and a very large proportion of the hits of the next 20 years had their origins in the movies.

The new medium required new artists. Bing Crosby, Eddie Cantor, Dick Powell and Fred Astaire were the great song salesmen of the early movies, but the girls tended to lag behind until the appearance on the screen of Alice Faye helped to re-dress the balance.

Born Alice Leppart on May 5th, 1912 in Brooklyn she started her career in the chorus line of the Capitol Theatre in 1929. From there she progressed via local radio to a job as featured vocalist with Rudy Vallee, who was at the height of his fame as a crooning band leader. When Vallee was called to Hollywood to star in *George White's Scandals of 1934* Alice went along. The studios had signed Lillian Harvey for the female lead, but she walked out a few days before shooting was due to commence. Through Vallee's intervention Alice was given the part and made a good enough impression to be awarded a long-term contract. For the next few years she played in an average of four or five films a year and her parts became bigger as her popularity increased. By 1937 she was a star and from then until her retirement from the screen in 1945 she was the Queen of the Box Office.

Perhaps the most accurate description of Alice Faye would be to say that she was the Doris Day of the '30s and '40s. She combined a generally underrated acting ability with a sympathetic personality, in addition to which she was a cuddly blonde with the type of good looks to attract the men without alienating the women. But her greatest asset was her voice, a warm velvety contralto with a comfortable two-octave range combined with excellent diction, good intonation and an above average feel for the meaning of a lyric.

None of her closest rivals in musicals (like Betty Grable, Ruby Keeler, Ginger Rogers and Dorothy Lamour) relied on their singing for their fame. To put it another way, Betty Grable was a dancer who also sang a little, Alice Faye was a singer who danced a little. Practically every film in which Alice appeared produced at least one memorable song: eg *King Of Burlesque* (1935), from which came *I'm Shooting High*; *Stowaway* (1936), which produced *Goodnight My Love*; and *On the Avenue* (1937), with an Irving Berlin score which included *This Year's Kisses* and *I've Got My Love To Keep Me Warm*. *Wake Up And Live* in 1937 contained *Never In A Million Years* and in 1938 another Irving Berlin musical *Alexander's Ragtime Band* found her bringing new popularity to a whole raft of his old hits as well as a new one, *Now It Can Be Told*. Among the songs she popularised in the 1940s one could cite *No Love No Nothing*, *Tropical Magic*, and perhaps her best remembered song of all, *You'll Never Know*. In her earlier days she could handle rhythmic numbers like Berlin's *Slumming On Park Avenue* and *He Ain't Got Rhythm* with some flair, but it was ballad singing that was really her forté; no other female screen star before or since can lay claim to as many hits.

Her song-selling ability is the more surprising when one realises that she achieved it almost entirely with her screen appearances. Her recording career was limited to a handful of 78s made before she hit the peak of her career. The majority are included in an American CBS album *Alice Faye In Hollywood* and one LP made in 1962 for the Reprise label (recently re-issued on Valiant), where she re-creates some of her earlier successes. This shows a slight diminution in vocal range but no loss of charm and, if anything, an increase in depth of interpretation.

In her heyday Alice Faye was essentially a crooner and her simple, uncomplicated readings which allowed the songs to speak for themselves were a major influence particularly on the band-singers of the era, eg Edythe Wright (Tommy Dorsey) and Pat Friday (Glenn Miller). Possibly because of her lack of affectation, her work wears well and only the backings sometimes sound dated.

CE

# Dinah Shore

Of all the outstanding female singers of the 1940s, the one who typified the period most aptly was Dinah Shore. Aside from her agreeable appearance and wholesomely fresh, non-slick personality, she really had (and still has) one of the most naturally distinctive voices in the whole of popular music. Anyone who recalls the '40s at all should have no trouble remembering how often Dinah's silky light-as-air tone, with that pecularily unique fluttery vibrato, dominated the air-waves. Yes, Dinah Shore certainly belonged to the '40s and, in terms of record sales and air-play, one might just as easily say that the '40s belonged to her.

She was born Frances Rose Shore on March 1st, 1917 in Winchester, Tennessee. As a child she sang in local church choirs and later, while attending Vanderbilt University, she sang on a local radio station in Nashville. On these broadcasts she invariably used the song *Dinah* as her signature tune, later adopting the name professionally and legally.

In 1937 she went to New York to see what her chances were of becoming a professional singer. The going was far from easy and, naturally, when the opportunity presented itself to sing on a local radio station she grabbed it with both hands – even though there was virtually no fee involved. She sang purely in the hope that the exposure would be helpful to her career (during this period she rubbed shoulders with another equally hopeful young vocalist named Frank Sinatra, who was also broadcasting under similar conditions). She went back to college; then, after getting her degree in sociology, Dinah returned to New York in 1939 more intent than ever on succeeding as a singer.

She did more broadcasting under the same unprofitable conditions, at the same time picking up some solid experience – and a little eating money – with various bands. One night in 1939, while she was working with the Peter Dean band at a Greenwich Village club, journalist George T. Simon came in with bandleader Woody Herman, who was looking for a new singer. Simon suggested that Dinah would be ideal for the Herman band, but the bandleader felt otherwise. Years later Woody admitted to Simon that he had probably made a mistake in not hiring her. She was hired, though, by well-known bandleader Ben Bernie (part composer of the song *Sweet Georgia Brown*), who asked her to sing on his regular sponsored radio show. Bernie, who liked her singing, tried hard to keep her on the show, but one of the sponsors didn't care for her singing because she didn't sing loud enough. She was out! But not out of radio completely, for she had been filling in on a regular Sunday afternoon radio series for NBC (unsponsored and poorly paid) called 'The Chamber Music Society of Lower Basin Street'.

Dinah also sang briefly with Latin bandleader Xavier Cugat, with whom she made her first recording for American Columbia. When the disc was released her sub-credit on the label read: 'Vocal chorus by Dinah Shaw'. But nothing deterred her and despite all these various setbacks, Dinah (who was sometimes affectionately referred to as 'Fannie from Tennessee') kept right on trying. Her philosophy seemed to be very simple: any opportunity to sing was better than no singing at all. Eventually, through sheer tenacity, she hit the success target with a string of weekly appearances on the popular Eddie Cantor radio show (sponsored and well paid), which over the weeks had a cumulative effect on the public at large. A healthy recording contract followed and soon her unique voice was recognised by millions via discs, juke boxes and, of course, radio. Her first big hit was *Yes, My Darling Daughter*, a pop adaptation by songwriter Jack Lawrence of an old Russian folk melody. This was followed in 1941 by the hugely successful Harold Arlen/Johnny Mercer classic *Blues In The Night*, which became her first million seller.

With this increasing stream of commercial success came offers from Hollywood and she made her film debut in an all-star variety film vehicle called *Thank Your Lucky Stars* (1943). This was followed by a star part opposite Danny Kaye in *Up In Arms* (1943), in which she sang another attractive Harold Arlen composition called *Now I Know*. Her other films included *Follow The Boys* (1944), *Belle Of The Yukon* (1944), a guest appearance, singing *Smoke Gets In Your Eyes*, in the so-called biography of Jerome Kern entitled *Till The Clouds Roll By* (1946), *Fun And Fancy Free* (1947) and *Aaron Slick From Punkin Creek*

(1952). Her voice only was heard singing *Two Silhouettes* in Walt Disney's musical cartoon extravaganza of the mid-'40s, *Make Mine Music*.

In later years she proved a natural for television and drew perhaps even more acclaim from mass audiences in America through her extremely successful and perennially popular TV show. She became the female counterpart of Perry Como and even today with her voice and looks still more or less intact she remains a powerful attraction on US TV.

Of late she has not been particularly active as a recording artist and there is very little of her work on disc that is immediately available. One album, however, from her Capitol days (circa 1959) is still obtainable from World Record Club. Entitled *Dinah, Yes Indeed*, it presents her in company with the fine Nelson Riddle orchestra and can be recommended highly – especially for the sheer musical brilliance, both vocal and orchestral, of *Falling In Love With Love*. This track must rank as the most imaginative performance she has ever given on record, and is the highspot of what is probably her best LP.

In the 75th Anniversary edition of the famous American publication *Billboard* (December 1969) it was written:

"No girl singer has earned more money than Dinah, And she is an unbeatable tennis player as well."

And just to round things off, she became a grandmother in 1970.

KB

# Jo Stafford

There's a popular but quite fallacious conception of Jo Stafford as a cold, academic singer. Precise, yes! Immaculate, certainly! And definitely academic in the sense that she was incapable of singing a bad note or turning a wrong phrase. But there was also a richness of tone and marvellous musicianship, plus an unsuspected vein of humour in this apparently unbending lady.

A native Californian, born in Coalinga around the end of World War I, Jo started singing in a family act. The Stafford Sisters were in a country groove and made their radio debut in 1935 with the Crockett Family of Kentucky. In January, 1941 Jo joined the Tommy Dorsey band and was featured both as soloist and as lead voice of the Pied Pipers vocal group. It was, in fact, her voice with its pure tone, distinctive timbre and total freedom from vibrato that gave the Pipers their special sound.

Branching out as a single Jo made some excellent records for Capitol, including her first gold disc, gained almost anonymously. The gorgeous hillbilly version of *Temptation* by Red Ingle and the Natural Seven featured a goofy voice by Cinderella G. Stump, and it was only after the disc swept the world in 1947 that the mad Miss Stump was revealed as Jo Stafford having a day off. The last hit for Capitol was *Shrimp Boats* in 1950, but on joining CBS Jo soon followed up with *You Belong To Me* (1952) and *Make Love To Me*, two years later. More important, this was the start of a period in which Jo Stafford made some extremely fine albums of standards, bringing to them the warmth and maturity which the years had added to her singing. She proved an adept TV performer when she came to England in 1960 for an ATV series which introduced *inter alia* such guests as Bing Crosby, Mel Torme and Rosemary Clooney.

One far-reaching result of her spell with Dorsey (apart from the technical inspiration she, like Sinatra, gained from TD's trombone playing) was her marriage to Paul Weston, the band's arranger, who has been her MD ever since.

In the mid-'50s Paul did a few piano tracks as 'Jonathan Edwards', incorporating every cliché, every fumble and faked run of every amateur who ever ruined a canteen piano. These were hilarious enough, but when 'Darlene Edwards' got in on the act with wicked take-offs of every girl singer whose ambition outstripped her technique, it was obvious that Mr and Mrs Weston had pulled off the greatest musical satire of all time.

Cold? Academic? What do you think?

AJ

# Lena Horne

Whenever anyone writes about Lena Horne, adjectives like 'lovely' and 'beautiful' punctuate the prose. Her lasting beauty – is it unfair to the lady to reveal that she was born in Brooklyn, New York, on June 30th, 1917? – is only rivalled by her outstanding ability to mould a song in such a way that it becomes a creation that is entirely her own.

She has a feline approach and one can trace a long line back through Tina Turner, Shirley Bassey and Eartha Kitt to reach that combination of the sensual and the sensational originally formulated by Miss Horne. Like nearly every outstanding popular singer to arise during the '30s and '40s Lena gained much of her early experience with a big band. In her case it was the orchestra of Noble Sissle, with whom she toured and recorded from 1935 to '36, before which she had already gained more than a smattering of professional exposure as a dancer and singer at New York's Cotton Club.

With Sissle she carved herself an enviable reputation as a band singer and it came as no surprise to anyone when she was eventually asked to appear in an all-Negro musical quickie which Hollywood was contemplating. It was called *The Duke Is Tops* and apparently was a completely forgettable affair, though Lena herself was impressive enough to win a place in a further production entitled *Blackbirds of 1939*. A stint with the Charlie Barnet orchestra ensued and though the association lasted a mere six months Lena did make a couple of fine recordings in January 1941 – *You're My Thrill* and *Good-For-Nothing Joe*.

Next came a spell in cabaret at Cafe Society Downtown, during which time Lena recorded some excellent tracks with the Teddy Wilson band. It was about this time that she became a prominent worker in the Civil Rights Movement which made her, along with Paul Robeson and Hazel Scott, one of the first Negro entertainers to lend her name to the fight for racial equality.

A major film contract with MGM brought Lena's talent to a wider audience via such films as *Panama Hattie*, *As Thousands Cheer*, and especially *Cabin In The Sky* where her *Consequences* routine with Eddie 'Rochester' Anderson proved to be a real showstopper. In 1943 she was loaned to 20th Century Fox for their epic musical *Stormy Weather*. Whatever it may or may not have done for Fox it certainly provided Lena with a song that was to be associated with her throughout her career.

She was now an international star and when the London Casino inaugurated a season of variety shows in 1947, Lena Horne and her husband and arranger, the late Lennie Hayton, were among the first artists to appear. It was a total triumph and every evening Lena received a standing ovation.

One of Lena's long-standing ambitions was at last realised in 1957 when she appeared on the Broadway musical stage in Harold Arlen's *Jamaica*, a show that was to run for eighteen months on a score that was excellent but now strangely neglected.

If, during the '60s, Lena's talents were expected to fade then her detractors (if indeed there were any) were doomed to disappointment. Her stage, cabaret and TV appearances were just as warmly received as ever and her recordings were even more impressive than in the '40s and '50s. Indeed, *Here's Lena* (Stateside) – an album of protest songs sung as only Lena Horne could sing them – was one of the most outstanding vocal LPs of 1964, providing her with a single hit in *Now* (a Comden-Green-Styne re-write of *Hava Nagila*). Another notable, and even more musically impressive, LP was the 1962 production *Lena – Lovely and Alive* (RCA) – a set of great standards with exceptionally fine arrangements by Marty Paich. Not surprisingly there are many who believe this to be her finest recording. Her supremacy as a cabaret artist is well highlighted in the 1956 *Lena at the Waldorf Astoria* (RCA), which includes her popular *New Fangled Tango*.

Even today, Lena Horne is as valid as ever and has lately emerged with a collection of contemporary pop songs for the Buddha label that is truly soulful.

In retrospect, however, it is worth pointing out that Lena was one of the very first black artists to sing 'pop-soul', although in those days it was probably called 'torch-singing'. Whatever it was called then, whatever it's called now and whatever it will be called ten years from now, Lena Horne will always be one of its best interpreters.

FD

# Margaret Whiting

If a list were compiled of singers who never realised their full potential or received due recognition Margaret Whiting's name would be near the top. To the general public her name is no more unknown now that it was 10 or even 20 years ago. Yet at 20 she appeared with Billy Butterfield's band on a Capitol 78, in the song that is still identified with her, and although *Moonlight in Vermont* is now a much-recorded standard there's no doubt that Margaret Whiting did as much for the song as it did for her.

One of the things that may have sidetracked her was her partial neglect of singing in favour of music publishing, a not unexpected venture, for her father was Richard Whiting, composer of such great standards as *Louise, My Ideal, Sleepytime Gal, Too Marvellous For Words* etc. He died in 1938 when Margaret was fourteen (she was born in Detroit on July 22nd, 1924), leaving behind many songs in MS form which Margaret later did much to promote.

Whiting's lyricist Johnny Mercer started 'Madcap Maggie', as she was affectionately known, on her career in his radio show and on Capitol Records, which he had founded in 1942 with Buddy De Sylva and Glenn Wallichs. The *Vermont* song helped consolidate both her career and the new company's success. She earned more gold discs in 1948 for *A Tree In The Meadow* and the following year for *Slippin' Around*, a hillbilly duet with Jimmy Wakely. Hardly in the top class musically, these showed the way popular music was going at the end of the '40s and Maggie's increasing involvement in novelty songs, while no doubt commercially necessary, did little to increase her musical stature.

Later her recording activities became more selective. Probably the peak of her career came when Norman Granz signed her to take over from Ella Fitzgerald in his series of albums devoted to the great popular composers. *The Jerome Kern Songbook* produced the finest singing yet heard from Margaret Whiting as well as introducing a number of rarely-heard Kern songs. (Strangely enough it's about the only one in the series that has never been reissued.)

In her mid-forties Miss Whiting moved with the times in more ways than one, and an album of contemporary songs recently told the world by its title that *Maggie Isn't Margaret Anymore*.

AJ

# Pearl Bailey

The most difficult problem facing any vocalist is the problem of *originality*: how to achieve an identifiable sound or style and how to align it with one's own personality. Miraculously, this problem never seems to have existed for Pearl Bailey. Firstly because her own humorously unique personality reflects

– and sometimes even intrudes – on her singing, and secondly because it is impossible to confuse her actual vocal sound with any other singer.

These two points make her important as a stylist if not as an actual influence. Perhaps the reason that she has not been much of an influence on other vocalists is that people have always tended to think of her as a comedienne who sings a little, rather than as a vital singer with a sly and pointed sense of humour.

She was born on March 29th, 1918 in Newport News, Virginia (which means she was born in the same year and same town as Ella Fitzgerald). Pearl began her career as a dancer, but soon switched to singing in New York nightclubs in the early '40s. This led to her touring as a band vocalist with trumpeter Cootie Williams (1943 to '44). After starring in the 1946 Broadway musical *St Louis Woman* she developed her aptitude for comedy and in the late '40s became nationally known throughout America as a talented comedienne. Her singing, however, remained an essential part of her act and she always retained her in-born jazz qualities. In 1947 she made a memorable appearance in Paramount's all-star musical film *Variety Girl*, singing a song that is always associated with her – *Tired*, which is a pretty good description of her general image. And this is another point which makes her unique as an entertainer, because even her visual approach could never be confused with any other artist.

Over the years, Pearl's natural talent for comedy has proved to be both a blessing and a curse – a blessing because it has made her into a world-famous entertainer, but a curse because it has tended to obscure the fact that she is a superb song stylist with all the potential of a first-rate lyric interpreter and all the qualities of a classic blues singer.

Her rich deep-toned voice is an astonishingly expressive instrument. She herself often abuses its marvellous warmth by tossing the occasional spoken aside or comedy line into an otherwise moving performance. There is no doubt, of course, that she has completely mastered the art of comedy timing, but show business's gain is decidedly the vocal connoisseur's loss.

In 1952 she married drummer/bandleader Louis Bellson, who generally accompanies her in club and theatre engagements. Perhaps Pearl's most famous film appearance was in the 1954 box office success *Carmen Jones*. In this film she was the only member of the principal cast to use her own singing voice. The others like Harry Belafonte and Dorothy Dandridge used operatic 'ghosts'.

Other films in which Pearl Bailey has appeared include *That Certain Feeling* (1956) (which featured one or two memorable vocal moments), *St Louis Blues* (1958), *Porgy and Bess* (1959) and a particularly fine character role in *The Landlord* (1971). She still records from time to time and examples of her work can currently be found on EMI's Columbia and Saga's Eros labels respectively.

KB

# Kay Starr

When the *Wheel of Fortune* spun round and stopped opposite Kay Starr's name it not only guaranteed the girl from Oklahoma a share of the pop world's fame and riches, but effectively ruined any chances Kay had of being recognised as a great jazz singer.

For, until that fortunate day in 1952, Kay was a girl who sang with jazz musicians, performing jazz songs in a righteous, swinging, belting yet magnificently controlled style. In two words, a jazz singer – irrevocably so! Which occupation, as we all know, doesn't always pay the rent. So can we blame the former Katherine Starks for *Rock 'n' Roll Waltz*, *Changing Partners* and the other novelties that filled her successful career from then on? Ideals are great to have, but compromise is usually necessary to survive. But it worked both ways, and when Kay appeared at the London Palladium to perform her hits she also cunningly introduced a British music hall audience to what may well have been their first taste of real jazz singing.

But it's Kay's earlier musical life that earns her a place in this book. Born on July 21st, 1922, she was brought up in Dallas and Memphis, with the inevitable debut on the latter's 'Grand Ole Opry'. While still a 16-year-old schoolgirl she appeared briefly with Joe Venuti and Bob Crosby, and made a couple of singles as fill-in singer with Glenn Miller. After school she went again with Venuti before joining Charlie Barnet with whom she recorded several 78s. But it wasn't till she left dance bands and started recording with small groups that she emerged as a mature and inventive singer. Her accompanying groups read like a 'Who's Who' of jazz, but many of the recordings, done for transient labels, have long since vanished. Some she did in 1945 with the Lamplighter All Stars were reissued on a London LP in the '50s, there were some concert tracks on a Vogue EP which have also gone the rounds of the budget labels, but it was her sessions with the Capitol International Jazzmen and other Cap. studio groups that really made it. (One 78 coupling, *Steady Daddy*/*You Gotta See Mama Every Night*, is to this contributor worth more than gold.)

With this sort of background, even commercial success with musical junk couldn't satisfy Kay Starr permanently, and it was a great relief when in the early '60s she came swinging back with a couple of the brightest vocal albums in the Capitol lists, *Movin'* and *Movin' On Broadway*.

AJ

# Vera Lynn

Nostalgia is undeniably a potent, even essential, ingredient in the success of the more durable popular singers and this is especially true in the case of Vera Lynn. During the dark days of World War II her voice, deeply immersed in homely sentiment and glowing with optimism, earned her the shining sobriquet 'Sweetheart of the Forces'. Her appeal was just as solidly based on nostalgia then as it is today. To the homesick serviceman throughout those war-torn years she was the vocal personification of the sweetheart or wife back home. And today, with her still attractive appearance and a voice as good as ever, she remains a source of inspiration to her original admirers; the perfect panacea to the uncertainty of middle age, guaranteed to take minds off the spreading waistlines and thinning hair. Certainly she's corny, but oh how effective!

Her vocal style, magnificently uncomplicated, is aimed straight at that particular section of the public who do not look for great art in their singers – only a healthy voice and a warm personality. Not for Vera the hot jazz, wild rhythms and lowdown blues that typify the seamier side of life. After all, is she not the perfect sweetheart? If she does part from her lover in song – *Auf Wiederseh'n Sweetheart* – it is always on the strict understanding that *We'll Meet Again*. Her image is a sort of vocal amalgam of Mrs Miniver and Rebecca of Sunnybrook Farm. It is an image that would not sit well on any other singer, for there is really no other singer better equipped to handle this particular corner of popular music than Vera Lynn. Her personality is simple and clear cut and her voice, which was once described as 'a freak mezzo-soprano with an irresistible sob', has exactly the right *I'll-get-by-as-long-as-I-have-you* quality.

Born in East Ham, London on March 20th, 1919, Vera Lynn (real name Vera Margaret Welsh) started singing at the age of seven, was a principal member of a children's troupe at eleven and had her own dancing school at the age of fifteen. Singing, of course, was always her main activity and by the time she was seventeen her reputation as a cabaret singer ensured her a steady flow of work at local functions and concert parties.

After singing for a while with local bandleader Howard Baker, she did an audition for Joe Loss and landed her first broadcast. This led to her signing with pianist-bandleader Charlie Kunz, joining his band at Casani's Club in London and making regular broadcasts for some eighteen months before landing a top job singing with the famous Ambrose and his orchestra. In 1938 she made her first recordings for the Decca label and after working successfully for three years with Ambrose she decided, in 1941, to take a chance on a solo career.

Following a successful appearance in the revue *Apple Sauce* at the London Palladium, she launched her own radio series *Sincerely Yours*, which proved so immensely popular with servicemen – particularly those members of the armed forces who were serving overseas – that she soon became known affectionately as 'The Sweetheart of the Forces'. It was really during those war years that Vera Lynn's colourful reputation as a great vocal entertainer became firmly established.

In response to countless requests she made many tours abroad singing for the troops, was featured in a number of films and of course made a whole string of successful recordings including *Yours* (which became her signature tune) and

*We'll Meet Again*, which understandably was one of the most requested songs.

After a period of retirement which began in 1946 she returned to singing in 1951 and proved herself to be just as popular as ever. 1952 was a particularly successful year for her as far as record sales were concerned, for in that year she recorded *Auf Wiederseh'n Sweetheart*, which had the distinction of being the first British disc to top the best-selling lists on both sides of the Atlantic. Total sales of this recording were well over the two million mark, in those days an unprecedented achievement for a British performer. Personal appearances in America consolidated her success as an international entertainer and more hits followed, including a revival of her original 1941 recording of her signature tune, *Yours*, which provided her with a second gold disc.

In recent years Vera Lynn has kept her recordings and TV appearances to a shrewdly judged minimum. Being the show business perennial that she is, her occasional sojourns into the public eye are invariably greeted with joyous enthusiasm by critics (the less cynical ones that is) and public alike. But in view of the ridiculous simplicity of her material and delivery, is Vera Lynn really a great singer? Today's generation of pop fans may regard her as unfashionable and corny and by the same token there is nothing in her style that is likely to appeal to connoisseurs who prefer more subtle singers like Peggy Lee or Ella Fitzgerald. But Vera Lynn remains unchallenged in her particular field because of her obvious sincerity, an illuminating quality which goes hand in hand with her consummate professionalism.

So is she a great singer? The answer, whether or not one cares for her style, must be a resounding 'Yes'. For on the evidence of the last thirty years, wouldn't it be extremely difficult to describe her as anything else?

KB

# Frankie Laine

Laine's belting and forceful approach to such pot-boiling hits as *Jezebel*, *Cry Of The Wild Goose* and *I Believe* earned him a tremendous international following in the late '40s and early '50s, not to mention 13 gold disc awards and total record sales in excess of 80 million.

Born on March 30th, 1913 in Chicago, Laine (whose real name is Frank Paul LoVecchio) began his singing career in the early '30s with a four-piece group. In 1937 he took over from Perry Como as vocalist with the Freddy Carlone orchestra, after which he went into radio as a solo singer on the staff of a New York radio station. Shortly after this he teamed up with pianist Carl Fischer and built up a successful night club act. Not long after World War II, he signed with Mercury Records and in 1947 he recorded his first million seller, *That's My Desire*. A year later he notched up a second gold disc with *Shine*.

In the early '50s, Laine changed record labels and signed with American Columbia. These were indeed the boom years for Frankie Laine, for in addition to turning out a succession of massive hits he also starred in several popular musical films for Columbia Pictures. His voice was in great demand on film soundtracks, particularly in Westerns such as *Gunfight At The OK Corral* and *3.10 To Yuma*.

Although Laine's peculiarly individual style of singing has now dated, he has managed to survive the changing fashions of the last 15 years with more distinction than his vocal contemporaries of the '50s such as Johnnie Ray, Guy Mitchell and Eddie Fisher.

Never a significant LP artist, Laine's forté was really the singles market. There is, however, a reasonable selection of Laine albums on such well-known budget labels as Hallmark and Fontana-Special. His best album, from an artistic viewpoint, is a long-deleted item called *Jazz Spectacular* which he recorded in the mid-'50s for American Columbia in company with a fine all-star jazz unit led by trumpeter Buck Clayton. Although Laine could never be classed as a jazz singer, his style on this occasion fitted in agreeably with the happy and swinging surroundings, resulting in an album of considerable charm.

KB

# Rosemary Clooney

Rosemary Clooney, perhaps more than any other popular singer, typifies the spirit and the very feel of the '50s. An artist who could make the charts with novelty singles like *Come On-a My House* and *This Old House* without sacrificing the respect of more sophisticated listeners, she did equally successful 'quality' singles such as *Hey There* and *Tenderly*, as well as a number of albums that came down heavily on the side of musicianship.

As with many other stars, Rosemary paid her dues as a band singer, in this case with Tony Pastor. She and her sister Betty were featured with the band in the late '40s, this job in itself being the culmination of all the girls had worked for through their teens – amateur contests, local socials ('local' being Maysville, Kentucky, where Rosemary was born on May 23rd, 1928) and radio in Cincinatti where the family lived from 1941.

Again paralleling the careers of other band singers turned soloist, Rosemary went into films with a Paramount contract, making her debut in *The Stars Are Singing* with operatic opposition from the massive Lauritz Melchior and tiny Anna Maria Alberghetti that all but swamped her. *Here Come The Girls* with Bob Hope and Tony Martin showed up the holes in her acting technique; *Red Garters*, an impressionistic Western satire, was a fine film and an artistic success but a commercial failure; *Deep In My Heart* for MGM was only a guest spot, and her best performance was in *White Christmas*, where she held her own with Bing Crosby, Danny Kaye and Vera-Ellen. But by then musicals were on the way out, and she turned to TV where she attained her greatest success with a friendly personality and warmth that, allied to her fine singing, came over well on the small screen.

A personal appearance at the London Palladium in 1955 showed the *rapport* Rosemary Clooney could establish with an audience, and in real life she proved as warm and genuine a person as her public image. Like all too many quality singers she is heard little on records nowadays, but her last album, done for Reprise *circa* 1963, revealed that although the vibrato was a little more pronounced than of yore Rosemary had lost none of her tonal quality. Her sensitive phrasing, immaculate timing and, above all, her intense feeling for a song, were as impressive as ever.

AJ

# Part Four

# *Now You Has Jazz*

*If you have great talents, industry will improve them:
if you have but moderate abilities, industry will
supply their deficiency.*
                    Sir Joshua Reynolds (1723 – 1792)

Popular music and jazz, whether by fate or timing or for some reason known only to the gods, have been incontrovertibly linked since the beginning of the 1920s. And previously, ragtime – a North American musical form which was a direct predecessor of jazz as we know it – had attained a huge following as an offshoot of the popular music of the 1890s.

Jazz, of course, is mainly thought of as an instrumental form of expression, yet the earliest forms of jazz were purely vocal. Indeed, the vocal aspect has always been prominent right from the early days of the folk-blues singer-guitarists like Blind Lemon Jefferson, Robert Johnson and Sam 'Lightnin' Hopkins, through the great female blues artists like Bessie Smith and Ma Rainey, and later manifested in the work of such as Louis Armstrong, Billie Holliday, Jimmy Rushing and Mildred Bailey. Closer to the present, jazz vocal styles became more sophisticated and in the work of artists like Sarah Vaughan, Ella Fitzgerald, King Pleasure, Jon Hendricks and Mark Murphy, a more instrumental-like approach was stressed.

This particular section deals with the middle ground, the area of jazz that is closest to popular music and from which popular singing has most benefited. Selection and discrimination are always a major problem in cases such as this where a capsule approach is called for, but the seven artists whose work and careers are covered here can be said to represent the best examples of jazz in relation to popular singing. Or to put it another way here are seven jazz artists whose work was of direct benefit to the general flow of *popular* singing.

KB

# Mildred Bailey

To many listeners of the younger generation the name Mildred Bailey will convey nothing, but during her short life span (born Seattle, Washington February 27th, 1907 and died New York December 12th, 1951) she was one of the most highly regarded and influential singers around. Perhaps her chief claim to fame lies in the fact that she was the first female band vocalist, thereby starting a chain of succession that included most of the major girl singers of the '30s and '40s.

She first worked as a song demonstrator in a local music store in Spokane and then joined a touring revue on the West Coast. For a while she sang on radio station KMTR in California before joining the Paul Whiteman Orchestra in 1929. Her brother Al Rinker had been with the Whiteman band as one third of Whiteman's Original Rhythm Boys (the others were Bing Crosby and Harry Barris) since 1927.

Whiteman was then at the height of his fame as the world's foremost band leader and while with him Mildred became well known through the band's numerous broadcasts and public appearances. Where Whiteman led, everyone followed and soon every band had at least one resident female singer.

Her first record was made in 1929 with a small group drawn from within the Whiteman band under the nominal leadership of guitarist Eddie Lang, the song being an obscure Hoagy Carmichael composition *What Kind Of Man Is You*? She seems to have had a special affinity for Carmichael's songs and among her early records she included such soon-to-be standards as *Georgia On My Mind*, *Concentratin'*, *Lazy Bones*, *Snowball* and the song that was to become her theme, *Rockin' Chair*. The latter was such a success that when she left Whiteman in 1933 to start a solo career she carried the billing which she retained for the rest of her life, 'The Rockin' Chair Lady'.

For the next couple of years she sang on the air and in theatres with Ben Bernie's Orchestra and with Willard Robison, as well as appearing as a solo attraction and recording with the Dorsey Brothers Orchestra.

Towards the end of her stay with Whiteman she married xylophonist Red Norvo. From 1936 to '39 she co-led a band with him and they were billed as 'Mr and Mrs Swing'. During this period she recorded copiously both under her own name and as vocalist on discs issued as by Red Norvo and his Orchestra. As a series, these records can only be compared with the contemporary recorded work of Billie Holiday and Teddy Wilson.

In fact, many of the musicians appearing on the discs made under Mildred's name (and they included most of the top jazzmen of the day) also appeared with Billie. On a couple of discs she even had Teddy Wilson himself at the piano and many of the songs that she sang, eg *For Sentimental Reasons*, *More Than You Know*, *You're Laughing At Me* and *My Last Affair*, were also part of Billie's record repertoire.

In 1939 Mildred, whose health was never robust, tired of the continual touring life with a band, decided to concentrate on a career as a soloist. Throughout the '40s she played a series of residencies at various top-line night clubs around New York, including the Blue Angel, Cafe Society, The Famous Door, The Onyx etc, also doing occasional touring and continuing to broadcast and record regularly, but her health was failing and after a short spell in Chicago in 1950 and a tour accompanied by Ralph Burns in 1951, she died of a combination of diabetes and heart trouble.

Mildred Bailey belonged to that select band of singers who are equally at home in jazz or popular music. She was a big fat woman and it was always something of a surprise to hear emerging from that large body a small and rather high-pitched voice with a sweet, pure and very distinctive tone. Her phrasing owed much to Ethel Waters, Louis Armstrong and Bessie Smith, as did her use of vibrato and she could swing with the best of them. Apart from being the first band singer, her place in popular music history is assured by the influence she had on such other greats as Peggy Lee, Ella Fitzgerald and Kay Starr, and today her work sounds completely fresh and undated.

She was important enough for a three-volume album set of her best work from the '30s and 40's to be issued on the CBS label a few years ago and was probably the finest white female jazz singer of that period. Only Connee Boswell and Lee Wiley could hold a candle to her in the '30s and she did not find a serious rival until Peggy Lee joined Benny Goodman in the '40s.

CE

# Jimmy Rushing

The big, powerful, sometimes hoarse-sounding voice of Jimmy Rushing may not exactly fit the bill for those with inclinations towards the more gentle, sophisticated and delicate kinds of pop singing. But blues shouters aren't always noted for their ultra-subtlety – they don't need to be.

For when, as Rushing did for fifteen years, you're handling the vocal chores with an exciting, shouting band like Count Basie's, you've got to have lungs like leather and possess the stamina of a horse. In Rushing's particular art, subtlety comes with the use of dynamics, light and shading. And it almost goes without saying that you need to have the ability to swing with exceptional power.

Mind you, Jimmy Rushing does have his more mellow moments – it's not all shoutin' and screamin'. One of the most pleasing numbers which he has featured for many years now is the jazz ballad *I Want A Little Girl*, which the rotund singer invariably delivers with tenderness and no little charm. It can also be noted that Rushing hasn't always featured just jazz and blues numbers in his repertoire. Over the years, he has consistently featured standards like *Exactly Like You, When I Grow Too Old To Dream* and *You Always Hurt The One You Love* – and even excruciating novelties like *Mama Don't Want No Peas An' Rice An' Coconut Oil* (which he recorded with the Basie Band in 1938).

In fact, during the earlier part of his career, James Andrew Rushing, born in Oklahoma City, on August 20th, 1903, was as much a balladeer as a blues singer. Recalls Jimmy: "When the Basie and Kirk bands would have a week off after a string of one-nighters, we'd get together at Mary Lou's (Williams, composer-pianist), have some drinks, barbecued chicken, beer, and I'd play piano and sing. Or sometimes on a cold night, when there wouldn't be too many people in the club, we'd go up there and entertain each other."

The warm and friendly Mr Five by Five – an affectionate nickname bestowed upon him by his old friend and ex-colleague Basie – came from a very musical family. His father played trumpet and both his mother and brother were singers. As a youngster, Rushing took up violin and piano, both of which he learned to play by ear. He did, however, study music at Douglas High in Oklahoma.

Graduating from school in 1921, Jimmy worked for three weeks in a furniture store, and was then hired as intermission pianist at the Quality Night Club of Hollywood. One afternoon, a top blues singer, Carolyn Williams, heard Jimmy singing after one of her own rehearsals. She was impressed – so much so that she shocked him that very same evening by introducing him from the floor and inviting him to sing. He was twenty.

Rushing joined Walter Page's Blue Devils, an exciting small combo, with whom he made his first recordings (in 1928). Next stop (in 1929) was with the Kansas City band of Bennie Moten. Following this, when Count Basie took over the nucleus of the Moten band on the latter's death, Rushing commenced his long tenure with the Basie outfit. That was 1935.

He stayed with Basie until 1950, when he formed his own septet and went out on the road and theatre circuits. But he gave up the band two years later in order to do freelance night club work. He has continued to work with small combos right up to the present, apart from odd guest appearances with big bands like Basie's from time to time. During his lengthy career, Rushing – a man with a formidable reputation as a consumer of food – has appeared in a film (*Funzapoppin*, with Olsen & Johnson) and on various TV shows (including a 1953 appearance on *Omnibus*).

With his enviable ability to swing mightily at all times – and in an exciting, soulful, yet happy-making manner – Jimmy Rushing has been an important influence on fellow singers – popular as well as jazz or blues – for the past 40-odd years.*

SB

# Lee Wiley

Subtle, sensitive and sincere – three ways to describe the singing of Lee Wiley. A singer who has never quite made it in the same as, say, Ella Fitzgerald or Mildred Bailey, but who always has been immensely talented, if often a trifle under appreciated. Today, Lee still puts in an occasional appearance here and there – now a seasoned veteran, but still a highly-intelligent, much-skilled artist whose phrasing, tonal quality and timing are, as always, a joy to hear. Add to this an absolutely impeccable taste in picking the best in pop material, and you have someone who is very much a singer's singer.

Sadly, however, there is little recorded evidence available of the art of Lee Wiley. Which is more than regrettable, because over the years she has recorded

*The voice that Mary Lou Williams claimed "could be heard ten blocks away without a megaphone" was regrettably stilled on June 8th 1972 when Jimmy Rushing died in a New York hospital.

tracks which have long since been accepted by the hardest-to-please experts as minor masterpieces. (Anyone coming across a copy of *Lee Wiley Sings Rodgers & Hart And Harold Arlen* (Monument) is strongly advised to hold on to it for dear life. Recorded in 1940 (Side 1) and 1945 (Side 2), it offers admirable evidence of Lee's unique vocal abilities.)

Born in Port Gibson, Oklahoma, on October 9th, 1919, of part-Cherokee extraction, Lee Wiley ran away from home at 15, and within two years was a highly-rated singer in Chicago and New York bistros. At 18, came a major tragedy: riding a horse in Tulsa, she was thrown and blinded. After receiving special treatment for over a year, she gradually began to regain her eyesight, later resuming her singing career with the orchestras of Leo Reisman and Paul Whiteman; still later she sang with Willard Robison on CBS (with orchestrations provided by William Grant Still).

From 1939 onwards, she became closely associated with jazz, mostly of the white Dixieland kind, and particularly with the various aggregations led by Eddie Condon. It was in 1939 that Lee recorded the first of her show-time albums, wherein she saluted a superior set of songs by the Gershwins. On this album – as with subsequent recordings which saluted the works of some of the great Tin Pan Alley masters – her smoky, honey-toned voice was showcased beautifully, with ideally sympathetic accompaniments as an added bonus.

Musicians of the calibre of Max Kaminsky, Joe Bushkin, Bobby Hackett, Bud Freeman, Fats Waller, George Wettling and, of course, Condon took part in these and other sessions. Invariably, the combination of singer and musicians produced memorable music.

Said Max Kaminsky: "The *Lee Wiley* albums were years ahead of their time. Lee set the style for years to come with her marvellous phrasing and the haunting timbre of her voice and later everyone else copied her."

During the mid-'40s, Lee Wiley toured with a big band which ex-Goodman and Bob Crosby pianist Jess Stacy was leading – she and Stacy were married for five years during this period – and later on in that decade she worked as a solo artist, singing mostly in nightclubs. After that, her appearances gradually became less frequent and indeed at one time she retired from show business.

Thankfully, however, she decided not to turn her back completely on the music business, and today, even though her appearances are rather limited, those who remember her fondly from previous years and who are in the fortunate position of being able to see her in person, make a beeline to any club or hall where she might be singing.

In her time, Lee Wiley has done a little songwriting. Although she hasn't had a great deal of success, one of her songs – *Any Time, Any Day, Anywhere*, co-written with the late Victor Young – became an R & B hit several years ago via a recording by Joe Morris and Laurie Tate. It was also effectively recorded by the late Nat 'King' Cole.

It is doubtful if any of Lee Wiley's early recordings, made for the Columbia,

Allegro, Storyville and Decca labels, are presently available, which is a great pity, for one has the feeling that they would have strong appeal for today's more discerning listeners.

Fortunately she has just started recording again and the resulting album, released in the US in February, 1972, appears on the Monmouth Evergreen label. It was reviewed in *Billboard* (week-ending February 26th, 1972). The reviewer had this to say:

"It is good to hear Miss Wiley's new LP. It is her first in a while and her voice is easy, her phrasing subtle and well planned. She retains her individuality by not falling prey to the contemporary pitfall that many of her peers have fallen into. The material is standard, the arrangements straight, and the feeling cool."

So there you are. Her records – like her singing itself – have a quality that is timeless.

SB

# Anita O'Day

Although there have been any number of fine jazz singers (or singers who have operated on a definite jazz-pop fringe), it is perhaps curious that there have been comparatively few really distinctive, and thus unique, vocal stylists, whose work is at one and the same time both difficult to copy and completely individual.

Anita O'Day is certainly a unique individualist, whose cool-sounding, jazz-based singing has pleased millions, fans and musicians alike, for over 30 years and who, in turn, has inspired such other vocalists as June Christy, Chris Connor and Julie London. But though Anita has influenced these singers in many ways, particularly from the tonal standpoint, none has managed to equal her, technically speaking. (Sensibly, they have resisted the temptation to try and reproduce Anita's vocal eccentricities: in any case, some of her vocal contortions would certainly have been beyond the capabilities of the singers mentioned.)

Perhaps significantly, the influential O'Day voice itself is free from the trademarks of others, with the exception of Billie Holiday. For not only did Anita grasp the essentials of Billie's style at an early stage in her career, but she adopted – on ballads in particular – some of the husky quality of 'Lady Day'.

This apart, Anita O'Day is her own vocal mistress. With complete individualism, she combines a commendable ability to swing easily with an almost instrumental-like technique which, when it is not over used, can be startingly effective. Not that she is all technique. Thankfully, she often exhibits a deep commitment to the mood and lyric of a song – particularly so on ballads.

Conversely, there are times when her quirky phrasing and a natural inclination to invert the melody line lead to a loss in lyrical quality and interpretation. Overall, though, Anita O'Day remains an important voice, appealing to both jazz and pop lovers alike.

The singer was born Anita Colton, on December 19th, 1919 (she adopted the name O'Day because it was a pig-Latin expression meaning 'dough' – the financial kind). Before her singing career hit the big time, she had another, rather exhausting, occupation. She was a regular participant in innumerable 'walkathon' contests (remember Jane Fonda in the harrowing *They Shoot Horses, Don't They?*), held in and around her native Chicago. During one contest, Anita walked for 2,228 hours yet she only finished second! In fact, she never ever won a single walkathon competition. Incidentally, her regular partner was another aspiring young singer: Frankie Laine.

During these contests, Anita got the chance – in between walks – to climb on to the stand and sing and dance; the audience threw money to show its appreciation. But in 1939, the youngster got a job with the trio of vibraphonist-pianist Max Miller, at the Three Deuces, on New York's 52nd Street.

However, her big break came when she was invited to take the place of Irene Daye as vocalist with the big band of Gene Krupa. She soon made a tremendous impact. Three months after she joined Krupa, she recorded a vocal duet with trumpeter Roy Eldridge, *Let Me Off Uptown*. It was a great success. Other titles she recorded with Krupa during her stay with the band included *Georgia On My Mind*, *Drum Boogie*, *Green Eyes*, *That's What You Think*, *Thanks For The Boogie Ride* and *Murder, He Says*.

Anita left the Krupa outfit in March, 1944, to marry golfer Carl Hoff and also to join the progressive-minded Stan Kenton Orchestra. Almost at once she scored a hit with her recording, with Kenton, of *And Her Tears Flowed Like Wine*. But she remained with this band for less than a year. Rejoining Krupa for a while, and working briefly with Woody Herman, Anita decided upon a solo career. Since then, she has worked with her own small groups.

A poll-winner on several occasions, Anita made the first recordings under her name in 1947. Subsequently she has recorded for innumerable different labels, and in various settings, and has appeared in concert halls, clubs and at festivals in numerous spots throughout the world.

But for most people, the sight of Anita O'Day, clad in long dress and ridiculously wide-brimmed hat, singing *Tea For Two* and *Sweet Georgia Brown* at the 1958 Newport Jazz Festival, and included in the highly-praised film *Jazz on a Summer's Day*, is the one thing which registers more than any other single event during her distinguished career.

The former walkathon exponent has certainly come a long, long way since the days when she was a gangling teenager, trying desperately to attain her own place in the history of pop/jazz singing.

SB

# Dinah Washington

Dinah Washington's sudden death at the age of 39 came as a great shock to those who had followed her fortunes through many years as a blues-based pop singer. For Dinah – 'The Queen' they used to call her – seemed to be the very essence of life itself.

An often vociferous, outspoken and temperamental woman, and an always colourful personality in any context or situation, her powerful, emotive and most rewarding brand of rhythmic singing was usually a perfect mirror of the woman herself.

She lived hard, played hard and sang hard. There was never any pussy-footing kind of vocal work from the former Miss Ruth Jones, one-time child Gospel singer and seven times married. Her seemingly rugged and uncompromising style was rarely lacking in subtlety, however, and she constantly proved herself capable of handling all kinds of lyrics to most kinds of songs.

Stylistically, she was indebted to the classic Gospel singers, bore more than a trace of the Bessie Smith heritage but was nearest in basic style to R & B star, Ruth Brown. But whatever traces of other singers were sometimes present in her vocal make-up, what came out was pure Dinah Washington.

Born Ruth Jones in Tuscaloosa, Alabama on August 29th, 1924, she grew up in Chicago. Her earliest experience in the field of music came as pianist-accompanist and singer in her local church choir. This 'churchy' sound was to remain with her throughout her entire career, and from the very earliest evidence was an essential ingredient in her singing style.

When she was about fifteen years old she tried singing other types of material, but with little success at first. However, she did win an amateur talent contest which earned her a few minor nightclub dates, but nothing much of consequence resulted from these. Her ardour more than a little dampened, she returned to the church choir.

A visit to a club to hear the great Billie Holiday in 1942 rekindled her interest. It was at this time that she met Joe Sherman who gave her a break by asking her to sing in a stage bar. She stayed there for a year. She changed her name to Dinah Washington at the suggestion of agent Joe Glaser. Then came her first major breakthrough as she joined the famous Lionel Hampton orchestra.

Dinah's first recordings took place whilst she was a member of the Hampton unit, although American Decca (to whom Hampton was at that time contracted) had refused to record her with the Hampton band. She recorded for the Keynote label with a contingent from the Hampton aggregation – the leader himself sat in for a couple of numbers – including Joe Morris (trumpet), Arnett Cobb (tenor sax), Rudy Rutherford (clarinet) and Milt Buckner (piano). Of those early sides, *Evil Gal Blues* and *Salty Papa Blues* were the most successful and became forever associated with her name.

Those early recordings rank with her very best work on disc. Her natural affinity with the blues, plus her fiery preaching style and a most distinctive vocal timbre, stamped her as a vocal performer of the highest quality. Throughout her widely varied recording career it was always difficult to know just how or where to categorise Dinah Washington: she sang fine jazz, her style also fitted beautifully into the R & B field or she could handle standard popular material with equal ease.

Following her decision to leave Hampton and go it alone, she soon became a much-in-demand artist in cabaret and in concerts, not to mention recordings. She even made a memorable and incandescent single contribution to that much-praised film of the 1958 Newport Jazz Festival, *Jazz On A Summer's Day*, in which she sang a marvellous jam-session version of *All Of Me* and even fooled around on the vibes trading four-bar jazz phrases with vibesman Terry Gibbs.

Disc-wise, Dinah Washington recorded many titles for many different labels and in a wide variety of settings. Most of her successful single recordings were replete with string-laden accompaniments or with other even more obviously commercial trappings. Just think of *Fly Me To The Moon*, *What A Difference A Day Made*, *September In The Rain*, *Where Are You?*, *Baby, You've Got What It Takes* and *A Rockin' Good Way* (the last two titles had Dinah sharing the vocal spotlight with that excellent and sophisticated R & B singer, Brook Benton). But it was on blues, or at least blues-tinged material, and the more jazz-based numbers that her talent shone like a beacon, especially if there was a goodly complement of top-class musicians around to make the proceedings even more appetising.

Dinah Washington died on December 14th, 1963 following a tragic accident involving tranquilising tablets. Upon her death there was some talk of suicide, but those who knew her could never comprehend that living-for-life-Dinah could possibly have meant to take her own life.

Despite the fact that only a comparatively small number of her recordings could be classified as great, Dinah was still a real influential figure in vocal music from the mid-'40s right up to the time of her passing, and perhaps even beyond.

Possibly the best summation of Dinah Washington came a few years back from the distinguished jazz critic, Leonard Feather: "Though many called her a modern Bessie Smith, though she had made an album of Bessie's songs, Dinah was a more sophisticated singer; her diction was precise, almost emphatic, her voice higher pitched and more strident, her style more often laced with a bitter-sweet humour. She was a master of the art of splitting syllables into several notes and of bringing effective dramatic meaning to the tritest of songs, which was a challenge Bessie never was required to meet."

Frankie Laine, pictured in the early '50s with his accompanist the late Carl Fischer. Apart from his ability as a singer, Laine has also scored success as a songwriter. The team of Laine and Fischer were co-writers of that fine standard ballad *We'll Be Together Again*—which was recorded most effectively by Frank Sinatra and several other top-line singers.

The talented and personable Rosemary Clooney flanked by two famous musical directors Nelson Riddle (left) and Paul Weston. The occasion was a London press reception of the early '60s.

*/Richi Howell*

*Above left :* The magnificent Bessie Smith. To call her the greatest
blues singer of all time would not be an exaggeration. History
has dubbed her 'The Empress of the Blues'—and rightly so.
*/Melody Maker*

*Above right :* Mildred Bailey was perhaps the most significant
of the early white jazz vocalists. For one thing she was actually
the first female dance band singer, and for another she was the
first white pop singer to fully absorb and incorporate a jazz
feeling in her songs./*Melody Maker*

Jimmy Rushing, the classic blues-shouter who sang for 15 years with the original Count Basie band, has probably had more influence on today's 'soul' singers than they would care to admit. Some of them might claim that they have never heard of Jimmy—or Mr Five by Five as he is affectionately called—but the Rushing influence is there alright, though perhaps by osmosis. After nearly 50 years in jazz, Jimmy passed away in June 1972. /*Melody Maker*

Billie Holiday represented the absolute quintessence of jazz vocalising. Her style while still a teenager was remarkably mature, her approach to a song completely intuitive. She was perhaps the first vocalist to demonstrate how jazz values could be found in even the trashiest pop songs. But when she sang material of a more subtle nature each performance became an instant classic. Billie Holiday could very well be the only unique singer that jazz has produced. She died at the age of 44, at a time when most artists are just beginning to realise their full potential./*Melody Maker*

*Left :* Ever since the '30s the subtle yet commanding voice of Lee Wiley has remained a source of great pleasure for musicians and afficionados. Unfortunately, the public-at-large never quite cottoned-on to her. But that's their loss not Lee's, for she has never been short of work. And recently she has started recording again—so it's still not too late./*Melody Maker*

*Below left :* Anita O'Day's importance as a jazz vocal stylist can be judged by the amount of top singers who live in her shadow, stylistically speaking. She was, in fact, the hip forerunner of the 'cool' school as characterised by such as June Christy, Chris Connor, *et al./Melody Maker*

*Below :* As a song stylist, the ebullient Dinah Washington always seemed years ahead of her time. Since her tragic death in 1964, a large percentage of the world's female singers have acquired many of her vocal inflections and phrasing ideas. Outside of Ella Fitzgerald and Sarah Vaughan, Dinah was probably the best example of a female jazz singer who could contribute to the pop scene without losing the essence of her style./*Melody Maker*

The first truly significant vocal group was undoubtedly the Mills Brothers, seen here in the 1932 film *The Big Broadcast*. During this early period they were known simply as 'Four Boys and a Guitar'. Their own specialised brand of close harmony has never lost its basic appeal which may explain why the Mills Brothers are still active today as performers and recording artists.

/Paramount Pictures

The Deep River Boys were always a fine group who could handle spirituals with authentic conviction, as well as giving the public the latest jazz or pop pieces.

Undoubtedly the most famous and biggest-selling vocal group of the '30s and '40s were the Andrews Sisters. Here they are in typical '40s attire and full of enthusiasm.
/Music for Pleasure Records

An affectionate study of the Merry Macs. Led by Judd and Marjorie McMichael (top and bottom), this was undoubtedly one of the most creative groups around during the late '30s and early '40s. Baby Kelly McMichael, with the aid of a little trick photography, climbed into this picture to add a fifth voice to this famous group. Remaining members are Dick Baldwin (left) and Clive Erard./Courtesy of Arthur Jackson

The Delta Rhythm boys, an extremely polished and highly
exciting team, were one of the first vocal groups to convincingly
simulate the rhythmic character and feeling of a big band.
*/Courtesy of Arthur Jackson*

*Above:* Musicians and singers still rave about the Mel-Tones. Here they are in the '40s with mastermind and leader Mel Torme (centre). The singer on the far left is Les Baxter, who later became one of America's most important arrangers and a recording artist in his own right. The two girls are Betty Beveridge and Ginny O'Connor (who later became Mrs Henry Mancini). The fair-haired young man on the right is Bernie Parke. The group's version of *What is This Thing Called Love* recorded with the Artie Shaw Orchestra was hailed as a vocal/instrumental classic. It combined the joint-arranging talents of Mel Torme, Artie Shaw and Sonny Burke and was full of interesting ideas and innovations./*Melody Maker*

*Below left:* The superb singing talents of The King Sisters were an exciting musical mainstay of the Horace Heidt and Alvino Rey bands. Later they branched out as an individual attraction and created many musically rewarding performances on record.
/*Capitol Records*

*Below right:* The top commercial group of the early '50s, with million-selling singles like *Tell Me Why, Three Coins in the Fountain* and *Love is a Many Splendoured Thing* to their credit, were The Four Aces. By 1955 the group had sold over ten million records./*MCA Artists Ltd*

The great instrumental and vocal group The Four Freshmen, who first found fame through the enthusiastic promotional efforts of bandleader Stan Kenton. They are pictured here at an EMI press reception in London—with another famous Kenton alumnus, singing star June Christy./*Richi Howell*

Technically speaking, the Hi-Los were the most incredible vocal group in the whole history of popular music. Some critics dismissed them as being too slick and glib, but those who took the time to listen discovered in the group's work an endless fund of musical excitement combined with the most riotous sense of humour ever heard in any vocal group. Today, the Hi-Los are disbanded as a group but their collective and individual talents are constantly heard on American TV commercials. A great shame, for popular music needs them more then ever today.

*Above left:* Former jazz trombonist Ray Conniff made history in the '50s with his own individual method of scoring voices in an instrumental style alongside the instrumental sections of his orchestra. The effect was quite astonishing and made Conniff into a major star almost overnight.

*Above right:* With a fine voice, flexible enough to operate as either a baritone or tenor, backed up by first-rate musicianship and handsome features, former sax-player Tony Martin became one of America's most popular romantic singers of the late '30s and '40s.

Sincerly
Dick Haymes

Dick Haymes has sometimes been referred to as the 'greatest ballad singer of them all'. There was a time in the '40s when the former Harry James, Benny Goodman and Tommy Dorsey vocalist almost outstripped Sinatra's popularity. Certainly, his recording of *You'll Never Know* easily outsold the Sinatra version and earned a gold disc—which is something Sinatra never achieved in the '40s, despite his huge fan following.

Haymes made a big impression in films too. Here he is vieing with his former bandleader boss, Harry James, for the attention of the lovely Maureen O'Hara in a scene from the 1946 musical *Do You Love Me.*/20th Century Fox

Former trumpeter/trombonist and leader of one of the world's finest jazz orchestras, Billy Eckstine found international success and lasting fame as a popular vocalist. With superior songs like *Cottage for Sale* (1945), *Everything I Have is Yours* (1947), *Blue Moon* (1948), *Caravan* (1949), *My Foolish Heart* (1950) and *I Apologise* (1951) the unique *Mr B* notched up a most Impressive array of gold disc awards. Each of these quality performances actually topped the million-sales mark.

'This boy has the finest pipes in the business.' So said Frank Sinatra of Vic Damone's vocal quality. For several years, Vic was an unashamed Sinatra copyist but he eventually developed his own identifiable approach to a ballad and wound up in the million-selling class with songs like *Again* and *On the Street Where You Live./Ember Records*

Easy-going Dean Martin takes his cue from arranger/conductor
Nelson Riddle at a recording session for the Capitol label. The
always-likeable Dino has never claimed to be a great singer, but
his casual charm and pleasing tones invariably win the day.
'Look,' he says. 'I sing a song. If it takes, beautiful. If it doesn't,
we try again—why try to make it complicated? I sing the best I
can— you can't put me in jail for that.' His sustaining popularity
plus a long string of million-selling hits cancel out all arguments.
Dino sells charm—and the world buys!

*Left:* The epitome of vocal relaxation. A young Perry Como at a recording session in RCA's New York studios.

*Above:* Perry confronts Harry James and Vivian Blaine in a scene from the 1946 musical *If I'm Lucky.*/20th Century Fox

*Right:* The ever-casual Como as he is today. Still recording for RCA and still turning out hit records like *It's Impossible*... and still one of the world's finest interpreters of the love song. /*RCA Records*

Andy Williams is often referred to as one of today's great pop stars—and so he is—but very few people realise that his career extends back across thirty years of experience from being a childhood member of the Williams Brothers (they later backed Bing Crosby on his 1944 record of *Swinging on a Star* and did a lot of sound track work for Hollywood Films). Andy learned his craft the hard way, and because of this his stylists roots go deeper than most singers./*CBS Records*

The professional at work. Andy Williams at his happiest—in the recording studio.

# Bessie & Billie—Two of a Kind

Both Bessie Smith and Billie Holiday lived colourful, if sad, lives. Both died in tragic circumstances – Bessie in a Mississippi hospital, following a serious road accident, and Billie in a New York hospital, following a gradual deterioration in health, accentuated by her addiction to narcotics and drink.

In the field of blues singing, Bessie Smith was indeed the 'Empress'. Likewise, Billie Holiday is usually acknowledged as probably the greatest jazz singer of all time. Both Bessie and Billie have exercised an influence outside of blues and jazz.

Like that of Louis Armstrong, their singing styles – particularly the rhythmic and emotional aspects of their work – have often been a source of inspiration for generations of pop vocalists. Although Bessie Smith has been dead now for well over 30 years, she still continues to inspire singers not normally associated with blues. The late Janis Joplin – who, curiously, also died in tragic circumstances, in 1970 – often acknowledged Bessie as her prime inspiration. And Miss Holiday made a profound impact on the work of such pop artists as Frank Sinatra, Peggy Lee, Ella Fitzgerald, and Anita O'Day. (Miss O'Day, it must be admitted, is usually more associated with jazz than popular music, although her popularity hasn't been confined solely to the former.)

Like Billie Holiday, Bessie Smith was a Negress and throughout her career she experienced all the ramifications of life as a coloured person in the United States. The possessor of a majestic, rich-brown voice, Bessie Smith – christened Elizabeth, and coming from a family of five children – was born in Chattanooga, Tennessee, probably in 1898 – her official birthdate is uncertain. She appeared in school plays as a child and when she was nine years of age earned $8 for one theatre appearance in her home town.

A most important event in Bessie Smith's life came when she was about 14. She met Gertrude 'Ma' Rainey, who was probably the first of the great female blues singers. Then Ma Rainey's husband, Will, heard Bessie sing and invited her to join the Rainey troupe, an outfit called the Rabbit Foot Minstrels. For about two years, the young singer learned all about the tricks of the vaudeville circuit. One thing she learned was to really project her voice, without using a megaphone (needless to say, there was nothing as sophisticated as microphones to be used).

Bessie left the Rainey troupe around 1914 to go it alone as a singer/dancer. Subsequently, she worked innumerable engagements in theatres, dancehalls, *et al*, throughout the Southern States of the US. By 1919 she was earning as much as $75 a week, plus tips. In 1920, she joined a revue at the Paradise, Atlantic City. Thanks to promoter/bandleader Perry Bradford, she made a recording test for a label called Emerson Records of New York. But the label didn't sign her up.

Then a meeting with the legendary saxophonist/clarinettist Sydney Bechet enabled Bessie to obtain a part in the show *How Come*. The pair did a test recording for the famous blues and jazz label, OKey – but OKey already had more than its share of blues singers. Again, the young singer remained unsigned.

Finally, Frank Walker of Columbia Records, who had heard her sing several years before, arranged for her to record two numbers, *Down Hearted Blues* and *Gulf Coast Blues*. The date was February 16th, 1923. Walker became the singer's manager. Although neither track indicated the truly majestic way in which Bessie later sang the blues, it was the beginning. And, in fact, both numbers were hits. So, a mutually profitable recording career, lasting 10 years in all, was off to an excellent start.

During her recording career with Columbia, Bessie Smith cut 180 sides. Although the last recordings she made, in company with top-line jazz musicians like Jack Teagarden, Frankie Newton and Chu Berry, showed what her over-indulgence in alcohol was doing to her general health, the overall standard of performance was superbly high.

*Black Mountain Blues* (recorded 22/7/30), *Weeping Willow Blues* (26/9/24), *St Louis Blues* (14/1/25), *Jailhouse Blues* (21/9/23), *Midnight Blues* (15/6/23), *See If I'll Care* (12/4/30), *You've Been a Good Ole Wagon* (24/1/25), *Careless Love Blues* (26/5/25), *I Ain't Gonna Play No Second Fiddle* (27/5/25), *Nashville Woman's Blues* (26/5/25) and *J. C. Holmes Blues* (26/5/25) are exceptional examples of blues singing of the highest order. And, for this listener anyway, Bessie's version of *Nobody Knows You When You're Down & Out* (25/5/29) is one of the most moving vocal performances ever recorded.

Instrumental support on Bessie Smith's recordings, from the likes of Louis Armstrong, Ed Allen and Louis Bacon (cornets), Jimmy Harrison and Charlie Green (trombones), Fletcher Henderson, James P. Johnson, Porter Grainger and Clarence Williams (pianos), Fred Longshaw (harmonium/piano), clarinet-tists Buster Bailey and Coleman Hawkins and tubaist Cyrus St Clair was usually sympathetic – often quite magnificent. In the case of trumpeter Joe Smith (Bessie's favourite), the rapport between singer and instrumentalist was almost unsurpassable (viz *Lost Your Head Blues* (4/5/26), *Young Woman's Blues* (10/10/26), *Send Me To The 'Lectric Chair* (3/3/27).

Through all those 180 titles, that powerful highly-emotive and absolutely inimitable voice sang the story of the blues – sad blues, despairing blues, spirited blues, but *always* the blues – in a style and with an impact that can only be called definitive. No wonder her influence became, and continued to be, so widespread!

Superlative instrumental support, plus a unique vocal style, made Billie Holiday's recordings so appealing – and, in some cases, masterpieces of vocal-cum-instrumental jazz. Billie hadn't the deep richness of Bessie Smith, but she had a voice which, though in later years it became ravaged with her own personal excesses, was on the same emotional plane. Billie possessed a fine rhythmic sense, often phrasing just a shade behind the beat. Though her range wasn't at all exceptional, there was never any lack of shading and dynamics in her delivery.

Throughout her 26 years as a recording artist, Billie Holiday – known affectionately by the title 'Lady Day' bestowed upon her by an ardent admirer and musician named Lester Young – made humorous sides, singing all types of material. But even to the utter banality of the worst pop trivia of, say, the 1930's she brought a dignity, an artistry and a meaning that still remains unchallenged in its supremacy.

Billie was born Eleanor Gough McKay in Baltimore, on April 7th, 1915. Her father, Clarence Holiday, was banjoist/guitarist with the Fletcher Henderson Orchestra in the early 1930's. As a kid she had listened avidly to Bessie Smith and Louis Armstrong recordings. But even at a very early age, her life was mirrored with tragedy. By the time she was 10 her father had deserted Billie and her mother to remarry.

In the excellent book, *Hear Me Talkin' To Ya* (co-edited by Nat Shapiro and Nat Hentoff, published by Peter Davies), Billie gave a graphic account of how she and her mother were penniless and starving. And of how she got her first break.

"... Finally, I got so desperate I stopped in the Log Cabin run by Jerry Preston. I told him I wanted a drink. I didn't have a dime. But I ordered gin (it was my first drink – I didn't know gin from wine) and gulped it down. I asked Preston for a job, told him I was a dancer. He said to dance. I tried it. He said I stunk.

I told him I could sing. He said 'Sing'. Over in the corner was an old guy playing the piano. He struck *'Travlin'* and I sang. The customers stopped drinking. They turned around and watched. The pianist, Dick Wilson, swung into *Body and Soul*. Jeez, you should have seen those people – all of them started crying. Preston came over, shook his head and said: 'Kid, you win.' That's how I got my start . . . ."

But Billie was a street-walker by the time she was 13 and at an early age became acquainted with drugs. It certainly sounds melodramatic and presumptuous, but her appalling private life seemed to contribute considerably to the depth and feeling which were *the* most important ingredients of her vocal make-up.

But unlike Bessie Smith, Billie Holiday wasn't a blues singer. No more than a dozen, at the most, of her records were of blues. Yet Billie's work had all the *inner* qualities of the finest of blues singing, although it was only on rare occasions that she sang and phrased idiomatically in a more or less definite blues framework.

And not everything that Billie sang was low-keyed of self-pitying. She could swing and sing, happily, with the best, as items such as *Your Mother's Son-in-Law* (from her first-ever recording date, 27/11/33), *What A Little Moonlight Can Do*

(2/7/35), *I've Got My Love To Keep Me Warm* (12/1/37), and *On The Sunny Side Of The Street* (8/4/44) demonstrated admirably.

But unquestionably it was the sad, love-lost repertoire with which she was more closely associated – the sort of material which, when sung by Billie, could strike a chord in even the meanest of hearts (and as far as records go, it still can). From her earlier days, *He's Funny That Way* (13/9/37), *Why Was I Born?* (25/1/37), her own *Billie's Blues* (10/7/36), *You Go To My Head* (11/5/38), *I Can't Get Started* (15/9/38), and *Some Other Spring* (5/7/39) stand out. Later recordings like *Lover Man* (4/10/44), *Don't Explain* (14/8/45), *Easy Living* (13/2/47) – compare this version with Peggy Lee's on her *Black Coffee* LP for an obvious example of the Holiday influence on another singer – and the definitive, deeply moving *Porgy* (10/12/48) offer quite beautiful examples of the art of Lady Day.

By the time the 1950's had arrived, the voice was often a cruel croaky parody of its former self. But though the voice and the technique were severely diminished, the feeling became more intense – and certainly more embittered. Two of the better latter-day Billie Holiday recordings were the albums *Songs For Distingue Lovers* (World Record Club) and *Lady In Satin*. The former put Lady Day in her best environment: in the company of a small star-studded jazz combo. Harry Edison (trumpet), Ben Webster (tenor sax), Jimmy Rowles (piano) and Barney Kessel (guitar) were in the accompanying group, and although there were many moments on the Norman Granz-produced LP when, technically, the singer barely made it, there was a poignancy that even she had rarely captured in her previous recordings (Examples: *I Didn't Know What Time It Was*, *One For My Baby*, *Embraceable You*).

*Lady In Satin* (CBS-Realm) is different again. This time for her penultimate recording dates (for American Columbia), she had been presented with a collection of fine standard tunes (*End Of A Love Affair*, *But Beautiful*, *For Heaven's Sake*, etc) but with accompaniments that were singularly inappropriate – syrupy strings and cooing choir arranged and conducted by Ray Ellis.

But just as Charlie Parker had burst triumphantly through the shackles of a diabolical string section several years before, the voice of Billie Holiday conquered her almost bizarre surroundings. Her singing, although technically poor, was emotionally harrowing. One track sums up everything: the seemingly prophetic *For All We Know* (*we may never meet again*). Recorded on February 19th, 1958, it is performed with such intensity as to make one believe she really knew that she would be dead within a short time (she died almost seventeen months hence to the day).

For the very best of Billie Holiday, though, one must go back to the '30s and '40s. For session after session she made recordings which really have attained musical immortality. Then Billie was joined by such great instrumental stars as Buck Clayton, Roy Eldrige, Red Allen, Bunny Berigan, Harry Edison, or Cootie Williams (trumpets), Dickie Wells, Benny Morton, or Trummy Young (trombones), Irving Fazola, Edmond Hall, Benny Goodman, or Buster Bailey (clarinets), saxophonists Harry Carney, Johnny Hodges, Ben Webster, Chu Berry, Joe Thomas, Benny Carter, or Hilton Jefferson; pianists Teddy Wilson (often leader of Billie's accompanying groups), Claude Thornhill, Joe Sullivan, Joe Bushkin, or Clyde Hart; drummers Cozy Cole, Gene Krupa, Jo Jones, or Eddie Dougherty; bassists Walter Page, Artie Bernstein, Milt Hinton, or John Kirby; and guitarists Freddie Green, Dick McDonough, Lawrence Lucie, or Allen Reuss.

But above all other accompanying musicians, there was the tenor saxophone of the aforementioned Lester Young, truly a giant in his field and a major stylistic innovator. Young's warm, intensely rhythmic, utterly sympathetic accompaniments and solos were the perfect foil for Billie's singing. There are many, many examples of the Young-Holiday team working superlatively together, but the following will suffice to illustrate this point – *He Ain't Got Rhythm*, *This Year's Kisses* and *Why Was I Born?* (all recorded 25/1/37), *Mean To Me* (11/5/37), *Foolin' Myself* and *Easy Living* (1/6/37), *I Can't Get Started* (15/9/38), and, perhaps the finest of all, *I Must Have That Man* (25/1/37).

Billie Holiday recordings which fall into the slightly unusual category are *Strange Fruit*, first recorded April 20th, 1939, and *Gloomy Sunday*, which received its initial recording by Billie on August 7th, 1941. *Strange Fruit*, a song about lynchings of Negroes in the Deep South, proved successful for the singer as regards sales, but was quite understandably not much appreciated by certain persons living in this part of the US. *Gloomy Sunday*, a Hungarian suicide song, received a chilling, unforgettable interpretation by Miss Holiday.

Several of Billie's compositions have survived the years and are still remembered by other singers – *Don't Explain*, *Tell Me More* and in particular, the charming *God Bless The Child* (which has been latched on to in recent years by present-generation pop artists like Blood, Sweat & Tears and Judith Durham).

Although Billie Holiday was at her best singing with the small jazz group set-up, she could – and indeed did – sing with big bands. She sang and toured with the Count Basie orchestra in 1937, and was the first Negro singer to be permanently featured with a white band when she joined Artie Shaw the following year. She also broadcast with the Benny Goodman band on at least one occasion.

Billie Holiday was without doubt a unique talent. So, too, was Bessie Smith. Their respective talents were much too big to be restricted to one musical form alone. Their influence will, one would hope, remain for as long as listening to music – and in particular to gramophone records – continues as such a rewarding occupation. And their continued influence, even infinitesimally, on pop music can only mean that this musical form will be just that better for the experience.

SB

# Part Five

# The Vocal Groups

*An art can only be learned in the workshop of those who are winning their bread by it.*
    Samuel Butler (1835 to 1902)

Group singing has always had a hold on the public, from the madrigal singers of the Middle Ages, through the choirs of the Baroque period, the minstrel shows of the 19th century, the glee clubs and barber shops of the turn of the century, the male voice choirs beloved of the British working man; and, in popular music, the development from the syncopated rhythm singing of the '30s, through the smooth close harmony groups of the '30s and '40s, via the rock groups of the '50s to the pop music of today.

In our music the story of the vocal groups started when Paul Whiteman featured Bing Crosby, Al Rinker and Harry Barris as his Rhythm Boys in spirited arrangements of songs like *Mississippi Mud*, which became focal points of the Whiteman band's performances and recordings. The Rhythm Boys' 'hot' singing came as a revelation to a public fed during the late '20s on the novelty numbers and schmaltz of groups like the Happiness Boys and the Revellers.

After appearing in the film *The King of Jazz* in 1930 the trio went into the Coconut Grove in Los Angeles with the Gus Arnheim band, regular broadcasts from that venue establishing them as a number one attraction and giving Crosby the opportunity to carve out a solo career. Good for Bing: not so good for the group which promptly disintegrated after having made its mark on musical history.

*The Big Broadcast*, Bing's first starring film, also featured the group that made harmony singing universally acceptable. And the ract that the Mills Brothers are still singing the songs of today is a tribute to the durable talent of – as they were then known – The Four Boys and a Guitar. Quietly rhythmical, they consolidated their reputation with realistic vocal impressions of musical instruments between the vocal choruses. The Mills Brothers (one of the few real family groups) established vocal groups as a basic essential of the music scene and, despite the host of coloured quartets which followed, always retained their individuality and style.

They found little opposition at the time, and during the '30s no other influences appeared, despite the jazz-based work of the Five Spirits of Rhythm, The Three Peppers, Babs and her Brothers and the amusing jive antics of Slim (Gaillard) and Slam (Stewart), all of whom found an appreciative if somewhat limited audience. At this time harmony singing was more or less the province of coloured groups such as these, white groups being limited to the more vaudeville-styled performances of the Yacht Club Boys who were a hit with their comedy routines based on self-written material.

Around the mid-'30s, as popular music itself assumed a veneer of sophistication through the songs of the Gershwins, Cole Porter, Dubin and Warren, Harold Arlen, Gordon and Revel, *et al*, so vocal groups began to lose the 'vo-de-o-doh' image.

Even the Negro groups weren't immune; the Inkspots who had been featuring mainly jive novelties now added the high-pitched tenor of Bill Kenny, who sang schmaltzy ballads with remarkably corny phrasing, while bass singer Orville 'Hoppy' Jones intoned the 'middle-eights' of each chorus in a lugubrious recitative. This formula was applied to virtually every record they made and while many became best-sellers (*Whispering Grass, Bless You* or the happier-sounding *Java Jive*) discerning listeners were all too aware of the limitations of the formula.

It cannot be said (fortunately) that the Inkspots were much of an influence on group singing. Their brand of corn was ignored by other coloured quartets such as the Charioteers, the Deep River Boys and, to my mind the best of all, the Delta Rhythm Boys. This handsome well-mannered quintet, anchored firmly by the resonant bass voice of Lee Gaines and enhanced by the lyrical but never sugary tenor of Kelsey Pherr and the jazz-inflected tones of Traverse Crawford, not only produced some superb ballad performances but swung most convincingly.

All these groups had a connection, however tenuous, with jazz and/or gospel and/or race music; there was always a suggestion of vocal freedom and self-expression in their work. But for ultra-smooth and sophisticated close harmony singing, devoid of any jazz pretensions but eminently satisfactory in a commercially swinging way, the white groups cornered the market.

The road was signposted in the late '30s by the Merry Macs (three McMichael brothers with a procession of girl singers in the lead role). The Macs set a style that the others followed unvaryingly, although for many years their arrangements and unique vocal timbre made them the supreme example of the *genre*. Reduced to fundamentals, the Macs and their contemporaries reproduced the time-honoured vocal set-up of soprano or counter-tenor leading the alto-tenor-baritone/bass harmony. In essentials, that is. What they and the other groups did within those confines bore no resemblance to the medieval consorts or the barber shop quartets, but the generic thread was there, as it still is in the latter-day work of the Hi-Los, Beach Boys and many other pop groups. The only surprising aspect of the situation was that so many groups, utilising what was basically the same style, should have produced so many individual and colourful permutations of sound. Six Hits & A Miss were also early in the field, though their work was mainly confined to radio, and ensuing years resounded to the teamwork of a myriad of harmony groups many of which sprang from the ranks of the big dance bands.

The Swing Era lasted from about 1935 to 1945, during which time the big bands reigned supreme. During the '30s the music of the bands themselves was their main selling point but later the need for escapism and glamour to offset the strains of wartime brought the vocalists to the fore. Goodlookers like Peggy Lee, Jo Stafford and Helen Forrest and personable youngsters like Frank Sinatra, Dick Haymes, Perry Como and the Eberles graced the bandstand and assumed an importance comparable with that of the bands with which they worked.

With this spotlight on singers, many maestros supported their efforts with their own harmony groups often drawn from the ranks of the sidemen. From the highest to the lowest the bands sprouted their trios and quartets. Les Brown had his Town Criers, Charlie Spivak his Stardusters; Bob Crosby produced the Bob-o-Links, Claude Thornhill the Snowflakes; Sammy Kaye's group vocals were by the Three Kaydets and the Kaye Choir; Ted Fio Rito featured the Debutantes, followed by Kay Swingle and her Brothers (one of whom eventually turned up in France with the Bach-swingin' choir). Even the big swinging jazz bands weren't to be left out: Jimmie Lunceford had vocals by the simply-named 'The Trio' (Trummy Young, Willie Smith and Sy Oliver), Stan Kenton experimented with the Pastels, and Woody Herman's Blue Moods later found a separate existence as the Skylarks.

Some leaders went all the way in giving their audiences glamour with all-girl vocal groups. Vaughn Monroe backed up his own stentorian pipes with the Norton Sisters and the Moon Maids; Tony Pastor had the Clooney Sisters, Ralph Flanagan the Young Sisters, Ina Ray Hutton featured the Kim Loo Sisters, while the King Sisters began with Horace Heidt and went with Alvino Rey when he left to form his own band. Inevitably, few of these purely functional groups offered much in the way of genuine talent or outlived their stint with the bands in question.

A handful did, though, and lasting fame came to Tommy Dorsey's Pied Pipers, Glenn Miller's Modernaires and Artie Shaw's Meltones. The Pipers probably reached the highest peak of all, with a superb blend and polish that testified to the musicianship of Hal Hopper, Chuck Lowery and Clark Yocum. June Hutton was the female lead in later years, but the voice that gave the quartet its individuality in the Dorsey days was Jo Stafford, whose accurate intonation and vibratoless tone were ideal for the job. Although Frank Sinatra wasn't a member of the group his voice was scored as part of their harmony on memorable records like *I'll Never Smile Again*, *This Love Of Mine* and *Stardust*. The Modernaires, out of a job when Glenn Miller joined the USAAF (their parts in the Miller scores were taken over by the Crew Chiefs), found a niche for themselves as a solo act. Group member Ralph Brewster became a choral director, and in the '60s singer-arranger Alan Copeland was in charge while the Mods revised their old hits in modern style.

The group that musicians still rave about appeared on Artie Shaw records of the mid-'40s. If they had never done anything else Mel Tormé and the Meltones would be remembered for *What Is This Thing Called Love*, which for advanced ideas and a superb conception of solo and group singing has never been equalled.

Tormé, at 19, was already a veteran and though the Meltones may have been a momentary diversion (briefly revived on record two decades later for nostalgia's sake) the brevity of their professional career is in inverse ratio to their reputation in vocal group history.

With the advent of the '50s the shift from ensemble to solo sounds was under way. Frankie Laine and Guy Mitchell were just coming into sight with their mule trains, riders in the sky and assorted sea shanties, a motif reflected by two of the few vocal group records to make the charts at this time.

These were *Goodnight Irene* and *On Top Of Old Smokey* by the Weavers, marking the introduction of the Folk theme later to be pushed to even greater success by the Kingston Trio, the Limeliters, Peter Paul and Mary and the New Christy Minstrels. But this was merely a by-product of the mainstream of popular music. The Inkspots split up and each member formed his own 'Original Inkspots', which began to get a little confusing. The intimate, swinging style of the King Cole Trio lapsed as its leader's solo potential was realised. Although Nat became one of the greatest and best-loved singers of all time, many of us remember with affection his little group which sparked off a host of imitators. Nat Cole did, however, make one or two records with the Starlighters, a vastly under-rated quartet which at various times included ex-Artie Shaw singer Pauline Byrnes and a 17-year-old Andy Williams, and whose tremendous *Night And Day* is one of my all-time favourites – a record which perhaps more than any other shows what close harmony singing is all about.

Vocal group singing went off at various tangents, despite courageous attempts by such short-lived ensembles as the Honeydreamers and the Axidentals, who did superb work which a decade earlier would have been acclaimed and richly rewarded. But now there was no time, no room for it and only musicians took notice. As public tastes changed the field was open for all-male groups who tended to parody the extrovert performances of Frankie Laine and Johnnie Ray, whose lachrymose style was echoed in the tear-jerking efforts of the Four Aces – maybe not the best quartet of the early '50s, but surely the most successful, with a seemingly endless string of gold discs for *Tell Me Why, Love Is A Many Splendoured Thing, Stranger In Paradise* and other big ballads calling for undiluted vocal histrionics.

Rather more musically masculine were others like the Four Lads, the Ames Brothers and Williams Brothers, and the Kirby Stone Four whose witty and irrepressibly rhythmic arrangements featured the quartet singing against a girl chorus and infectious shuffle rhythms. Though they finally merged into the pop scene in the '60s the Stone Four had a good run and were the most durable group of the era.

It was the last of good-humoured quality music we were to hear for a while. Two things happened between 1954 and 1956: Bill Haley and Elvis Presley. And in their wake came the period of emergence of coloured groups whose rock 'n' roll was merely a bowdlerised version of their own 'race' as it had been known for years.

This was an ultra-commercial form of it, decked out with piano triplets (a soon-to-be-dated trademark), over-emphasised rhythm with a thunderous off-beat, honking tenor saxes and vocal styles that owed more to a clamorous demands of the teenage market than to any real identity with the blues which had been the basis of 'race' music. This holds true today, as the white groups achieved domination over the originators of the music (by virtue of the pre-dominantly white audience) with firstly a plagiarism then a complete adoption of the rhythm and blues style.

But how ephemeral it all was – and is. Can anyone now recall the Chuckles, Cheers, Diamonds, Coasters, Fleetwoods, Dominoes, Clovers and a few thousand others who turned out hit after hit, and flop after flop? Even the titles of their gold discs are forgotten. But not all were instantly forgettable. Bill Haley and the Comets pursued a steadily successful path; the Crew Cuts were accorded the honour of a public debunking on a Stan Freberg comedy record; the Platters, notable more for showmanship than for good singing, had a long run with their formula of an extrovert and highly erratic solo voice against group harmonies; the Everly Brothers kept their simple two-part C & W rock harmonies going (in some respects they predated the Beatles, some of whose early work is remarkably Everlyish); the Jordanaires were more capable per-formers than their many accompanying roles might have indicated; the Hill-toppers veered between corn and rock, but are now best known for their arranger, Billy Vaughn, who went on to fame as an orchestral conductor.

It was a tough time for groups trying to make it on the basis of 'quality' music yet, emulating nature's attempts at preserving a natural balance, the onset of rock 'n' roll also saw the re-birth of hope for lovers of good singing. Jackie Cain and Roy Kral persevered with the stylish jazz-based singing they had originated with Charlie Ventura's late '40s bop band, the Brothers Four took a new look at folksy themes and swing music came back with the three outstand-ing groups of the decade. 'Rugged individualists' does, I suppose, best describe Lambert, Hendricks and Ross who conceived the idea of setting lyrics to jazz themes, emulating instrumental passages and working almost entirely in a jazz context. Formed by the late Dave Lambert (who had previously formed what strictly speaking *could* be called a group in his bebop duets with Buddy Stewart in Gene Krupa's band), the trio included Jon Hendricks and Annie Ross, later replaced by Yolande Bavan. Too way-out for general public acceptance, L, H & R occupy a place in the jazz books even if strictly on a love-'em-or-hate-'em basis.

There emerged also a quartet who set a standard that has not been challenged to date. Being extremely subjective about it, I unhesitatingly claim the Hi-Los as the greatest vocal group of all time. Others may put in their vote for the Four Freshman. I don't agree, but I won't object. Both all-male groups set out on a course charted long ago by the Macs and the Pipers, in the absence of a female voice reverting to the traditional use of a counter-tenor or falsetto lead. In Clark Burroughs the Hi-Los had a truly remarkable lead with a voice of fantastic range. Normally working in a conventional tenor role, Burroughs was now and again called on to provide shock effects in leader-arranger Gene Puerling's magnificent scores. These were usually done tongue-in-cheek and so audaciously that they could leave the listener in a state of complete disbelief. Vocal tricks apart, the Hi-Los swung most convincingly and with a rare sense of humour, and on ballads achieved a rich tonal blend that I thought the most beautiful sound I had ever heard from human voices. In contrast, the Freshmen were too academic, their harmonies too cold and deliberately contrived in search of effect; there was too much attention to the notes and too little to the lyrical sense and melodic feeling. But they moved with the times and are still exploring the modern pop repertoire, proving more likeable than when purveying static arrangements of quality songs. The Hi-Los, despite brief flirtations with folk songs and bossa nova, refused to compromise with pop in order to survive, and finally and sadly passed out of the business altogether.

# The Distaff Side

'Sister' acts were always a part of show business, although in most cases their appeal was more visual than aural, and with only two exceptions they have always taken second place to the mixed or all-male groups. It could be because most of the girl groups were trios, which meant a lack of harmonic fullness, allied to the absence of variety in female voices as compared to the greater tonal range of the others.

The early sister acts were aimed at the '20s equivalent of the admass, with vaudeville as the spiritual home of the Duncan Sisters, Williams Sisters, and the Brox Sisters (best known for their work with Whiteman and the Rhythm Boys in *The King of Jazz*). It wasn't until the advent of the Boswell Sisters that girls achieved musical equality. Martha, Connee and Vet (Helvetia) were three youngsters from New Orleans who could sing hot choruses with the best of them, and usually recorded in company with leading jazz musicians. It is possible to regard them as the inspiration of every girl trio for the next twenty years, and though their singing and swinging style was often emulated no other group possessed their affinity, their intuitive musicianship. Echoes of the Boswell Sisters were even heard in Britain, and the Rhythm Sisters, Carlyle Cousins and Southern Sisters all performed diffidently in their style with too-English accents.

The Andrews Sisters were next in line – also the end of the line for really big name reputations. Sparked by their 1937 million-selling record of *Bei Mir Bist Du Schoen*, Patti, Maxine and Laverne more or less cornered the market through the '40s and early '50s, But they were generally non-swingers, performing boogie novelties and schmaltzy ballads alike in a brassy style that appealed more to the general public than to those who looked for a little more sensitivity. During the war years they appeared in almost every 'B' musical film ever made – or it seemed that way. An attempted reunion in the mid-'60s was sadly halted by the death of Laverne.

The monumental Three Peters Sisters did a great visual act but achieved little musically, and the Dinning Sisters had one big hit (*Once In A While*), but little to offer other than pretty faces and pleasantly innocuous voices. It was the old story of gaps in the harmony, a problem which didn't face the Clark Sisters and King Sisters, both quartets. The Clarks first sang with the Tommy Dorsey band as The Sentimentalists (remember *On The Sunny Side Of The Street*?) and went off on their own with a musicianly approach to good material and a quite vibrant delivery of rich harmonies. As did the King Sisters, alumni of the Horace Heidt and Alvino Rey bands, and for my money the best all-girl group to emerge since the Boswells.

Britain's response was the Beverly Sisters, of erratic harmony and suspect pitching, and the Kaye Sisters, sometimes equally suspect. While they were making the most of BBC-TV variety programmes the 'sister' style was fading in the USA. The McGuire Sisters provided charm and a touch of quality, and Lawrence Welk's Lennon Sisters offered family appeal, but we were heading towards the female equivalent of the rock groups mentioned previously. It was the day of the Ronettes, Shirelles, Chordettes, Chiffons, Crystals, etc. These were all more or less interchangeable in sound and appearance and it took Tamla Motown to introduce, with the Supremes and the Vandellas, the era of 'soul'-ful soloist with decorative and only nominally harmonising support. The fact that the groups eventually appeared under the names of soloists Diana Ross and Martha Reeves only served to show how much the musical world had changed since the group ideal first expressed so beautifully by the Boswell Sisters 30 years before.

# Second Class Powers

The discerning reader may have noticed that, current or recent pop groups apart, discussion so far has been mainly confined to American groups. Logically, I feel, because in the pre-Beatle era Britain always followed the American lead. Certainly vocal group singing was a never-discovered art in this country until the '50s.

In the '20s and '30s we had the songs at the piano of Layton and Johnstone – who were Americans anyway; we had a music-hall act of harmonists and impressionists called the Four Aces, who twenty years later became the Radio

Revellers; we had the Kentucky Minstrels and Steffani's Silver Songsters and weren't we lucky? By the mid-40's we had the Ray Ellington Quartet who would do the King Cole Trio, Louis Jordan or Phil Harris bit at the drop of a stylus. Not that things were any better on the Continent. Pre-war Germany produced the Comedy Harmonists, who specialised in twee and generally unswinging 'popular' versions of light classical themes. And that was it until the Compagnons de la Chanson came along after the war and brought a fresh, individual approach allied to an energetic stage act.

When the '50s arrived British groups finally caught up with the American close harmony sounds of the '40s, and we got Pied-Pipers-and-Water from the Keynotes, Coronets, Kordites, Kentones and Stargazers, all operating in a very laboured manner (replaced in the '60s by the Fraser Hayes Quartet, Polka Dots – probably the best British quartet – Raindrops, Morgan-James Duo and Sounds Bob Rogers, who also managed to reach the American standard). There were the singing rhythm sections like the King Brothers and the Hedley Ward Trio, whose self-accompaniments were generally more interesting than the singing; and pop-of-the-period acts like the Dallas Boys and Jones Boys. And in a class of its own the Lonnie Donegan Skiffle Group, depending more on the leader's brazen renderings of folk and music-hall songs than any sort of group activity. This sort of folksy-pop was later developed by the Springfields, Seekers and New Faces. The same segment of the public (or a later version of it) which had taken to its hearts the belligerent vocalising of the lusty-voiced Five Smith Brothers in the '50s showed equal appreciation of the equally lusty Bachelors, which only went to prove that the public always had the last word – and to hell with music.

This was where the Continent, usually so far behind even by British standards, finally caught up. Various groups combining traditional close harmony with the modern swing style emerged in France, and the Blue Stars and the Double Six of Paris led to the commercially and artistically successful work of the Swingle Singers, who set Bach to a swinging beat with a scat style of vocalese that – if you looked closely enough – spanned the years from Whiteman's Rhythm Boys to Lambert, Hendricks and Ross. Lately I have heard two splendid albums by the Jumping Jacques and the Valente Singers, a one-session-only group dreamed up by Caterina Valente, both using unconventional vocal effects, split-second timing and a superb sense of rhythm. Will these groups exploit their possibilities or leave their audiences? It depends on whether they want to make history or money. What happened to the Gunther Kallman Choir should be an object lesson: some marvellously produced and brilliantly sung albums of evergreens and light music, discovery by the pop pundits and then a rapid descent into routine performances of pop banalities.

# King Size Groups

One of the most useful adjuncts to the record industry has always been the 'heavenly choir'. There can't be many solo singers who haven't had full choral backing at some time. In fact during two AFM (American Federation of Musicians) recording strikes the 'vocal chorus' proved indispensible. The 1943 strike was well under way when Frank Sinatra and Dick Haymes made their recording debuts, and both stars were first featured with *a cappella* backings by the Ken Lane Singers and the Song Spinners respectively.

Ken Lane, Lyn Murray, Jack Halloran, Ken Darby, Ralph Brewster, Jud Conlon (and in this country, Rita Williams, Johnny Johnston, Peter Knight) and many others were chorus masters experienced in vocal accompaniments, using *ad hoc* choirs specially assembled. like the backing musicians, for the particular recording session. Obviously the maintenance on a full-time basis of anything from 10 to 30 singers was hardly an economical proposition – unless one had the reputation of Fred Waring, who turned choral singing into a thriving industry!

Waring's Pennsylvanians started in the '20s as a college dance band, which the leader enhanced in the early days of radio with specially arranged vocal routines. Now in his 70s, he is still conducting what is probably the most immaculate choral group in popular music – maybe a little square, but an aggregation of beautifully balanced and tonally compatible voices directed with precision and a great sense of dynamics.

Equally good choral performances have been heard from the Norman Luboff Choir in their explorations of every conceivable angle of popular music; Gordon Jenkins' Singers, who brought choral-orchestral integrity to a fine art thanks to Jenkins' brilliant scoring; the Roger Wagner Chorale, a completely academic group who never ventured very far into the middle of the road; the Harry Simeon Chorale, led by a Waring alumnus; the long-lived Robert Mitchell Boy Choir; the Ray Charles Singers (no relation to the other Ray Charles), a warmly swinging combination who brought intimacy to the massed vocal sound; and possibly the most unique of all, The Voices of Walter Schumann, whose blend, technique, precision and enormous range of expression made them one of the wonders of the musical world.

As always, Britain fell more than a little short of paralleling all this choral magnificence, though there were highlights. No one (other than millions of non-critics) takes the Mitchell Minstrels seriously, but when the George Mitchell Swing Choir first emerged from its khaki dress after the war it had more than a little to commend it. Tight section work, a genuine sense of rhythm, and a diligent study by George Mitchell of the tenets laid down by Fred Waring made the choir the finest outfit in British music. Since its musicianship dissipated in the waves of applause that greeted its gallery-fetching minstrelsy, only the Mike Sammes Singers achieved a similar standard. Sammes' arrangements blend humour and swing in equal proportions, and even by American standards this group (smaller than the usual choir) is worthy of the highest plaudits. The Cliff Adams Singers mirror to a certain extent the sterling work a decade ago of Mitch Miller, who brought the 'sing-along' to millions of American homes, a banal type of performance redeemed somewhat by the robustly masculine tones of his lusty balladeers.

The biggest success stories of recent years belong to the Johnny Mann Singers, a versatile chorus who combine modernism with remarkable group precision, and Ray Conniff, who proved the leading influence of the last decade and a half. Though the current output of the Conniff Singers is strictly pop in character, the former jazz trombonist made history with his method of scoring the singers in vocalese fashion along with the instrumental sections of a big swing-style band. When other maestros jumped on the Conniff singing-bandwagon with inferior copies the sound fell out of favour, but for a few years it did give the record business some of the quality it so badly needed.

## FOOTNOTE

Vocal groups served as a sound training ground for aspiring soloists and it might be illuminating to re-cap on some of the vocal group members who went on to stardom in other directions: Conductor-arranger Les Baxter (Meltones). Actresses Priscilla, Rosemary and Lola Lane, and comedienne-authoress-MGM vocal coach/arranger Kay Thompson (Fred Waring's Pennsylvanians). Comedian-actor Art Carney (Donna and Her Don Juans with Horace Heidt's band). Singers Bing Crosby (Whiteman's Rhythm Boys), Rosemary Clooney (Clooney Sisters), June Hutton and Jo Stafford (Pied Pipers), Connee Boswell (Boswell Sisters), Mel Tormé (Meltones), Andy Williams (Starlighters and Williams Brothers), Blossom Dearie (Blue Reys). Vocal group leaders like Mike Sammes and Bill Shepherd (George Mitchell Choir).

AJ

## Part Six

# *A Bunch of Balladeers*

*We poets of the proud old lineage who sing to
find your heart . . .*
    J. E. Flecker (1884–1915) – from the prologue
    to *The Golden Journey To Samarkand*

# Al Bowlly

Al Bowlly is probably the most unusual performer to be featured in this book. In recent years his recordings have been flooding the market on the Music For Pleasure, Ace of Clubs, Encore, World Record Club, Eclipse and other labels, and appreciation of his singing has at times assumed the form of a cult.

Unusual? Yes, considering that the man has been dead for more than 30 years and that many of those who collect his records never heard him in person. Bowlly was essentially a ballad singer of the '30s; his attempts to swing must have sounded contrived even then, while some of his ballad embellishments involving a sort of 'twee-twee-twee' vocalese sound rather embarrassing in this day and age. For older listeners nostalgia is an essential part of his appeal. Bowlly's recordings are often the definitive performances of 'evergreens', done when they were the pops of the day. *Let's Fall In Love, Everything I Have Is Yours, Guilty* and the Ray Noble standards like *Goodnight Sweetheart* and *The Very Thought Of You* – these are the songs, so well known today, that Al Bowlly introduced. People of more mature years relive in these recordings their own youth, their first experience of these songs, and the time when Bowlly's broadcasts were an integral part of their formative years – in much the same way, in fact, that younger listeners will in time regard Presley's *Heartbreak Hotel* or the Beatles' *She Loves You*.

Al Bowlly was a South African of Greek descent, born in Lourenco Marques, Mozambique, on January 7th, 1898, who worked with bands in Johannesburg, Calcutta, Singapore and Berlin before coming to London to join Fred Elizalde at the Savoy. He moved to the Monseigneur with the respective bands of Roy Fox and Lew Stone, augmenting his income and reputation alike by recording with the HMV house band directed by Ray Noble. These recordings, with Noble's advanced orchestrations and the cream of London musicians, achieved fame on both sides of the Atlantic, and are still widely sought by collectors.

Such was their impact at the time that Noble was invited to New York to lead a band at the Rainbow Room at Radio City. He took with him his drummer Bill Harty and Al Bowlly and left the formation of the band to Glenn Miller (it later became the first Miller band when Noble went to Hollywood). Yet despite the stellar line-up (Claude Thornhill, Charlie Spivak, Bud Freeman, Will Bradley *et al*) it was Bowlly who turned out to be the star attraction. Returning to England for a variety tour he remained on the outbreak of war and teamed up with Jimmy Mesene in an act subtitled 'Two Greeks and Their

Guitars'. Bowlly was 43 when he was killed in an air raid on April 17th, 1941.

It may not be so easy to pin down his appeal to those not of his era, except that Al Bowlly was an individual stylist and a thorough musician (he was a fine guitarist, playing effectively in the Fox, Stone and Noble rhythm sections and accompanying himself with great skill). He was a crooner pure and simple and never tried to exceed his limitations. He was influenced by no-one and no other singer has tried to emulate him, and his voice had a distinctive quality that made him instantly recognisable.

In short, Al Bowlly was an original, and for this alone, in a world of hand-me-down singers, he would have deserved acclaim.

AJ

# Tony Martin

Although his singing was never touched by even the slightest jazz influence, and his name never springs immediately to mind in any discussion on 'quality' singers, Tony Martin's contribution to the school of romantic balladeers should never be underrated. He was the principal of the school with physical attributes to match the rich lyrical quality of his singing.

Martin operated equally well as a baritone or tenor with a wide technical range that he exploited most discreetly unlike other belters of, say, the Lanza school who could all too easily overpower lyric and listener alike. One fault which became more pronounced in later years was a tendency to use falsetto a little too frequently, a futile proceeding for a singer who had the range and ability to sing naturally in the upper register had he wished.

Born in Oakland, California on Christmas Day 1912, Martin began his career under his real name of Al Norris in the saxophone section of Anson Weeks' band at the Mark Hopkins Hotel in San Francisco. After other band jobs alongside contemporaries like Woody Herman and Ginny Simms he made his vocal debut on the Lucky Strike Hour on radio with Walter Winchell. Encouraged into a movie career by Frances Langford he soon hit the top, starring in a series of Twentieth Century Fox musicals of the mid-'30s, with such diverse leading ladies as Alice Faye and Shirley Temple.

He guested with Ray Noble's band on a few Columbia recordings before signing with Decca, at the same time moving to MGM films where he introduced such songs as *You Stepped Out Of A Dream* in *Ziegfeld Girl* and *Tenement Symphony* in the Marx Brothers comedy *The Big Store* (both 1941). His career was halted temporarily by service in the Far East with the United States Army Air Force, which earned him a Bronze Star and a Presidential citation.

Back home again he starred in many more MGM musicals, and joined Mercury Records for whom he notched up a million sales in 1946 with *To Each His Own*. When screen musicals began to fade Tony and his wife Cyd Charisse formed a successful night club act which showed the fine showmanship that British audiences had previously seen when Martin had starred at the London Palladium in 1951, interspersing his songs with comedy, dancing and clarinet solos.

A true professional, he continues to work as a top club attraction in the States and even records a little from time to time.                                                    AJ

# Dick Haymes

As a singer of popular ballads, Dick Haymes has probably been Sinatra's greatest rival. With his deep brown baritone voice he pervades an aura that is all male, and back in the '40s when he sang a love song, women dreamed of hairy-chested men and were left limp awaiting just one more reprise of *You'll Never Know*.

Haymes is not a muscle-bound beach boy by any stretch of the imagination – just a normal fellow with an anxious-to-please face and now greying hair; whilst he is not physical perfection his voice is pure Charles Atlas and then some.

As a song stylist he has only one major fault: his inability to swing. Often he turns his tonsils on to some bewildering belter, monotonously matching a swinging big band phrase for phrase – almost as though he were afraid of losing touch with the tempo – and the result could be described as something less than exciting. But framed by sympathetic ballad arrangements, such as those provided by Ian Bernard on his superlative Capitol albums of the mid '50s – *Rain Or Shine* and *Moondreams* – then Haymes displays an untouchable artistry and the masculine hormones in his voice are projected with arm-around-her-shoulder tenderness as he communicates in a way that turns a large concert hall into a lounge with just two people on a sofa.

Born on September 13th, 1916 in Argentina of an English father and an Irish mother, Haymes first entered the USA at the age of two. His cosmopolitan background was enhanced by an education that encompassed schooling in four different countries and a final flirtation with Paris provided Haymes with a fluent understanding of the French language. Trained as a singer by his mother, a vocal teacher, he soon developed a keen love of popular music. While still a teenager he joined the Johnny Johnson orchestra as featured vocalist. After a spell as a radio announcer, he did more singing stints with the Freddy Martin and Orrin Tucker bands. In addition to these he gained valuable musical experience singing with the great Bunny Berigan's brassy little outfit. For a while he had his own radio show on Station KHS, played some bit parts in Westerns, then headed for New York's Tin Pan Alley, where he hoped to sell some freshly written songs. He failed in his primary aim but, as a singer, managed to impress trumpeter Harry James who was about to form a new band.

James wasted no time in signing the young baritone for his aggregation and

Haymes then began the task of proving himself the finest band vocalist in the business despite some heavy competition from a fellow named Frank Sinatra – a former singer for Harry James – who was then singing with the rival Tommy Dorsey outfit. Such Varsity recordings as *How High The Moon*, *The Nearness Of You* and *Fools Rush In* established the Haymes-James combination with the record-buying public and their 1941 waxing of *I'll Get By* sold as fast as the Columbia record company's distribution could get copies into the shops.

In 1941 Haymes left James to form his own orchestra, but conscription in 1942 forced him to disband the project. Engagements with the Benny Goodman and Tommy Dorsey bands followed, then he was introduced to Helen O'Connell's manager, Bill Burton, who set him on the path to success as a solo artist. His film debut in *When Irish Eyes Are Smiling* (1944) proved Haymes to have potential box-office appeal and later films such as *Diamond Horseshoe* (1945), *State Fair* (1945) and *Do You Love Me* (a 1946 film in which he co-starred with his old boss, Harry James) established him as a rival to even the perennial favourite, Bing Crosby. The film scores also provided him with some marvellous songs and his interpretations of *The More I See You* and *I Wish I Knew* rank with the very best in popular vocal music.

The '50s found yet another change-around in the Haymes fortunes and trouble with tax and immigration officials found him facing deportation from the USA. Neither his film nor his recording activities continued to be particularly lucrative during this period and eventually both Haymes' personal life and his professional career plunged to an all-time low.

During the '60s he sought to carve out a new career for himself and moved to England, which he now uses as a base for concert and cabaret appearances both here and on the Continent. Sometimes he sings badly, but on a good night he can still create the magic of former years.

He still claims that he can reach the top once more (this, despite a further recent appearance in the bankruptcy court) and even though the dice is heavily loaded against him who can deny his chances when he can still display such undoubted talent? Certainly his recent (1972) successes on US television and in cabaret would suggest that his determination is already starting to pay off. And not just from a nostalgia standpoint.

Recordings of Haymes are rare these days, but it is still possible to find the occasional album if one cares to look hard enough. *Love Letters* (Ace of Hearts) is a splended compilation of songs recorded during Haymes' most successful period, the '40s, but the aforementioned *Moondreams* and *Rain Or Shine* albums on Capitol, made during one of his many come-backs, still remain as the supreme examples of the Haymes art. Yet another LP originally from the American Hollywood label (featuring the piano of Cy Coleman and arrangements by Maury Laws) has been released in Britain in various re-programmed guises. Much more recently Alan Dell, one of Britain's more musically conscientious disc-jockeys who sometimes works as a record producer, arranged for Haymes to record an excellent album for Philips entitled *Then And Now*, but it was shamefully and inexplicably neglected by their publicity and promotion people and was therefore fated for early deletion even before it was released.

FD

# Billy Eckstine

Trumpeter, trombonist, leader of one of the first big bop bands, but above all, 'Mr B', the baritone whose rich tones have been likened to molasses, chocolate cream and all those other similes used by writers possessing descriptive rather than critical powers.

Right now it's difficult if not impossible to credit that Eckstine topped the singles charts eight times in as many years, and always with top quality songs like *Cottage For Sale, Prisoner Of Love, Everything I Have Is Yours, Blue Moon, Caravan, My Foolish Heart, I Apologise* and *No One But You*. That he has never, even in his recent affiiliations with such pop labels as Tamla Motown and Stax, lowered his standards of performance is a tribute to the genuine musical feeling that informs his every move in the profession.

Born in Pittsburgh on July 8th, 1913, William Clarence Eckstein (he altered the spelling of his name when he entered show business) made the big time at 26 when he joined the famous Earl Hines band, with which he recorded jazz classics like *Stormy Monday Blues* and his own *Jelly Jelly*. He brought Sarah Vaughan into the band, finding with her a musical affinity that has lasted for more than a quarter of a century. On leaving Hines, Eckstine formed his own big band that included such embryo jazz giants as Dizzy Gillespie, Charlie Parker, Howard McGhee, Gene Ammons *et al*, but hit by an AFM recording strike and the atrocious recorded sound of such discs as the band was able to make, it never really got off the ground. What we have heard, though, suggests that had it happened a few years later alongside the Gillespie big band, Kenton, Herman etc, the band might have had a vastly different history.

From then Eckstine eschewed jazz in his own performances and blossomed forth into one of the best and most distinctive of all ballad singers. Purists may have resented his commerciality, some critics may have found his singing mannered, but his musicianship never faltered, and the fact that he appealed to the public (*vide* all those gold discs) while retaining the respect of other musicians speaks for itself. His voice had a sonority and richness, marked by a distinctive vibrato, that have seldom been equalled. His penchant for melodic variations was realised in the unique codas which gave his recordings a touch of distinction that raised them far above the norm, and his albums for MGM and Mercury (some latterly reissued on the Music for Pleasure, Fontana, Saga and Ember budget labels) are worthy additions to any popular collection.

AJ

# Dean Martin

Unless one happens to be a hard-faced cynic, it's difficult not to like Dean Martin. Musically, he isn't a particularly impressive singer nor could he ever be described as a subtle interpreter of lyrics, but he certainly scores on personality and charm. And with more than twenty years of recording behind him there can be little doubt that Martin knows how to give the public what it wants.

Born Dino Paul Crocetti in Steubenville, Ohio, on June 7th, 1917, he enjoyed a somewhat checkered career, as a filling station attendant, steel worker, prize fighter and croupier dealer, before entering show business. His first singing job was as vocalist with the Sam Watkins band in Cleveland. Later changing his name to Dino Martini he branched out as a solo club singer with initial engagements in New York. His Crosby-inspired style was nothing original in those days, with just about every other singer thinking and sounding the same, but with his pleasing appearance and easy-going charm he did at least manage to keep his audiences happy. There followed a second name change – to Dean Martin – and he continued to play clubs and theatres as a solo act until 1946, when he teamed up with gramophone record pantomimist and comedian, Jerry Lewis, whom he had met some four years previously in New York.

Initially their act was a flop until they started indulging in wild slap-stick routines which soon put them into the $15,000-per-week class. They appeared with great success on CBS-TV. They were signed by Paramount Pictures and made their first film, *My Friend Irma*, in 1949. Subsequent films featuring the pair made the team of Martin and Lewis world famous. But it was Jerry Lewis with his rubber-faced clowning who drew all the applause, while Dean Martin was regarded as little more than a stale 'straight' man. When the team broke up in 1956 the so-called show business experts predicted an uncertain future for Martin. He soon proved everyone wrong with a tolerably good performance – against opposition from experienced actors Marlon Brando and Montgomery Clift – in the 1958 film *The Young Lions*. The following year he gave even finer performances in *Rio Bravo* and *Some Came Running*. While his film career continued on a steady upward trend, he enjoyed similar success in his vocal activities with such hits as *Volare* and *Return To Me*.

His recordings in latter years have consisted of mainly unsophisticated Country-and-Western material which has certainly kept him in the commercial stakes, even though such a policy must have alienated him from the more discerning listeners. As a stylist, Martin falls somewhere between Crosby and Como. While he may be a less distinguished singer than either, it is to his credit that he manages to sound like no one but himself. Sometimes his singing can be uncomfortably sloppy, but at other times he can be warmly compelling. At all times, though, Dean Martin manages to conquer his audiences with a bland personality and an all-consuming charm. With such tools as these, Martin's longevity in the singing business is assured for many years to come.

Undoubtedly the best overall collection of Martin's work on record is a well-produced six-LP package available (on subscription only) from World Record Club. His latter-day work can be found on the Reprise label.

KB

# Vic Damone

Blessed with one of the best natural voices in the business, Vic Damone is generally recognised as a very, very good singer but not *quite* a great one. Damone, born Vito Rocco Farinola in Brooklyn on June 12th, 1928, initially suffered because of a tonal and stylistic resemblance to Frank Sinatra, which he admitted at an interview in 1958 when he said: "Sure I copied Sinatra. Who didn't? I used to save my money for those 25 cent Record Your Voice machines and practise singing just like Frank." So, at a time when the public was busy buying millions of 78's by Sinatra, Cole, Como, Haymes & Co, Vic's first few Mercury records went largely unnoticed.

Eventually his stage and club appearances at NY venues like the Paramount and La Martinique, and his steady radio work, opened the market for his discs, and with top sellers in *Again* and *You're Breaking My Heart* Damone entered the '50s as an established record star, and embryo actor in the MGM musical *Rich, Young & Pretty*. At this time Vic realised the futility of being a second Sinatra. There was nothing he could do about the tonal resemblance which was quite uncontrived, but to compensate he increased the tenor range of his voice to achieve top notes outside the compass of the average crooner.

Fine technique and his inherent knowledge of the popular music idiom ensured that Damone's upper register was at all times under complete control, and he remains (except perhaps for Gordon Macrae) the finest example of a singer who could handle popular songs and more legitimate material with no sense of anachronism. He could probably be called the latter-day counterpart of Tony Martin and almost certainly he's probably the sole survivor of the school of great romantic ballad singers.

Maybe the fact that the school and style are out of favour at the moment explains Vic Damone's lack of stature as one of the 'greats' of popular singing. He has kept up with the times by recording contemporary material but his heart obviously isn't in it, and it's all too obvious that he never was a swinger. But, in his early forties and developing as an actor, he is still there singing as well as ever when others have dropped out. The many quality albums he made for Capitol (*Linger Awhile* and *Strange Enchantment* reissued on World Record Club are really all-time greats), CBS and Ember (under affiliation to his own record company) over the years are the very epitome of taste and talent.

AJ

# The Two Giants
# of the Small Screen

*A singer, like a songwriter, must be judged by*
*his staying power. You can't point to one or two*
*hit records that he made. You must ask 'How good*
*has his average been over the years?' Perry Como's*
*record (no pun intended) will show that he's been*
*up there on top for a good many years and I know he*
*will remain there for a good many more.*

Irving Berlin

## Perry Como

Perry Como, surely one of the most durable singers in the profession, apparently sees himself as the exception to one of show business's most solid and seemingly unbendable rules. As Como himself once put it: "I've heard it said that you never get anywhere by copying someone else. Well, I copied Bing Crosby and I got somewhere." A bold statement indeed, particularly from such an established artist, but it won't really do. The last twenty-five or so years have given Como enough independence for him to merit recognition for his own talent and style – a style which, incidentally, is quite easy to distinguish from Bing Crosby's.

Naturally, this apparent case of plagiarism – strongly supported, as it is, by the singer's own statement – cannot be brushed off lightly. In fact, it even bears a little investigating. Firstly there *is* a certain tonal similarity between the two voices (but nothing short of a surgical operation could alter this). Secondly there is Como's unabashed admiration for Crosby's way with a song (but there were literally thousands of other singers throughout the '30s and '40s who felt the same way – and they didn't achieve anything like the success that Como has). Thirdly there is that supreme air of relaxation which typifies the work of both singers. It is perhaps on this point that the case is at its strongest. Crosby, after all, was the first to adopt and perfect this 'lazy' style of singing. So in this instance it is quite fair to say that Como was influenced by Bing Crosby, but his style is not, and never has been, a direct copy. Indeed, if the sum total of

171

Como's impressive achievements in popular music over the last quarter of a century rested solely on plagiarism he would scarcely qualify for inclusion here.

So to get down to basics, Perry Como is quite simply one of those singers who is capable of standing on his own merits. His track record clearly reveals him as one of the great popular singers of our time, not just because he happens to have sold a huge number of records but also because of his sheer musicality, warm approach and the fact that in an almost indefinable way he is something of an *original*. Not, perhaps, in quite the same positive terms as Crosby, Sinatra, Cole or Presley: but Como's voice and style certainly do carry elements that would be impossible to confuse with another singer. And isn't that originality?

Born into a large family in Canonsburg, Pennsylvania on May 18th, 1912, Pierino Ronald Como was perhaps destined for success from the very beginning. That is, if one subscribes to the fabled tradition surrounding 'a seventh son of a seventh son. And being blessed with this rare distinction, Perry Como certainly turned out to be a fortune teller's delight.

Young Como had a built-in drive to succeed even at the age of ten when he set his heart on becoming the best barber in Canonsburg. To earn pocket money he had been working after school in the local hairdresser's and by the time he was fourteen he was already making plans to buy his own shop. His father, however, felt that this was rushing matters somewhat and he talked the boy into delaying such plans until he had at least completed high school at the age of seventeen. Perry went along with his father's wishes and agreed to suspend his high-blown ambitions for three years.

By 1933 Como had established himself in Canonsburg as a barber and in a relatively short time had come close to achieving his early ambition, but being of classic Italian stock he also had a natural aptitude for *bel canto* which was expressed in a gentle and casual way whilst cutting hair. His singing was agreeably received by the customers, many of whom urged him to consider taking it up professionally – no reflection on his ability as a barber, of course. Since he was planning to get married, it occurred to Como that singing might be a good way to make a little extra money. After successfully auditioning for Freddy Carlone, a popular local bandleader, he was offered a good salary to join the band on a full-time basis. This posed a rather serious problem, he was obliged to choose between hairdressing and singing. After giving the matter some careful thought he plumped, somewhat reluctantly, for the singing job on the grounds that it would substantially increase his income for a while, at least. His intention was that after the wedding he would quit singing and return to the more stable business of cutting hair.

That, according to the publicity handouts, is how Perry Como got started as a professional singer. How he developed from band vocalist into an internationally famous recording star was a long and much more complicated process taking more than ten years. A far cry from today's 'instant stardom' syndrome.

Como spent more than three years touring the Mid-West as vocalist with

Carlone's band. One night in 1936 while the band was playing in Warren, Ohio, Como's singing caught the attention of Ted Weems, who was then one of the nation's most popular bandleaders. In the George T. Simons book *The Big Bands* there are two interesting and somewhat contrasting quotes – from Como and Weems – regarding that particular night. First, the Perry Como version: "I was singing with Freddy Carlone's band in a gambling casino. Ted came in and played the 'double oh' in roulette and it came in. Then he came downstairs where we were working and he heard me sing. Art Jarrett had just left him, so he offered me the job."

Perry had modestly attributed Weems' offer to the fact that the bandleader had been in a good mood following his success at the roulette table, and that he needed a new vocalist anyway. But the Ted Weems version was somewhat more complimentary to the singer: "Como was introduced in the floor show and had to do about six encores before the audience would let him go – a scene I was to see repeated many times in clubs and hotels throughout the country. I talked to Perry about joining my band, and he was interested. I believe Paul Whiteman's manager phoned from New York for an audition, which he didn't want to do."

After serving out his notice with the Carlone band, Como joined Weems some weeks later. "We were on stage when he arrived," recalled Weems, "and during the show I saw him standing in the wings. I interrupted our regular programme to tell the audience about my hearing Perry in Warren and I would like them to hear his first song with us. He came on stage and sang one number to a wonderful hand."

The response to Como's singing ability, however, was not totally complimentary during his first year with the band. For instance when the Weems outfit performed at the Palmer House in Chicago, radio station WGN actually threatened to discontinue the band's broadcasts if the new singer didn't improve. As Weems recalled: "I had recordings made of a number of Perry's songs taken from air shows, and one night I had Perry stay and listen to them. He commented, 'I can't understand what I'm saying.' I told him that he had been endowed with a fine voice and there was no need to embellish it with vocal tricks. Just open up and sing the words from the heart. From then on his enunciation improved and so did his professional stature."

Como remained with Weems until 1942, when the latter entered the armed forces. After this Como signed with General Amusement Corporation as a solo artist appearing in night clubs and theatres. During this period he was developing an enthusiastic following which had been steadily growing since his days as featured vocalist with the Weems band – but, more important, he was also building a fine musical reputation as a really first-class ballad singer.

In 1943 he signed a recording contract with RCA Victor (for whom he still records to this day). His disc sales in the early stages were steady but unspectacular and it was not until 1945 that his first really major hit materialised.

Also in 1943 he was signed to a seven-year film contract with 20th Century Fox, from which he was released at his own request in 1947. While under the film contract, however, Como did appear in a number of pleasant though rather ordinary musicals, *Something For The Boys*, *Doll Face* and *If I'm Lucky*. While they proved fairly conclusively that he was no great shakes as an actor they did at least allow fans a chance to see Como on screen and his warm voice and agreeable personality made a pleasant impression. 1945, though, was the year in which Perry Como took his first significant steps towards long-term stardom by recording two songs – *Till The End Of Time* and Rodgers and Hammerstein's *If I Loved You* (from *Carousel*) – which were to make him the first singer in the history of popular music to have two million sellers at the same time.

Como's entry into the million-selling stakes was due to several elements not least of which was the enormous popularity, in 1945, of the music of Chopin. This was perhaps mainly attributable to a successful film called *A Song To Remember* – a highly fictionalised Hollywood-style biography (if that's the right word) of Chopin – and two popular recordings of Chopin's *Polonnaise in A flat* (a rhythmic version by Carmen Cavallaro and a straight piano solo of the original work by José Iturbi). So it was inevitable that there would also be a demand for a vocal version and Como's recording of *Till The End Of Time*, a lyricised adaptation of the *Polonnaise* by Buddy Kaye and Ted Mossman, met that demand on a spectacular level. This recording and *If I Loved You* both hit the million sales mark in the same week. Perry Como, his barber shop days now far behind him, had well and truly "arrived" commercially. But what most people overlooked was that it had taken him almost twelve years of hard work and solid experience to earn the glowing appellation, 'sensational *new* singer!'

The Como voice in the mid '40s was a beautifully controlled instrument with a full, rounded tone and an exceptionally even vibrato. These qualities plus his lightly casual sense of humour and darkly handsome looks put him on a commercial par with those two vocal giants of the period, Bing Crosby and Frank Sinatra. In fact, Como's record sales were noticeably in excess of Sinatra's.

Como's only drawback in an otherwise perfect vocal armoury was an occasional tendency towards stiff phrasing (something which he certainly did not inherit from listening to Crosby). But this fault may very well have been induced by the kind of arrangements with which he was working at this time. A typical example was the totally unsuitable choral setting he received on his recording of Jerome Kern's *Long Ago And Far Away*. Happily though, this slightly irksome aspect of his singing began to disappear as the quality of his accompaniments improved.

Apart from the occasional novelty number like a *A Hubba-Hubba-Hubba* (which had been written by Jimmy McHugh and Harold Adamson for the Como film *Doll Face*) most of his successful recordings of the '40s were concerned with revived standards such as *Temptation* (originally made famous by

Crosby in 1933), *Prisoner Of Love* (a Russ Columbo hit of 1931) and *When You Were Sweet Sixteen* (a ballad written as far back as 1898 by James Thornton, a drinking companion of famous heavyweight boxer John L. Sullivan). Como, in fact, was given the title 'Maker of Songs' by *Variety* in recognition of his success with revivals.

At the start of the '50s, the general temperature of popular music was changing drastically and romantic ballad singers generally were being nudged out of favour by more strident performers such as Frankie Laine, Guy Mitchell and Johnnie Ray. While Dick Haymes and, particularly, Sinatra suffered sagging record sales and loss of prestige, Como managed to adapt to the commercial needs of the period by choosing different material like *Don't Let The Stars Get In Your Eyes* and *Papa Loves Mambo* and picking up more gold discs.

Perry Como's success in television is, of course, legendary. His cosy fireside personality proved ideal for the small screen and his casual manner provided a prototype for other singers to follow (today's most notable example being Andy Williams). He started out by starring on a thrice weekly TV show which later led to *The Perry Como Show*. Between 1952 and 1957 he was awarded all manner of accolades and honours for his contributions to television and home entertainment. And in his home town of Canonsburg – Third Avenue, where the Como family lived, was re-named Perry Como Avenue.

In recent years, Como has been enjoying a kind of self-induced semi-retirement, making the occasional record and doing the odd TV guest spot. His 1971 hit, *It's Impossible*, was certainly the surprise success of the year as far as the British record market was concerned. Why? Because he had not had a hit in this country for over ten years and *It's Impossible* made absolutely no concessions to contemporary trends. It was like hearing a hit from the '40s. By all the rules of the modern market it should not have been a hit at all. A fluke then? No, just further proof that the famous Como chemistry (when coupled with the right song) could be just as potent as ever after twenty-five years.

In February, 1971, Como was interviewed via the trans-Atlantic telephone by Laurie Henshaw of the *Melody Maker*. The results, which gave a good impression of the contemporary Como (if that's not a contradiction in terms), were published in the February 27th issue of that paper. The following quotes are extracts from the interview:

"*What have you been doing since your BBC-TV series?*"
"Like everything else, Laurie, you get tired, you know. You get to a certain point, a certain age where you take it a little easier.

I've been trying to do as little as I can get away with. I've been recording a little and doing one or two shows a year. I've got involved in a Vegas thing which I enjoy very much.

It's kind of a club thing. More of a challenge really. I haven't worked a night club in about 27 years. And after saying 'no' to the people at Vegas

– at the International Hotel – for four or five years, I finally said 'yes'.

I'm supposed to be there once a year for the next two or three years. I've already been there twice. We're going back in July for another three weeks.

So between that a couple of times a year, a little recording and very little television, I got to a point where I felt I was doing the same show over and over.

Even when I watch other shows today I feel I've already done that.

Where else can you go, you know. I feel I've walked around all the bushes in the world, climbed all the walls . . . I've been doing very little golfing, but I've done an awful lot of fishing. We live now in Florida. The kids all got married. I have three children and we have six grand-children."

"*How did you come to make* It's Impossible?"

"Some years we would release two or three singles. I just didn't like to keep throwing them out. Some years they'd release one, then after a couple of years they didn't release any. That recording has been in RCA for about six to eight months.

I didn't want to do what you call real hard rock stuff. I feel – as the youngsters say – it wasn't my bag. So rather than go into that I just laid off a little.

When a good song came along I would do it, but nothing much would happen. Actually that kind of music just wasn't selling.

Then we did four or five in one day, *It's Impossible* was one of them. It sold an awful lot of records here."

"*Would you now contemplate doing a follow-up with a bit more beat to it?*"

"We have one – I think it's out now, Laurie. But it's also a ballad. It is a very pretty thing. They seem to think now the trend is going that way."

"*You must have sung hundreds of standards in your time. Would you say the quality of songwriting is as good as it was?*"

"A lot of it, yes. A lot of it, no. And I think the kids know that themselves. They were looking for a beat, and they put anything to a beat. But some of the songs are pretty good – the Jim Webb things. Paul McCartney. Things like *Something*. These are all fine pieces of music.

We – who are a little older – tend to put it down a little. But after you listen to it, it's pretty damn good."

"*Do you think that people like Cole Porter and Rodgers and Hart had a little more sophisticated approach to lyrics than the contemporary lyric writers?*"

"I think that's putting it very nicely. I think so. When you listen to some of the lyrics, you wonder why some people bother.

But the ear is attuned to more rhythmical songs, and that's what they want to hear. You find out if you don't do what they want or get close to it, you can go on for years without doing anything.

It wasn't that I didn't want to do it; I felt it just wasn't my place to do it. I'd come home once in a while with something that had a little beat to it – something a little out of my line – and my kids would say, 'Dad – not for you!'

But when *It's Impossible* came out, my daughter was the first one to say, 'Boy, that's really good.' Now I couldn't figure out why. But the kids in our neighbourhood felt the same way. . . . They have all kinds of Top 40s – their own private little stations they listen to.

How they grabbed on to this is a little beyond me. I'm happy they did. And I kind of get along with them. Oh, I put them down a little, but they know I'm joking."

## RECOMMENDED RECORDINGS

**THE SONGS I LOVE** (RCA): Generally speaking this 1963 release is one of the finest all-round albums Como has ever recorded. The songs in the main are the kind that he sings so well – *Days Of Wine And Roses, Carnival, This All I Ask, What Kind Of Fool Am I* – and the arrangements for orchestra and choir, written by the late Mitchell Ayres (for many years, Como's regular MD) are models of good taste. Note, for example, the perfectly understated orchestration for *I Left My Heart In San Francisco*. It is an ideal framework for Como's every phrase in that the large orchestra is used sparingly – even in the instrumental passage where the emphasis is thrown mainly onto a softly played guitar and muted trumpet – until the climax when the entire orchestra is unleashed in a thrillingly designed crescendo (which is never overpowering) trailing off to a neat *pianissimo* close. The Como vocal is tenderly expressive throughout this track, and nowhere else in his recorded repertoire is there a more subtle combination of voice and orchestra. Another clever touch by arranger Ayres is the gently humorous quote from Rodgers and Hammerstein's *Younger Than Springtime* at the end of *This Is All I Ask*.

**LIGHTLY LATIN** (RCA): A warmly romantic excursion into bossa nova territory, this album must also rank amongst Como's best work. The latin-styled accompaniments may be far from authentic, concentrating as they do on harmonic, rather than rhythmic, atmosphere but Como responds effectively to what rhythm there is and delivers excellent versions of such first-class songs as *How Insensitive, Quiet Nights of Quiet Stars, Meditation* and *Once I Loved* (all composed by that master of Brazilian music, Antonio Carlos Jobim). Another highlight is Como's fine reading – complete with introductory verse – of Johnny Mandel's lovely song *The Shadow Of Your Smile*.

**WE GET LETTERS – Volumes One & Two** (RCA): These two albums – long deleted – are worth hunting for since they offer excellent representation of Como's work on a wide variety of standard songs and in an equally wide variety of settings (all directed by Mitchell Ayres). The first volume has Como in a small jazz group setting, in which he sounds eminently happy and only slightly less skilful than Bing Crosby would have sounded in a similar situation. On the ballads, though, Como has the edge over Bing, being blessed with a wider vocal range and better breath control. The second volume has full orchestra and chorus alternating on some tracks with small piano and rhythm accompaniments. Apart from the mainly excellent material – and generally good recording quality – these two LPs constitute a first-class memento of the kind of performances he gave on his fondly-remembered TV shows of the '50s.

**IT'S IMPOSSIBLE** (RCA): A pleasant example of Como in a contemporary bag. His huge 1971 hit *It's Impossible* certainly entitles him to join the race again, and with his voice still in good shape – why not? There are one or two highspots here, notably an excellent *We've Only Just Begun*, a smooth *Something* and a commanding version of Bacharach's lovely *A House Is Not A Home*. Some of the other tracks are not quite so strong but the overall effect is reasonably satisfying and entertaining.

**PERRY COMO IN PERSON AT THE INTERNATIONAL HOTEL, LAS VEGAS** (RCA): Recorded for the first time in front of a 'live' audience, in June, 1970, Como proves conclusively that he has lost none of his vocal magic or personal charm. His natural musicianship and timing reveal a true professional at work. His handling of ballads (like *Everybody's Talkin'* and, especially, *Without A Song*) and swingers (*I've Got You Under My Skin*, *Hello Young Lovers*) show how flexible he still is. Only once does he come rather badly unstuck rhythmically. It happens in *If I Had A Hammer* where his phrasing takes on a rather clumsy feeling that tends to drag the arrangement down. Not to worry, listening to Perry is still good entertainment. One of the real highspots, not just of the album but of the Como career, is a wry and warmly humorous piece of original material titled *If I Could Almost Read Your Minds*, in which he pokes fun at his own image and relaxed exterior. Great fun and good listening.

**THE BEST OF PERRY COMO** (Reader's Digest. 6-record boxed set): Here without doubt is the most comprehensive collection of Como ever gathered together in one package. The recordings cover 26 years of the Como career from his first million-seller *Till The End Of Time* (1945) to his recent hit *It's Impossible* (1971). It comes in an attractive box with informative notes on the whole of the Como career and a track by track review of each of the 72 titles. There are one or two moments when the material is rather poor but by and large the set is elegantly produced. This package, then, is really an absolute must for Como fans. It cannot be too highly recommended.

KB

*Andy's voice has a beautiful tone quality*
*and he handles it like a musician would*
*handle an instrument. Pitch doesn't bother him.*
*He's just a complete natural singer.*

Marty Paich

# Andy Williams

To point out that Andy Williams has achieved a musical and commercial greatness similar to Crosby, Como, Cole, Bennett and Sinatra is to proclaim the obvious. But Williams differs from the others in one notable respect. He never set out to be anything but a singer. Crosby, as a young man, studied law; Como was a barber, Cole a jazz pianist; Bennett a commercial art student, and Sinatra finally settled on a singing career after working at various jobs. Williams, on the other hand, was born into a family of singers and cannot clearly remember a time when he was not a working vocalist.

These days, of course, he is very definitely something more than a working vocalist. Through the shrewd distribution and investment of his considerable earnings from records, television, concerts and clubs, etc., he has gathered around himself a vast business complex worth an estimated $15 million, much of which is unconnected with show business. The personal fortune of Andy Williams today puts him in a similar financial class to such well-heeled super stars as Bob Hope, Crosby and Sinatra. But the most incredible aspect of the Williams success story is that he achieved his present position of super-opulence virtually within the last ten years. Before that he was just another fairly successful recording and cabaret artist whose roots belonged in the 1930s and '40s. But even if Williams had not accumulated such wealth, he would probably still merit a place in this book on purely musical grounds.

Vocally, Williams is a more than capable performer. He never gives less than a good account of himself in any kind of musical surrounding and more often than not his particular treatment of a song stands favourable comparison with any of his rivals. All the major singers, of course, have their faults and Andy Williams is no exception. But like Ella Fitzgerald, his faults are stylistic rather than musical and like Sinatra, he occasionally displays a lapse of taste but never technique.

Howard Andrew Williams was born on December 3rd, 1929 in the small town of Wall Lake, Iowa. He was the youngest of four brothers, all of whom had a keen passion for singing; a passion which found its first outlet in the local church choir and later at parties and social functions. Encouraged by their father, Jay Williams – who played piano – the brothers Bob, Don, Dick and Andy worked out special harmony routines so as to get the best out of their voices, collectively and individually. Andy usually carried the melody and Dick would sing tenor while Bob and Don filled in the complementary harmonies.

In 1936, Mr and Mrs Williams with their family of four sons and younger daughter, Jane, moved to Des Moines, a somewhat larger township about 100 miles south east of Wall Lake. This was one of several moves that Mr Williams, who was a railway worker, made with his family during the late '30s and early '40s. It was in Des Moines that the Williams Brothers did their first broadcast on the local radio station. The popularity of their singing earned them further broadcasts and engagements. From 1939 to 1940, the Williams family lived in Chicago and it was there that the boys worked as staff artists on local station WLS which meant they were on the air six days a week. This was followed by two years on the staff of station WLW in Cincinnati. It was during this period that the boys were sponsored by a shoe polish company resulting in their own series five mornings a week and an extra show on Saturdays.

When the family moved to California in 1943, the prospects at first didn't look too bright for the Williams Brothers. Competition was fierce and singing jobs were scarce, but as soon as the word got around that they could read music, sing in tune and – more important – sell themselves as an act, the work began to flow in. They got radio work, studio calls and within little more than a year they had made appearances in films for Republic and Warner Brothers.

During the family's first year in California, Andy was still in high school. The quartet's activities suffered some temporary interruptions when Don and Dick, being mindful of the war effort, joined the Merchant Marine. In 1945, Andy also joined the Merchant Marine for a year while elder brother Bob entered the Army.

When they finally got back together, the brothers resumed their studio activities which included choral work for MGM. It was at this time that they met Kay Thompson, a talented and dynamic woman who was tired of being constantly involved with choral work and soundtrack sessions. She suggested that if the brothers were to team up with her in a specialised club act, it might be profitable for all concerned.

Jay Williams, who had been acting as the quartet's manager, opposed the idea. "I was convinced it wouldn't work out," he said in an interview with Leonard Feather in *Billboard*, "but I was overruled. I was afraid that they would never get back together again – and, of course, after the act broke up, they never did."

The combination of talent, not to mention hard work, that went into the Thompson-Williams merger resulted in an act that was to become internationally successful. It was an act so unique, relying not only on vocal perfection but on clever and intricate choreography too, that it is still talked about today as one of the most imaginative combinations in the history of modern show business. The experience which Andy gained from this memorable association was to prove invaluable to him when he later embarked on a solo career.

According to publicity stories, the Thompson-Williams act stayed together for five years. This is not strictly true, as Andy himself attests: "Actually we broke up twice with Kay. We worked together for about two and a half years. Then there was an interim period when I did nightclub work alone."

Being in a solo spotlight after spending so many years as one of a group must have had its daunting moments, but as his father pointed out, "Andy was courageous. He had lots of drive. As a matter of fact, in my opinion, the quartet was built around him."

Commenting on the break-up, Don Williams had this to say; "Andy and my brother Dick each wanted to do a single. Kay said that she'd help all of us. Dick didn't want any help; he wanted to do it alone. Kay worked with Andy on his first act. We all went to see him in his first engagement, and we cried. It was beautiful."

Said his brother Bob: "Andy made it as an individual. Bing Crosby, Perry Como and Vic Damone were among his favourite singers but he had been singing so long before stepping out on his own that I'm sure he didn't pattern himself after anyone. . . . He listened to everybody."

Anyone compiling an Andy Williams discography would discover several fascinating facts surrounding the early part of his recording career. For instance, the first commercial recording Andy ever made turned out to be a million-plus seller. The session took place on February 7th, 1944 in company with his brothers – and a certain solo singer. Of course, Andy was not really able to claim credit for the record's success because the solo singer happened to be Bing Crosby and the song was the Academy Award-winning song of 1944, *Swinging On A Star*, introduced by Bing in the film *Going My Way*. "We were on that date with Bing," recalls Andy, "and Decca gave us label credit. Our fee was $100. Not $100 each – that was the grand total for the four of us."

It is also interesting to note that, in spite of the popularity of Kay Thompson and the Williams Brothers, the recording companies seemed to show very little interest in committing them to wax. Although the act's success was based to a fair degree on its visual impact, it certainly contained enough vocal talent to justify the cost of an occasional recording session. Columbia was the only label to approach and even this resulted in only one session in December 1947. The titles were *Jubilee Time* and *Louisiana Purchase*. Around this same period, Andy also put in a little time with another excellent vocal group called The Starlighters, which was often employed as an accompanying group on recording sessions.

The first solo efforts Andy ever recorded were for an RCA subsidiary named – rather oddly – Label X. In Leonard Feather's *Billboard* feature on his career, Andy recalled his early experiences with this label:

"Around that time I was thinking in a sort of folk bag and did a lot of research on folk songs. I found that quite a lot of this material tended to sound quite monotonous melodically, but there was a thing I liked called

*Groundhog*, which I recorded for Label X. A group of Negro children were on this track. At the same session I recorded *There Is A Time*. Harry Geller wrote the arrangement. Nothing came out of this date, though; the two numbers are still on the shelf. As I recall it, I re-did one of the tunes in another key, and the a & r man, who had no sense of pitch, spliced together two takes in two different keys!

I cut one other session for Label X with Van Alexander arranging and conducting. The songs were *I Don't Know Why I Should Cry Over You*, *Here Comes That Dream Again*, *Now I Know* and *You Can't Buy Happiness* . . . . I realised that what I had done for Label X wasn't the right kind of product – in fact the proof of this is that even years later, when I was selling big on Columbia, those sides were never re-issued on RCA."

After his misadventures with Label X, his subsequent attempts at breaking into the record market were more fruitful. They could hardly have been less so! It was in 1955, while he was appearing as a resident singer on Steve Allen's *Tonight* TV show alongside Eydie Gorme and Steve Lawrence, that Kay Thompson brought Andy to the attention of Archie Bleyer. As a result, Andy signed a contract with Bleyer's Cadence label on December 1st, 1955 and made his first recording for that company on the same day. His initial recordings were not successful, but Bleyer continued to show faith in Andy's talent and they eventually scored a reasonable triumph with his fourth release, *Butterfly* (which was actually a successful cover version of a song that was already a hit for another singer).

This disc, helped by his regular appearances on the Steve Allen show, paved the way for a string of quite respectable hits and near-hits such as *I Like Your Kind Of Love*, *Hawaiian Wedding Song*, *Lonely Street*, *In The Summertime* (an early Roger Miller composition) and *Village Of St Bernadette* (this last title was written by Eula Parker of the well-known British vocal group of the '50s, The Stargazers).

Having established a niche in the singles market, Andy next moved into the more sophisticated field of albums (in those days an artist had to justify his worth commercially before he could graduate into the more expensive LP market. A far cry from today's scene when albums of obscure artists pour into the stores in even greater quantities than single releases). His first LP, a collection of Steve Allen compositions, was indeed a project to be proud of. It turned out to be much more satisfying vocally than his later album of Rodgers and Hammerstein songs, which hasn't stood the test of time too well.

Without doubt Andy's best album on the Cadence label (and possibly his best ever album) was *Under Paris Skies*, a brilliant collection of French-flavoured songs which he recorded in Paris in 1960 with quite outstanding arrangements from Quincy Jones and Billy Byers.

In 1961, Andy – who was now married to French actress, Claudine Longet –

decided to live in California and because of this it became necessary to end his association with Cadence, which was essentially a New York based label. His relationship with Archie Bleyer had always been a friendly one. So friendly that Bleyer, who respected Andy's wish to move to the West coast, turned a blind eye to the fact that the Cadence contract still had two years to run and released him without obligation. Of his association with Bleyer, Williams said:

"He is a wonderful, very fair, very honest man, and he had a great influence on me. He would sit around for hours philosophising about what made a record good, and how you went about making it communicate.

. . . I also hope to have a record company some day. If I had one now, I'd like to operate it rather the way Archie Bleyer ran Cadence . . . Archie ran his company wonderfully; it was small enough so that everyone got attention. . . . It becomes dangerous when you have an enormous roster of artists."

Andy Williams officially left the Cadence label on July 31st, 1961 and on moving to California, signed with American Columbia (which appears as CBS in Britain to avoid confusion with EMI's Columbia label). Due to the tremendous exposure that Columbia were able to give him, Williams eventually became a leading force in the album market. His first LP on the Columbia imprint, *Danny Boy*, was the least successful in a long line of commercially profitable albums; even so, the sales figures on this were in excess of 400,000 copies. His most successful album is undoubtedly *Moon River & other great Movie Themes*, the sales of which are said to be approaching two million copies.

It is in the years since 1961 that Andy Williams has achieved his meteoric, yet somehow steadily measured, rise to super-star status. It started when he signed with Columbia Records and it continued when his manager, Alan Bernard, switched Andy's agency representation from General Artists Corporation (who apparently were not geared to handle TV packages) to Music Corporation of America (who were). MCA went straight ahead and sold the first Andy Williams weekly TV series in 1961 and it went on the air the following year.

As a fireside personality, Andy Williams clicked almost immediately. And he has been clicking constantly ever since! Success on records, TV, concert tours and even a film – the 1964 musical *I'd Rather Be Rich* – all of these activities contributed to his upward progress. Business investments, too, have played a very important part in his overall success. His companies include Barnaby Productions, Barnaby Music, Claudine Music, Noelle Music and Andy Williams labels, which produces the labels that go into Andy Williams sweaters. He also controls various important property holdings and there is a golf tournament named after him.

An impressive success story by any standards. But what of Andy Williams the singer? Having traced his climb to the top and outlined the perfection of his commercial operations, let us take a look at his faults. He certainly doesn't have many, but nobody's perfect, not even Andy Williams.

On a technical level, Williams is clearly beyond reproach. The clean accuracy of his intonation, the rhythmic urgency of his phrasing and the warm smoothness of his delivery – all these points stand out in his favour and stamp him as a remarkable and even unique singer. That he has talent is unquestionable. But the way he chooses to employ that talent is sometimes highly questionable.

His current fascination for following juvenile trends couldn't be more out of keeping with a singer of his apparent intelligence. We know it is part of a popular singer's job to give the public what it wants and if certain people want to hear such childish ditties as *Good Morning Starshine*, then Williams is perfectly justified in singing them. But, in concentrating almost entirely on such a narrow policy of trivia as he does these days, he is surely disappointing the more adult listeners who would like to hear him perform songs which are more worthy of his fine technique: the kind of listeners, in fact, who purchased his *Moon River* LP. Even Andy Williams shouldn't try to argue with sales figures of almost two million!

This particular situation was explained by Jack Elliott, musical director on the Williams TV series: "Andy constantly wants to do new material. If anything, the only professional criticism I would have is that I think he reaches too hard for today's stuff. He tends to forget or negate the fact that he is, in my opinion anyway, the best male singer around today. But he tends to feel that unless he's doing something new, he's not going to hit the kids, and this is a hard point to argue. He may be right, but I don't think it's the kids that have made him. I can get more out of Andy when he's just being Andy, singing good songs, whether they are Harold Arlen's or Burt Bacharach's."

Another point of criticism that certainly irks many listeners is Williams' constant and questionable use of his falsetto register. This dubious practice serves no good stylistic purpose, nor does it enhance the lyrics of a song. Admittedly, it can occasionally create a feeling of excitement in an instrumental context (rather like Mel Tormé's vocal 'trumpet-shake'), but this is a vocal feat that should be used with discretion or not at all.

When Andy Williams was in London in May, 1968, I attended his press reception at the Savoy Hotel and spoke, first to Jack Elliott and then to Williams himself. I found Elliott, tall, heavily built and bearded, a gently unassuming person ever eager to talk of matters musical. I enquired of Andy's unusual vocal range. How high can his voice go? G, certainly. A, perhaps?

"Higher than that," said Elliott with a casual upward gesture of his hand. "Andy can reach B – or even C – on a good day. Of course, it all depends on which voice you're talking about. He has two voices, you know. In order to go up to B or C, he goes into head tones. But in the tenor register, you're right, he reaches A. He has a very healthy two octaves plus."

On speaking to Andy Williams, I asked him why his records carried so much echo. It seemed to me that his voice didn't need it.

"Echo is a matter of personal taste," he said. "Personally I like a little echo on my records. It gives the sound more body. I admit, however, that sometimes the recording boys overdo things a little. The echo is not there while I'm recording – it is added later. Mostly I record in Hollywood, but when I can manage it I prefer to record in New York at the CBS 30th Street Studios. Of all my albums, I think *Born Free* has the most natural sound. We did that in New York."

Since he signed with CBS, I had read that Williams had purchased all his old Cadence recordings and I asked him if he intended to reissue any of them.

"Well, first of all, I not only bought my old masters, I actually purchased the entire Cadence catalogue. The main reason for this was that I wanted to have control of all my old sides. Not necessarily to reissue but, in many cases, to *destroy*. I made some awful discs in those days and buying them was the only way to make sure they wouldn't appear again. Some of the better ones, however, will be reissued. *Hawaiian Wedding Song*, for instance, has already reappeared. As for the rest of the Cadence catalogue, there are some nice items which are still marketable. Not long ago we put out a Don Shirley piano album on CBS."

I asked him if he intended to reissue *Under Paris Skies*, an album which many people feel was his best.

"I don't know. It was a nice disc but it didn't sell very well."

But wouldn't the sales be better today?

"I'm not sure. I wasn't happy with the sound on that album because I balanced it myself. Since then, I've left that sort of thing to experts."

(Not everyone would agree with Williams that the balance on this album is bad. In my own opinion, it has a much more natural sound than his recent albums.)

Andy Williams today represents a high pinnacle of achievement in modern-day show business. He is as talented as he is successful. But the pity of it is that he seems to have allowed his talent and good taste to take second place to his commercial instincts and business interests. Much the same thing happened to Frank Sinatra, but he usually managed to shake himself free of the executive boardroom and produce an occasional recording of distinction.

Perhaps the key to Williams' present attitude lies in something his brother Don said in the November 1967 issue of *Billboard*:

"Andy hasn't changed much through the years. About three years ago he seemed to gain an assurance and freedom that he didn't have before. One day I asked him what had happened. He replied: 'I just realised that nobody was going to fire me.'"

In the days when he was faced with the possibility of unemployment, Andy Williams was clearly a more conscientious singer!

RECOMMENDED RECORDINGS

**UNDER PARIS SKIES** (Cadence, issued in Britain on London): With superb songs like *I Love Paris*, *I Wish You Love* and *Mademoiselle de Paris*, Williams has rarely been heard to such fine advantage (the breath control and phrasing on *April In Paris* reveal a true master at work). The sympathetic orchestrations which strike a subtle balance between smooth Gallic romanticism and lively big band swing are a credit to the perceptive musicianship of Quincy Jones and Billy Byers. On some songs – notably Michel Legrand's beautiful *La Valse De Lilas* – Williams makes creditable excursions into the French language and for these tracks he was coached by the well-known French singer/guitarist Sacha Distel. This delightful album has been unavailable for some years, but it is well worth searching for in the second-hand shops, particularly since Williams has shown little interest in re-releasing it.

**IN THE ARMS OF LOVE** (CBS): Williams is in excellent voice here with beautifully judged versions of first-rate songs such as *The Very Thought Of You*, *Here's That Rainy Day* and *A Man And A Woman*. There are also some pleasant representations of the more commercial side of Andy Williams, not least of which is the easy-going Henry Mancini title tune.

**CAN'T GET USED TO LOSING YOU** (CBS): An enjoyable album, this is worth getting for Andy's superb double-track version of *You Are My Sunshine* and for fine ballad selections like *What Kind Of Fool Am I?*, *Days of Wine And Roses* and *I Left My Heart In San Francisco*. The title track, one of his biggest hits, is nicely sung too. Most of the other tracks, though, suffer from rather dull arrangements.

**THE SHADOW OF YOUR SMILE** (CBS): This is one of the best, if not the best, Williams album from the mid-'60s and it serves as a good reminder of the days when Andy chose his material for its quality rather than its topicality. Thus, we can hear him singing what were then contemporary songs such as the Beatles' *Michelle*, Jobim's *Meditation* and the album's title song alongside well-loved standard material like *That Old Feeling*, *Bye Bye Blues* and *Peg O' My Heart*. Robert Mersey's arrangements on this album are perhaps more influenced by Kaempfert than they should have been, but Andy sings with an insouciant charm that is somehow missing from much of his latter-day work.

**LOVE STORY** (CBS): One of the best examples of the latter-day Williams in that the song content seems to be better chosen than usual and is certainly more suited to Andy's smooth delivery. Alongside the popular *Where Do I Begin* (theme from the film *Love Story*), there are standout performances of *If You Could Read My Mind* and a lovely item called simply *Autumn*.

KB

# Index

* Brother of Ray Eberle, Bob altered the spelling of his name to avoid confusion.